Praise for *Your Money or Your Life*

"I've read this classic book three times—first when I started my financial journey, again after I achieved financial independence, and once more after I 'retired' at the age of thirty-four. Each time, it has revealed new gems that have helped me live a happier and more fulfilling life. If you want to invest in your financial future and (more importantly) your long-term happiness, I can't think of a better investment than *Your Money or Your Life*."
> —Brandon Ganch, *Mad Fientist*

"Now as never before, it's time to stop trying to 'get ahead' in a race that is both fixed and futile, and figure out how to organize your life so that it can be your life. Your one precious life lived for yourself, for your community, and for your planet. *Your Money or Your Life* shows you how to make the shift."
> —Bill McKibben

"Vicki Robin's *Your Money or Your Life* offers readers the gift of meaningful, applicable advice so that they can achieve true financial independence on their terms. It is deservedly one of the most acclaimed and referenced financial advice books of our time and will undoubtedly continue that legacy for generations."
> —Farnoosh Torabi, bestselling financial author and host of the award-winning podcast *So Money*

"Can you save your money and life? Yes, and Joe and Vicki's approach offers even more. Those who use their money carefully generate incredible benefits beyond the obvious gains for themselves. First, their use of natural resources drops, since they consume far more thoughtfully: bonus point for the world's ecosystems. Second, they may be able to work less: bonus point for other people's employment opportunities. Third, they spend their money on necessary, worthwhile products: bonus point for the economy of goods, rather than that of bads. Fourth, they are freeing their time and are now able to spend time volunteering with nonprofits, playing with their own and others' children, running for office, or just helping out where people are in need: bonus point for our communities. Fifth, they now have time to bring their dreams alive: bonus point for creativity, vibrancy, and joy. What are you waiting for?"
> —Mathis Wackernagel, CEO, Global Footprint Network

"Bless Penguin and Vicki Robin for re-releasing this timeless, exquisite, and classic work on our relationship with money. With clarity, incisiveness, and brilliance, *Your Money or Your Life* gives every reader, no matter what their circumstances, the keys to living a fulfilling and financially free life. This is one of the best and most truthful books you will ever read about money."

—Lynne Twist, author of *The Soul of Money*

"Most money books are full of the same trite tactics, tricks, and tips. This book blows past all of that to do what's most important: Radically transform how you think about, relate to, and ultimately use your money. If you read only one book about money, this book is it. You'll never see your money (or your life) in the same way again."

—Jesse Meacham, founder of You Need a Budget

"*Your Money or Your Life* is the rare book that is both map and compass. As we enter hard economic times, this visionary book provides eminently pragmatic and effective maps to reduce the costs of your life and increase your savings net. Of equal importance, it's a compass that can guide you to your true values—nonmonetary values such as community, friendships, and deeper relationships to your place and nature."

—Kenny Ausubel, CEO and cofounder, Bioneers

"*Your Money or Your Life* is nothing less than a clear and profoundly practical path to financial freedom. If you want to bring sanity, stability, and security into your money life, get this book and follow its advice. You will be very glad that you did."

—John Robbins, bestselling author, president of the Food Revolution Network

"*Your Money or Your Life* is a classic that has stood the test of time, and this new version adds much more to its already powerful value. In an era when conspicuous displays of wealth are promoted, even at the highest levels of government, we all need constant reminders that simplicity, frugality, community, and freedom from being possessed by our stuff are the best things in life."

—John de Graaf, coauthor of *Affluenza* and *What's the Economy For, Anyway?*

PENGUIN BOOKS

Your Money or Your Life

VICKI ROBIN, author of *Blessing the Hands That Feed Us* and coauthor of the best-selling *Your Money or Your Life*, is a prolific and well-known social innovator, writer, and speaker. In addition, she has been at the forefront of the sustainable living movement, launching projects such as Sustainable Seattle, the 10-Day Local Food Challenge, Transition Whidbey, and the Center for a New American Dream. Robin has been featured in hundreds of media stories in various outlets, including the *New York Times*, NPR, *The Oprah Winfrey Show*, *People*, and many more. She lives on Whidbey Island, in Washington.

JOE DOMINGUEZ (1938–1997) was a successful financial analyst on Wall Street before retiring at the age of thirty-one by devising and following the step-by-step program presented here in *Your Money or Your Life*. His teaching also lives on through his audio course, *Transforming Your Relationship with Money and Achieving Financial Independence* (Sounds True). From 1969 on, he was a full-time volunteer and donated all proceeds from his teaching to transformational projects.

PETER ADENEY, better known as Mr. Money Mustache, is an influential financial blogger who retired financially independent shortly after turning thirty, and now writes about how to live a frugal life of leisure.

Vicki Robin
and Joe Dominguez

YOUR
MONEY
OR YOUR LIFE

9 Steps to Transforming Your Relationship with Money and Achieving Financial Independence

Foreword by
MR. MONEY MUSTACHE

PENGUIN BOOKS

PENGUIN BOOKS

An imprint of Penguin Random House LLC
375 Hudson Street
New York, New York 10014
penguin.com

First published in the United States of America by Viking Penguin,
a division of Penguin Books USA Inc. 1992
Published in Penguin Books 1993
Revised edition published 2008
This second revised edition published 2018

Portions of this work first appeared in Joe Dominguez's audiotape course
and workbook titled *Transforming Your Relationship with Money and Achieving
Financial Independence*.

"Purpose in Life" test reprinted by permission of Psychometric Affiliates.

LIBRARY OF CONGRESS CATALOGING-IN-PUBLICATION DATA
Robin, Vicki.
Your money or your life : 9 steps to transforming your relationship with
money and achieving financial independence / Vicki Robin and
Joe Dominguez.—Rev. ed. / rev. and updated with
Monique Tilford and Vicki Robin
p.cm.
Includes bibliographical references and index.
ISBN 9780143115762
1. Finance, Personal.   I. Dominguez, Joseph R.   II. Title.
HG179.D624 2008
332.024'01—dc22 2008044048

Printed in the United States of America
30   28   26   25   27   29

Set in Meridien

To Joe Dominguez (1938–1997), of course!

Treasured mentor and companion

on the great adventure.

And to all he loved.

Why Read This Book?

Ask yourself these questions:

- Do you have enough money?
- Are you spending enough time with family and friends?
- Do you come home from your job full of life?
- Do you have time to participate in things you believe are worthwhile?
- If you were laid off from your job, would you see it as an opportunity?
- Are you satisfied with the contribution you have made to the world?
- Are you at peace with your money?
- Does your job reflect your values?
- Do you have enough savings to see you through six months of normal living expenses?
- Is your life whole? Do all the pieces—your job, your expenditures, your relationships, your values—fit together?

If you answered no to even one of these questions, this book is for you.

Contents

Foreword

There is really only one reason to read any book about money: to give yourself the gift of a better life. Money is not really the thing you're after—after all, would you lock yourself in a dark, silent box forever in exchange for becoming a billionaire?

It seems obvious when put into such stark terms, but the truth about money is that money alone won't solve most of your problems. In fact, a healthy relationship with money is most often just a by-product of living a happy, healthy life.

Instead of a dark box billionaire, you are probably hoping to become a lighthearted, productive, free person who just happens to never have to worry about money again.

This gigantic distinction is where most of the books, magazines, websites, TV shows, and podcasts ever created on the subject of money seem to fail. It's also the reason most people in the United States and other rich countries, despite our record income levels, remain just about broke, with many in record levels of debt. We're chasing more money and more of the things it can buy, without questioning the big picture of exactly what we are buying and why.

And this is the reason why this book, *Your Money or*

Your Life, remains a standout classic after more than twenty-five years in print, with its message still echoing strongly enough through our society to keep new generations thinking about the ideas and to bring Vicki Robin out of her peaceful island retirement to write this updated version. Robin's unique approach is what gives this book its unusual unprecedented staying power, and this update takes the same approach and applies it to the significantly changed world in which we now live.

The standard money advice is too meek, claiming that we all have different personal values and we need to follow our hearts. If I love hundred-dollar dinners out and you love expensive cars, that's fine! You can spend on those things you love, as long as you budget carefully to afford it and work hard to make enough money for it.

The reality is that most of this is nonsense: We're all humans, much more similar than we are different. Through centuries of philosophy and recent decades of more formal research, we've learned that there are a few genuine, universal human happiness buttons that can be pressed—the same basic factors such as friendship, health, community, overcoming challenges with your own ingenuity, and feeling in control of your life. These work for everyone.

At the same time, most of us are tempted by the ideas of convenience, status, and luxury, and buying ourselves treats to satisfy these temptations. And we're really good at justifying some of these trinkets as our true passions. The only difference is in which things—and how many of them—we choose to justify. With just a few of the more expensive "true passions," you can lock up almost any lifetime's income, sometimes eliminating your chance of claiming the bigger and more universal happiness prizes previously mentioned.

Even the most well-known finance and business gurus repeat some version of this "spending money equals happiness" myth. Follow their advice and you may just end up with a really well-polished conveyor belt of personal desire. Your skilled hands will be throwing goals onto one end of it and pulling satisfied bucket list items off of the other, but you can still end up standing in the same place you started. Endless desire is one of the pitfalls of human nature, and one of the first things you need to cure if you want to get ahead more quickly.

It is for this reason that *Your Money or Your Life* talks so much about so much more than money. It is a personal development guide to help you figure out what you really want out of your life, while also training away the money-wasting habits that you have probably developed that are getting in the way of it. And "training" really is a good way to think about it: You get better about this stuff slowly, by repeating small steps every day, which build naturally into bigger accomplishments. It all seems gradual until you look back and barely even recognize your past self: "How was I wasting that much of my time and energy every day without even realizing it?" The result of all this training is not just an improved financial picture—it's an improved you. This is the reason the book remains so popular.

There's a bigger picture here too, of course: the entire world and all the people and living things who share it. Far too often we are taught that our spending decisions are simply a matter of our personal choices. If there's enough money in our wallets and room for the resulting debris in our garbage or recycling bins, we are clear for purchase.

The reality is that almost everything we buy comes with a bit of unseen destruction somewhere else, and that damage has been adding up in recent decades. Facing the conflict between our lifestyles and the now-constant news headlines about their consequences is a source of stress. The great news, as you are about to learn in this book, is that streamlining your lifestyle for happiness will also dramatically cut down the amount of destruction that is done in your name.

Make no mistake—it's almost impossible to read this

book thoroughly without also drastically improving your financial situation for the rest of your life. The money part is definitely here. But the unique power of the method comes from working on the root of the problem—your personal beliefs and habits—rather the just the symptom of your monthly bank and credit card statements.

If you've never read this book and taken this journey before, brace yourself, take your time, and take it seriously. Your entire life is about to be transformed.

Mr. Money Mustache

Introduction to the New Edition

Welcome! From millennials to Gen Xers to boomers, this makeover of *Your Money or Your Life* is for you. Since its initial publication, this book has become an enduring classic, helping hundreds of thousands of people transform their relationship with money. The tools are evergreen but the world has changed, and I've brought together the best team possible to make it relevant for today and many years to come. And for you.

Of course you wonder, can it help you? Now? In your situation?

Can it help you get out of consumer debt, revive delayed dreams, get a place of your own, leave a job that doesn't suit you anymore, have enough money to afford some extras, increase your income, make the savings you have last longer, and even liberate you from working for money entirely?

It can. Or better said, you can—if you use these tools.

Because hundreds of thousands of people have indeed used these tools, I can make these promises:

- You'll spend less money and enjoy life more.
- You'll save more money than you ever thought possible.

- You'll flatten your debt and develop a natural resistance to spending more than you have for things you don't want to impress people you don't like (to paraphrase Robert Quillen).
- You'll have more time for what matters most.
- You'll learn a lot about yourself—relatively painlessly.
- You'll be at ease talking about finances openly and honestly.
- You'll forgive yourself for your past money mistakes and get on with it.
- You'll save for retirement and get there, possibly a lot earlier than you can now imagine.
- You'll put your life in service to your values rather than putting your time in service to money.

Financial Independence

The purpose of the nine-step program in this book is to transform your relationship with money and help you achieve Financial Independence. The result is liberating your most precious resource—your time—to make room for more happiness, more freedom, and more meaning.

What does it mean to "transform" your relationship with money? It doesn't mean getting more money or less money; it means knowing how much is *enough* money for you to have a life you love, now and in the future. It means shifting from being a victim of money and the economy to making conscious choices. Anyone can do this.

What do we mean by "Financial Independence"? At the most basic level, Financial Independence means no longer having to work for money. More than this, *Your Money or Your Life* takes you through a process of liberation that starts with freeing your mind from the illusion that buying stuff will make you happy or that more is always better. You see with such clarity the thoughts driving your money patterns that the patterns themselves evaporate. As you do the steps of the program, your debt melts away. With debt receding, you naturally build up savings. You no longer hit the panic button with unexpected expenses. Saving becomes a habit. You save more. And more. Eventually you can choose whether you work for love or money. This is how it's gone for many people—and how it can go for you.

As you read this book and work through the steps, you'll see that you need not be resigned to devoting the majority of your waking hours to making money. The nine-to-five grind may be the societal default, but you can steer your life down different highways—with off-ramps to your true calling and a more pleasing future. What will you do when you no longer have to work for money? You may not know right now, but by doing the suggested steps, you'll have enough clarity, focus, and confidence that the dreams waiting for you to find them will start to appear.

As one *Fler* (our term for a person who has applied the steps to achieve Financial Independence) says, "This isn't really a book about money. It's a book about life."

How This Book Came into Being

Meet Joe Dominguez, the originator of this nine-step program. Latino by descent, raised on "welfare cheese" by a mother who never learned English, he grew up in Spanish Harlem in New York City. He was a runty guy and wicked smart. He couldn't use brawn to survive, so he became the brains of his gang, learning to make explosives and plan strikes on rivals with successful getaways. His survival instinct was sharpened by necessity, and in part *Your Money or Your Life* comes out of his canny ability to assess threats and opportunities and emerge from anything alive. As Joe saw it, the money system was like the welfare system and the justice system and the poverty system: How do I get through this on my own terms, in it but not of it? He never graduated from college but stumbled into a job in a Wall Street firm. Not satisfied to just learn the ropes, he analyzed the game, eventually developing some of the first tools of technical analysis in the early 1960s, when computers were the size of a city block. He did not invest his own money but rather sold his expertise to one of the illustrious investment banking firms, and he saved with one goal in mind: Retire by thirty. Exit the money game. Be in life, not in the prison of a job.

Joe and I teamed up in the 1970s in life and work. We were well matched in our purpose in life: to leave this world a little better than we found it. While our differences sometimes grated, they more often produced a flinty creativity that generated our nearly two decades of teaching, writing, speaking, and—we hoped—world changing. He was an introvert. I was an extrovert. He was systematic. I was improvisational. He was a big-picture thinker. I was more like a racehorse, taking the work by the bit and running with it, depending for strategy on his wider view.

The culmination of our work, *Your Money or Your Life*, surprised us and everyone else by achieving instant success. By the time Joe died of cancer in the first weeks of 1997, we were at the top of our game. *Your Money or Your Life* had been a *New York Times* best seller as well as spending five years on the *BusinessWeek* Best-Seller List. We believed that if enough people used the tools, *Your Money or Your Life* would be a "lever long enough to change the world."

After Joe's passing, I continued the work with a strong eye toward movement building, forming a common cause with the leaders of the flourishing simplicity movement and bringing our shared message to the halls of power and to global networks working on sustainability. By 2004, when I was diagnosed with my own spreading cancer, my racehorse was spent, and the lofty dream Joe and I had of "transforming the way Americans think about, earn, spend, and save money" had not really panned out, despite hundreds of thousands of grateful readers. I retired, moved to a village of a thousand on an island in the Pacific Northwest, and turned my attention to making a difference here in this small patch of the planet.

A dozen years later, though, I heard the call again. I happened to be in a large circle of earnest people gathered to talk about money. Each in turn shared their confusion and fears. There was a well-off eighty-year-old who did not know if he'd run out of money before he ran out of years and a mid-career professional in a rut but afraid to leave. Several consultants confessed their inability to help clients with money issues because they weren't any clearer themselves on the subject. Lastly, a young college sophomore revealed she was already $20,000 in debt. To get anywhere in her field, she assumed she'd need a master's and likely a PhD. She was worried about the gamble she was already taking, about whether her degree would be worth enough to ever repay her loans.

The old fire in me started to rekindle. What kind of society requires everyone to depend for their very survival on something so unstable, unreliable, and out of their control? What kind of society turns its young people into a profit center for the debt industry? I checked around the circle whether people were familiar with *Your Money or Your Life*. The yeses came mostly from those with gray hair; the noes, from those under thirty-five. Knowing how much *Your Money or Your Life* had liberated one generation, I thought perhaps it could help another one break the spell of consumer culture and be free to give their considerable gifts in these decisive times. That's when I sought out young people to help me understand their circumstances and perspectives, and when I discovered how far the FIRE (Financial Independence, Retire Early) ideas had spread. With much encouragement from many friends, I undertook the careful work of updating a classic to be in tune with a new time.

And so this makeover was born. For those who read

the original version, rest assured that nothing of the bones of this program has changed, and all of the ideas you've come to love are still there.

Changing Times

There's no denying, however, that you live in a very different reality from the one in which Joe Dominguez and I, Vicki Robin, became financially independent. Boomers entered a stable world created by parents who'd survived the Great Depression and World War II. Government institutions such as the progressive income tax and the GI Bill fostered a growing middle class and a sense of social cohesion.

For those navigating the workforce in the twenty-first century, the corporate landscape has changed. Pensions are in their death throes, and the thought of retirement is a pipe dream for young and old alike. Nearly a fifth of all Americans over sixty-five depend solely on Social Security, with more than 50 percent getting half of their income from it.[1]

Young people fledge into a world where their bachelor's degrees don't guarantee incomes sufficient to ever pay off their debts, where everyone—no matter what their job—is in the YOYO class: You're On Your Own.

Today, more than at any time in history, the old rules have become fluid enough that you can move freely wherever you want—in location, in career, in your personal life, and in your purpose in life—no matter where you started. It's scary—and exciting. People from all walks of life are navigating these rapids of change, some better than others.

Adapting to a New World

How well is this new crop of humans in these new times doing? I got curious, so I talked to every person in their twenties and early thirties I met—anywhere. I hosted a focus group. I perused Reddit and Facebook groups. I was surprised—and impressed. The people I found had already incorporated the broken promise of the old American Dream into their lives and were designing their lives not around a ladder of success but around meaning, creativity, flexibility, and a sort of rapid prototyping not just of jobs but of entire careers. Many are getting their education from a range of channels—technical training, skill development workshops, community colleges with name-brand universities as finishing schools, digital MOOCs (massive open online courses), apprenticeships—as well as traditional degrees. Gap years are more common. The growing percentage of people who don't have traditional jobs work on their computers and set up shop in coworking spaces and makerspaces, in cafés and on unmade beds, never knowing whether they are onto the "next big thing" or just the next interesting step. They build networks, teams, start-ups, and proficiencies as they go, and they take breaks for travel or babies or self-reflection if they have a kit bag of skills that are portable and in demand. Not only that, Gen Xers and boomers are learning from younger people how to navigate this changing landscape of work. Here are some stories about these innovative, adaptive young people:

Brandon is the youngest of six children. His family had some means to help his eldest brother attend college, but they were still short thousands of dollars every semester. To close the gap, his brother worked as a sales associate at a national grocery chain. By the time Brandon graduated from high school, his oldest sibling still worked at the same big-box-store job, for the same pay. College—the diploma and the debt—did not seem worth it, so Brandon went directly to working as a farmhand and then driving a tow truck. He's saving up to go to trade school to learn how to work in auto repair in an era of computerized systems, aiming to make $40 an hour.

Chris got a degree in engineering, paid off his college debt in one year working at a major aerospace company, then saved up enough to take a year off to do service projects and travel. At the end of the year he went back to work in a new and exciting role with a great pay package.

Melody works in customer service at a rental car desk, saving up to get a nursing assistant degree at a two-year college. From there she'll see which new training she wants to take to move up or sideways in the medical field—and how long it will take at a new pay scale to pay off the cost of the certificate.

Naomi did Running Start in high school, peeling a year off her college requirements, then did her second year at a community college before transferring to a university to finish her degree in social work—all without accumulating crushing debt. Truly maximizing their potential, some students do two years of college in high school through the Running Start program.

Older people already in the workforce are exercising this kind of fluidity and creativity as well. Doctors become carpenters. Carpenters become architects. Social workers become farmers. Art lovers leave office jobs and become tour directors for the great museums of Europe. Biologists leave the laboratory and lead people on naturalist trips to the remaining jungles of the world. Teachers become massage therapists. Soldiers apply their military training to a range of post-service professions—some highly technical and highly paid.

Some find their passion and path early in life and become financial planners or real estate agents or doctors or professors for life. But more and more people, according to the Bureau of Labor Statistics,[2] zigzag through a dozen jobs, moving up, moving sideways, moving down . . . but always moving.

What about that more than 50 percent who get half their income from Social Security, who thought the good times would roll forever and failed to save and plan? They adapt through extending their working years, perhaps until they die. Others downsize or move closer to their children to reduce the burden of hiring help around the house. Many take advantage of social services, matinees, and free activities. They are involved in their communities, having fun by volunteering. And, taking a page from millennials, they have entered the gig economy as handymen, bloggers, or Airbnb hosts, turning their only asset—a house—into a source of income.

Whether you're a senior in college, mid-career worker, or soon-to-be retiree, the tools in this book can support you wherever you are in the spectrum of life and experience.

Who Is This Book For?

This program works for anyone who earns or spends money—not because anyone can be rich, but because everyone can discover for themselves how much is enough . . . and have that. It helps you transform your *relationship* with money—and we all have one.

In fact, "enough" is the radical promise of *Your Money or Your Life*. Having more is an endless horizon. No matter how much you have, that voice of "more would be better" drives you to make acquisition the name of your game. Greed is one of the many strings in the human heart, and it can be pro-survival, but unchecked by a sense of fairness, balance, and love, it can gut our capacity for joy. Defining "enough" requires you ask yourself some crucial and pertinent questions:

- What makes you happy?
- What's most important to you?
- What values will you never compromise?
- If you had $1 million right now, what would you do with your time?
- What's one thing you could get rid of to make yourself happier? (A person doesn't count.)
- Will you ever have enough money to retire?
- If someone today erased all your debts, would you dig yourself into that hole again? How or how not?

Nobel laureate and best-selling author Daniel Kahneman, in his research on money and happiness, found that beyond a certain level of sufficiency (currently about $75,000 a year in the United States), more money doesn't buy more happiness. In our early seminars in the 1980s we'd collect data from participants and analyze it on the spot to reflect the audience back to itself (using paper and pencil because it was long before laptop computers). Correlating participants' income with "how much would it take to make you happy," almost everyone, in every income bracket, said: 50 percent more than I have now. When asked to rate their happiness on a scale of 1 to 5, there was no significant difference between the top and bottom earners. You could hear a pin drop as people realized that the person in the row ahead of them probably had the "more" they thought would make them happy—and it made no difference.

This data suggests that a conscious, clear, empowered relationship with money is the real key to success, not your "number" (that dollar amount picked out of thin air and set as a goal).

When *Your Money or Your Life* came out in 1992, there were few books that spanned money and happiness in any practical way. Now there are hundreds of thousands of FIRE aficionados who, like the FIers I've known, seem to share two powerful qualities:

1. A purpose for their lives that's greater than their current limited circumstance—including their jobs
2. A willingness to do the work of change, to tell the truth, to be accountable, and to persist

These qualities are like the kindling that lights the FIRE desire in people.

As I've studied this FIRE movement I've seen in its bones three strands—frugality, simplicity, and self-sufficiency—that have woven through people, societies, and religions for thousands of years. These values appeal to people of diverse financial means and across every political, cultural, and geographical spectrum. Christians have seen the teachings of Jesus in the pages of this book. Buddhists have seen Buddhism. Atheists have found the program's rationality trustworthy.

While no two conscious money mavens are entirely alike, they do seem to follow certain trends. These aren't the only way to go, but it's useful to know what others out there are doing. I refer to the current crop as Ninjas, Minimalists, and DIYers.

Ninjas: Personal finance Ninjas love to run the numbers, optimize systems, exploit niches, study personal finance blogs, mess with investments, hack the system to get free flights and hotel stays. Subcategories are the Frugalistas, who love bargains, clipping coupons, free-cycling, and deal making; and the Supersavers, who love beating last month's percentage of salary saved. Saving money is an all-American sport.

Minimalists: It's not about the money; it's about the meaning, about clearing away clutter to get to the marrow of life. These are Thoreauvians, more likely to prioritize experiences over things. They minimize stuff to maximize something nonmaterial but more precious: the life of the mind, the soul, and so on. They could be called the Soulfulists. Simplicity has been a perennial value of this land from before the colonialists arrived— and since.

DIYers: Money's not the point. Dinking around with the material world is where all the fun lies. Building, farming, tinkering, making, cooking, gardening, designing, creating, painting, or inventing. Unlike with minimalists, having junk around is part of the creative process for DIYers. These are conscious materialists— making the most of every scrap of life. A can-do attitude is as American as apple pie.

You don't have to identify with any of these to *want to* transform your relationship with money enough to overcome your inertia and be drawn ever onward—but you have to want something more than the status quo. Common to all people who do succeed are accountability, self-awareness, and empowerment. They actually do the steps.

Turtles and Hares

How fast people move toward their own Financial Independence varies. I call it a spectrum from turtles to hares.

The turtles use the program to slowly, steadily, methodically dig out of debt, moderate spending, and build savings with the assurance of arriving at some ripe middle age able to retire. They don't care how soon; they care that on the way they've built a family and served their community and their boss with integrity—and visited all the national parks.

The hares like speed, and often, like Joe, set an FI goal of age thirty. Having a deadline is motivating, like a sprint to the finish line. They see that the more they save, the sooner they are free, and they often become fixated on increasing the percentage of each paycheck squirreled away. They beg forbearance from friends and spouses, promising them gobs of attention on the other side.

Overall, whatever type you may or may not be, the key is to start—and keep going. True, the starting line isn't the same for everybody: There's a gradient of privilege in the USA, and factors such as upbringing, race, and gender can make this much, much more difficult for some than for others. Still, whether it's dreams of adventure and travel, of making a difference, of loving relationships and family, of self-knowledge and transcendence . . . the strength of your dreams and the grit of your commitment will move you forward.

Through the thousands of communications from fans we've received, we know some of the ways people's lives have been enriched by following this program:

- They finally understand the basics of money.
- At a tangible level, they settle their debts, increase their savings, and are able to live happily within their means.
- They reconnect with old dreams and find ways to realize them. With a great sense of freedom and relief, they learn how to distinguish between the essentials and the excess in all areas of their lives and how to unburden themselves.
- On average, people at all income levels reduce their expenses by 25 percent—and most feel happier, even if for the sake of their sanity they forsake a bit of income. They find that their relationships with their partners and children improve.
- Their new financial integrity resolves many inner conflicts between their values and their lifestyles.
- Money ceases to be an issue in their lives, and they finally have the intellectual and emotional space to take on issues of greater importance.
- They increase their free time by reducing expenses and the amount of time on the job.
- They stop buying their way out of problems and instead use these challenges as opportunities to learn new skills.
- Overall, they heal the split between their money and their life, and life becomes one integrated whole.

The Four FIs

This program is designed to liberate your mind and life from the thrall of the consumer culture. You don't just use a different strategy. You think differently. We call this FI thinking, which is being ever conscious of and curious about the flow of money in your life. Just reading this book will initiate FI thinking in your life, but there is more. Actually doing the simple steps outlined here will transform your relationship with money. You will master four FIs: Financial Intelligence (FI1), Financial Integrity

(FI2), Financial Independence (FI3), and Financial Inter-dependence (FI4). All of these will cascade naturally from applying these tools to the flow of money and stuff through your life.

Financial Intelligence

Financial Intelligence is the ability to step back from your assumptions and your emotions about money and observe them objectively. Does money really buy happiness? Does everyone really "gotta make a living"? Is money really something to fear or covet, to love or hate? If I sell the ma-jority of my time for money, will I really be secure?

Gaining Financial Intelligence begins with knowing how much money you already have earned, what you have to show for it, how much is coming into your life, and how much is going out.

But that isn't enough. You also need to know what money really is and what you are trading for the money in your life.

One tangible outcome of Financial Intelligence is get-ting out of debt and having at least six months of basic living expenses in the bank. If you follow the program presented in this book, it will lead inexorably to Finan-cial Intelligence.

Financial Integrity

The dictionary defines *integrity* as "1: firm adherence to a code of especially moral or artistic values: incor-ruptibility; 2: an unimpaired condition: soundness; 3: the quality or state of being complete or undivided: completeness."[3]

Financial Integrity is achieved by learning the true impact of your earning and spending, both on your im-mediate family and on the planet. It is knowing what is enough money and material goods to keep you at the peak of fulfillment—and what is just excess and clutter.

It is having all aspects of your financial life in alignment with your values. If you follow the program presented in this book, it will lead inexorably to Financial Integrity.

Financial Independence

Financial Independence encompasses a lot more than having a secure income. It is also independence from crippling financial beliefs, crippling debt, and a crippling inability to manage modern "conveniences." Financial Independence is anything that frees you from a dependence on money to handle your life.

Financial Interdependence

Along the way you realize that the independence we crave is a separation from dead-end routines, jobs, relationships, and ways of thinking—not from one another. Our happiest moments come from love and contribution, and we want more time for what makes life truly meaningful. Our interdependence—doing for one another, receiving from one another, creating with one another—is part of what makes our lives rich. Our interdependence is also a fact of life. We all depend on the services of the natural world. We all depend on shared institutions—from roads to airports to libraries to myriad safety nets to money itself—for a viable life. We float in a sea of interconnectedness. In fact, after achieving Financial Independence, most people (once they get enough rest and indulge some long-standing dreams) actually want to spend their time helping to make the world a better place.

What's New in This Edition

I've made literally thousands of adjustments to the prior edition of this book to reflect today's reality—and two chapters in particular have been significantly revised.

The advent of smartphones and the blogosphere and

the myriad of Internet tools for shopping and investing required a deep update of chapter 6 ("The American Dream—on a Shoestring"). The heaviest lift, though, was to remake chapter 9 ("Where to Stash Your Cash for Long-Term Financial Freedom"). The investment strategy that served Joe and others very well for twenty-five years is no longer the only or best way to create a steady passive income stream. With input from wonderful colleagues across several investment philosophies, chapter 9 now presents a range of strategies people in the FIRE movement use, resting on the same foundation of "think for yourself."

Readers of earlier versions will also notice a brand-new tool: **Money Talks**. The nine-step program necessarily focuses on what individuals can do to free themselves from the work-and-spend treadmill. No one but you can take responsibility for transforming your relationship with money. For Joe and me and many of you, though, social support has been a big key to waking up and making changes. In the new epilogue, I present the simple Money Talks methodology, a proven way to talk with friends and strangers about big subjects—and money is one of the biggest. In each chapter I offer a few potent questions you can raise in such conversations, whether in the privacy of your own journal, with a loved one, or in groups. When we talk with others about our dreams, confusion, fears, and persistent questions, change happens.

Let the Transformation Begin!

I hope that reading this introduction has whetted your appetite for learning about the nine-step program; such an appetite for change will get you to take the first step. I hope your curiosity has been piqued; curiosity will surely keep you moving. I hope your belief that you can change your future has gotten a boost. Next, read the whole book from start to finish. After that, come back to chapter 1 and begin your step-by-step journey toward transforming your relationship with money and achieving Financial Independence.

Repeat readers, welcome back, welcome home. And new readers, welcome to a set of tools that has liberated hundreds of thousands of people, with my sincere hope that you will be one of them. The world needs you to show up and follow your dreams.

YOUR MONEY
OR YOUR LIFE

1

The Money Trap:
The Old Road Map for Money

MONEY: THE TENDER TRAP?

"Your money or your life."

If someone thrust a gun in your ribs and said those words, what would you do? Most of us would turn over our wallets. The threat works because we value our lives more than we value our money. Or do we?

Rachel Z. worked seventy hours a week as a successful saleswoman, but that wasn't It. She reports, "After reading books like *The Poverty of Affluence* [by Paul Wachtel] I realized that my feeling that 'something was missing' wasn't something only I experienced. I began to talk with others and found they often felt similarly let down. Having gotten the prize of a comfortable home with all the trimmings, there was a sense of 'Is this all?' Do I have to work and work and then retire—worn out—to be put out to pasture? To do nothing then but to try to spend money I saved up and to waste my time till my life is over?"

Don M.'s love was music, but his life was working in data processing, and he'd all but given up the hope that love and life could go together. Unsure of what it meant to be a man, he'd assumed all the trappings of

adulthood and waited for the day when they'd cata-
pult him into manhood. He'd graduated from college
and gotten a wife, a skill, a job, a car, a house, a mortgage, and a lawn to mow. Instead of feeling like a
man, however, he felt increasingly trapped.

Elaine H. just plain hated her job as a computer
programmer. She did the bare minimum in order to
keep her job, but did it so well that she couldn't be
fired. She accumulated all the symbols of success—a
sports car, a house in the country—but they barely
balanced the boredom of her job. She went on to travel
and participate in a variety of workshops, but none of
these pleasures countered the doldrums of the workweek. She finally decided that this must be how the
rest of her life would be—with her job biting the center out of her life.

Kristy and her husband were classic DINKs—
double income, no kids—in high-paying tech jobs.
They were young, rich, and good-looking—what
could not be perfect about that? But then Kristy
watched her coworker collapse from stress and almost
die at his desk. In Japan they have a name for this:
karoshi (death by overwork). When Kristy saw this
same person come back to work a week later, acting
like nothing had happened, she knew something was
deeply wrong. Then her boss was hospitalized with a
blood clot, and her best friend was fired. Kristy started
popping anxiety meds and bolting awake at three a.m.
from stress. She thought, "I can't do this anymore. This
isn't worth it."

Nicole followed her father's script. He was a lawyer
and encouraged her to also get professional training,
bugger the cost, because she would easily pay it off
through her career. So Nicole got an advanced family
nurse practitioner degree, which took more than eight
years and left her well over $100,000 in debt. But it
wasn't 1969, the year her father graduated from law

school. It was 2011 and her net earnings after paying staff, office rent, overhead, insurance, and continuing education was not enough to pay her debt faster than the interest built up. She was sliding backward, even with a degree in one of the top in-demand professions. She admitted to a friend, "I don't think I will ever actually pay it off."

Brian's old friend Kevin stopped by on his way through town. In high school Kevin had been that middle-of-the-pack guy nobody noticed. Now he was raking in six figures annually from an online educational product business. Brian grilled Kevin about every detail because he wanted to support his family, be a stay-at-home dad, teach people effectiveness tools, and, truth be told, have it all be easy and quickly lucrative. He wanted what Kevin seemed to have. But while the online education business has a very low bar entry—anyone can piece together a few web services and, voilà, have paying students—success is not a guarantee. So Brian spent money learning from the best and more money buying the best tool, and the business actually took many more hours than he anticipated to set up and run. The expensive goose has, to date, failed to lay any golden eggs.

Even though some people really like their jobs, very few of us can say with honesty that our work lives are perfect. The perfect work life would offer enough challenge to be interesting. Enough ease to be enjoyable. Enough camaraderie to be nourishing. Enough solitude to be productive. Enough hours at work to get the job done. Enough leisure to feel refreshed. Enough contribution to feel needed. Enough silliness to have fun. And enough money to pay the bills . . . and then some. Even the best jobs have trade-offs. Midlife comes and we discover we've been living our parents' agenda. Or worse, we've been filling teeth for twenty years because some seventeen-year-old (was that really me?) decided that being a dentist would be the best of all possible worlds. We've joined the "real world," the world of compromise. For all the hype about "going for the gold," we're so weary at the end of the day that going for the sofa is as good as it gets.

Most of us cling as long as possible to the notion that there is a way to live that makes more sense, that brings more fulfillment and has more meaning, but over time, as our jobs wear a groove into our lives and our days fill with to-dos, the idea that we could have a more reward-ing existence seems to fade. The people you'll be reading about in this book have found that there is another way. There is a way to live an authentic, productive, mean-ingful life—and have all the material comforts you want or need. There is a way to balance your inner and outer lives, to have your job self be on good terms with your family self and your deeper self. There is a way to go about the task of making a living so that you end up more alive. There is a way to approach life so that when asked, "Your money or your life?" you say, "I'll take both, thank you."

We Aren't Making a Living, We're Making a Dying

For so many working people, however, from people who love their work to those who barely tolerate their jobs, there seems to be no real choice between their money and their lives. What they do for money domi-nates their waking hours, and life is what can be fit into the scant remaining time.

Consider the average worker in almost any urban in-dustrialized city. The alarm rings at six forty-five and our workingman or -woman is up and at it. Check the phone. Shower. Dress in the professional uniform—suits for some, coveralls for others, scrubs for the medical professionals, jeans and T-shirts for construction workers. Breakfast, if there's time. Grab commuter mug and briefcase (or lunch box). Hop in the car for the daily punishment called rush hour or get on a bus or train packed crushingly tight. On the job from nine to five (or longer). Deal with the boss. Deal with the coworker sent by the devil to rub you the wrong way. Deal with suppliers. Deal with clients/customers/patients. E-mails pile up. Act busy. Scroll through social media feeds. Hide mistakes. Smile when handed impossible deadlines. Give a sigh of relief when the ax known as "restructuring" or "downsizing"—or just plain getting laid off—falls on other heads. Shoulder the added workload. Watch the clock. Argue with your conscience but agree with the boss. Smile again. Five o'clock. Back in the car or on the bus or train for the evening commute. Home. Act human with your partner, kids, or roommates. Cook. Post a picture of your dinner online. Eat. Watch an episode of your favorite show. Answer one last e-mail. Bed. Eight hours of blessed oblivion—if we're lucky.

And they call this making a living? Think about it. How many people have you seen who are more alive at the end of the workday than they were at the beginning? Do we come home from our "making a living" activity with more life? Do we bound through the door, refreshed and energized, ready for a great evening with family and friends? Where's all the life we supposedly made at work? For many of us, isn't the truth of it closer to "making a dying"? Aren't we killing ourselves—our health, our relationships, our sense of joy and wonder—for our jobs? We are sacrificing our lives for money, but it's happening so slowly that we barely notice. Graying temples and thickening middles along with dubious signs of progress like a corner office, a company car, or tenure are the only landmarks of the passage of time. Eventually we may have all the necessities, niceties, and even luxuries we could ever want, but inertia itself keeps us locked into the nine-to-five pattern. After all, if we didn't work, what would we do with our time? The dreams we had of finding meaning and fulfillment through our jobs have faded into the reality of professional politics, burnout, boredom, and intense competition. That sense of wonder we had as children, that sense of mission we had in college, those times when love connected our hearts to all beings great and small are forgotten—all filed under "We were so young."

Even those of us who like our jobs and feel we're making a contribution have a sense that there is a larger arena we could enjoy, one that is beyond the world of nine-to-five: the fulfillment that would come from doing work we love with no limitations or restraints—and no fear of getting fired and joining the ranks of the unemployed. How many times do we think or say, "I would do it this way if I could, but the board members of the Zilch Foundation want it done their way"? How much have we had to compromise our dreams in order to keep our funding or our jobs?

We Think We Are Our Jobs

Even if we were financially able to turn our backs on jobs that limit our joy and insult our values, we are all too often psychologically unable to free ourselves. We take our identity and our self-worth from our jobs.

Our jobs have replaced family, neighborhood, civic affairs, church, and even partners as our primary allegiance, our principal source of love and site of self-expression. Reflect on that for yourself. Think about how you feel when you respond to that getting-to-know-you question "What do you do?" with "I am a _____." Do you feel pride? Do you feel shame? Do you want to say, "I'm only a _____," if you aren't meeting your own expectations for yourself? Do you feel superior? Inferior? Defensive? Do you tell the truth? Do you give an exotic title to a mundane occupation to increase your status?

Have we come to measure our worth as human beings by the size of our paychecks? When swapping tales at high school reunions, how do we secretly assess the success of our peers? Do we ask whether our classmates are fulfilled, living true to their values, or do we ask them where they work, what their positions are, where they live, what they drive, and where they are sending their kids to college? These are the recognized symbols of success.

Along with racism and sexism, our society has a hidden hierarchy based on what you do for money. That's called jobism, and it pervades our interactions with one another on the job, in social settings, and even at home. Why else would we consider stay-at-home moms second-class citizens? Or consider teachers lower-status than doctors even though their desk-side manner with struggling students has equal merit to many doctors' bedside manner with the ill and dying? Whether we realize it or not, our daily interactions involve the unconscious sizing up of how each of us "makes a living."

The High Cost of Making a Dying

Psychotherapist Douglas LaBier documented this "social disease" in his book *Modern Madness*. The steady stream of "successful" professionals who showed up in his office with exhausted bodies and empty souls alerted him to the mental and physical health hazards of our regard for materialism. LaBier found that focusing on money/position/success at the expense of personal fulfillment and meaning had led 60 percent of his sample of several hundred to suffer from depression, anxiety, and other job-related disorders, including the ubiquitous "stress."[1]

Even though the official workweek has been pegged at forty hours for nearly half a century, many professionals believe they must work overtime and weekends to keep up. A 2015 study from the Organisation for Economic

Co-operation and Development (OECD) discovered that nearly 12 percent of Americans are working fifty or more hours per week.[2] In addition, a Conference Board study of the same year found that less than half of Americans are "satisfied" with their jobs.[3] We are working more, but enjoying life less. The result? We have developed a national disease based on how we earn money.

What Do We Have to Show for It?

Even if we aren't any happier, you'd think that we'd at least have the traditional symbol of success: money in the bank. Not so. Our savings rate has actually gone down.

According to the US Bureau of Economic Analysis, the US personal savings rate has hovered around 5 percent over the past four years, up from a low of less than 2 percent in 2007 but down from the pre-1980 days when Americans saved well over 10 percent.[4]

Making matters worse are stagnating wages for the vast majority of Americans. While those on top (and the corporations they work for) continue lining their pockets, wealth is siphoned from individuals at the bottom. In a 2016 report, the Economic Policy Institute discovered that wages for the lowest 70 percent of workers had grown a marginal 5.3 percent since 2000, while the poorest 10 percent of Americans saw only a 2.2 percent improvement in pay. How did the highest wage earners fare over that time period? Since the turn of the millennium, the 90th and 95th percentile of wage earners experienced 15.7 percent and 19.8 percent growth respectively.

With relatively lower wages and less savings, our level of debt has gone up—way up. By late 2017, consumer debt had topped $3.7 trillion, more than double the total at the end of 2000. That's more than $11,000 for every man, woman, and child in the country.[5] Debt is one of our main shackles. Our levels of debt and our lack of savings make the nine-to-five routine mandatory. Between our mortgages, car financing, student loans, and credit card debt, we can't afford to quit. More and more Americans are ending up living in their cars or on the streets.

In a time of increasing globalism and corporate mergers, layoffs in every sector from manufacturing to high tech are the new reality.

We Make a Dying at Work so We Can Live It Up on the Weekend

Consider now the average consumer, spending his or her hard-earned money. Saturday. Take your clothes to the cleaners and your car to the service station to have the tires rotated and the funny noise checked out. Go to the grocery store to buy a week's worth of food for the family and grumble at the checkout that you remember when four sacks of groceries used to cost $75 instead of $125. (Sure, you could cut costs by clipping coupons and shopping sales, but who has time?) Go to the mall to buy the book everyone is reading. Emerge with two books, a suit (half-price on sale) with shoes to match, and some new clothes for the kids—all paid for with a credit card. Home. Yard work. Oops . . . a trip to the nursery for pruning shears. Come home with two flats of primroses, some new pots . . . and, oh yes, the pruning shears. Fiddle with the toaster that's burning every slice, even on the lightest setting. Fail to find the warranty. Go to the home improvement store to buy a new one. Come out with shelves and brackets for the den, color samples for painting the kitchen . . . and, oh yes, the toaster. Dinner out with your partner, leaving the kids with a sitter. Sunday morning. Pancakes for the whole family. Oops . . . no flour. To the grocery store for flour. Come home with frozen strawberries and blueberries for the pancakes, maple syrup, Sumatra coffee . . . and, oh yes, the flour. Take the family to the lake for a swim. Buy gas; wince at the price. Drive to a cute restaurant in the country, paying for dinner with the credit card. Home. Spend the evening watching TV, allowing the ads to float you on fantasies of the really good life available if you'd only buy a Porsche or an exotic vacation or a new computer or . . .

The bottom line is that we think we work to pay the bills—but we spend more than we make on more than we need, which sends us back to work to get the money to spend to get more stuff—that sends us back to work again!

What About Happiness?

If the daily grind were making us happy, the irritations and inconveniences would be a small price to pay. If we could believe that our jobs were actually making the world a better place, we would sacrifice sleep and social lives without feeling deprived. If the extra toys we buy with our toil were providing anything more than momentary pleasure and a chance to one-up others, we'd spend those hours on the job gladly. But it is becoming increasingly clear that, beyond a certain minimum of comfort, money is not buying us the happiness we seek.

Participants in our early live seminars, whatever the size of their incomes, always said they needed "more" to be happy. We included this exercise in our seminars: We asked people to rate themselves on a happiness scale of 1 (miserable) to 5 (joyous), with 3 being "can't complain," and we correlated their ratings with their incomes. In a sample of more than 1,000 people, from both the United States and Canada, the average happiness score was consistently between 2.6 and 2.8 (not even a 3!), whether the person's income was under $1,500 a month or over $6,000 a month. (See Figure 1-1.)

FIGURE 1-1
Life Rating Scale

Select the list that most closely applies to your life right now.				
1	2	3	4	5
Uncomfortable	Dissatisfied	Content	Happy	Joyous
Tired	Seeking	Doing OK	Growing	Enthusiastic
Incomplete	Not enough	Average	Satisfied	Fulfilled
Frustrated	Relationships could be better	Acceptable	Productive	Overflowing
Fearful		Sometimes happy, sometimes blue	Relaxed	Ecstatic
Frequently lonely	Coping		Free of tension	Powerful
Angry	Getting better		Efficient	Making a difference
Need love	Not very productive	Stable	Time available	
Insecure	Need reassurance	Normal	Fun	
		Few risks	Secure	
		Fitting in		

Select the list that most closely applies to your life right now.					
Monthly income	$0–1500	$1501–3000	$3001–4500	$4501–6000	Over $6000
Average of quality-of-life rating for all participants in that income range	2.81	2.77	2.84	2.86	2.63

The results astounded us. They told us that not only are most people habitually unhappy, but they can be unhappy no matter how much money they make. Even people who are doing well financially are not necessarily fulfilled. On those same worksheets we asked our seminar participants, "How much money would it take to make you happy?" Can you guess the results? It was always "more than I have now" (by 50 to 100 percent).

So here we are, the most affluent society that has had the privilege to walk the face of the earth, and we're stuck with our noses to the grindstone, our lives in a perpetual loop between home and job, and our hearts yearning for something that's just over the horizon or perhaps entirely out of reach.

PROSPERITY AND THE PLANET

If this was just a private hell it would be tragedy enough. But it's not. Our affluent lifestyles are having an increasingly devastating effect on our planet.

In 1987, the United Nations World Commission on Environment and Development warned that consumption patterns in the developed world were one of the primary engines driving global environmental damage. Since that time, however, little in our lifestyles has changed—except better technology to impulse-shop.

Our failure to change is not from a lack of warning. Some tune out the data entirely, but even if we watch the news, we don't know what to believe anymore—or why we should care.

Environmentalists have been trying to make the data feel vivid and personal, so that we can feel the planet heating the way we feel chilly when the temperature drops.

The Ecological Footprint, a metric distributed by the Global Footprint Network, measures everything we buy—from cars to sofas—in terms of how much of the earth's resources are embodied in that purchase. You can take a quiz about your consumption and see what your footprint is. Even careful, conscious North Americans would learn that if everyone consumed the way they do, we'd need four earths. Oh, but we have only one.

Every year, in partnership with the World Wildlife Fund, the Global Footprint Network announces Earth Overshoot Day, the annual date when we've collectively used up the resources our planet can renew in a single year before going into ecological debt. In 1971, Earth Overshoot Day fell on December 21. Ten years later it was November 12. Then October 11 in 1991. In 2001 it fell on September 23. On and on, earlier and earlier. In 2016 it was August 3. Check it out. What is it now? The earth's stores are Mother Nature's cupboard. How long before an essential ingredient in the recipe for life as we know it is no longer available?

When we go into personal debt, we might lose our car, our house, or our ability to borrow at all, but as long as we are alive we can start filling the coffers again. With ecological debt, that doesn't work. We have only one planet.

The Biggest Loser in the Money Game

Sadly, many of us are not even aware of this ecological debt because our primary benefactors don't have a voice and we didn't even know we were borrowing from them. We haven't just borrowed from "the bank." We've borrowed from future generations, and from our very generous planet.

Everything we eat, wear, drive, buy, and throw away comes from the earth. As Annie Leonard vividly shows in her short film *The Story of Stuff*, our appetite for things drives a one-way trip for resources from the earth to factory to store to our house to the dump. We have ignored the fact that we enjoy our current level of affluence by the good (and free) graces of nature—soil, water, and air, which cost nothing yet are being taxed to the limit. As civilized and advanced as we may have become, we still depend on breathable air, potable water, and fertile soil for our daily existence.

No matter how often these facts are repeated, however,

we don't seem able to put the brakes on our consumption. Corporations have little incentive to encourage us to consume less. Politically it's still suicidal to propose consumption-limiting legislation. And personally, until everyone changes, few are willing to sacrifice.

The only way green corporations, local governments, and nonprofit organizations have been able to change us at all is to convince us that the three sirens of consumerism—comfort, control, and convenience—are better served by products that demand less from the earth. Once the cost of solar energy became competitive, adoption accelerated. As electric car charging stations become as convenient as gas stations, consumers will adopt this climate-friendlier way of personal transportation. We aren't changing our minds; we're just changing our technologies. Is this enough? Not according to Robert Ornstein and Paul Ehrlich. In their book, *New World New Mind*, they point out that our minds were designed to respond well to short-term threats—tigers and fires and the whites of our enemies' eyes. In today's world, however, piling debts (personal and national) and environmental threats like climate change are building up so slowly that the part of our minds made to respond to harm can't register the danger. We must, Ornstein and Ehrlich contend, learn to react to the early warnings of sophisticated environmental measurements with the same vigor with which we used to climb trees to escape the jaws of a tiger.[6]

Some consumers *are* motivated to change—they look at these ecological trends and become early adopters of green energy innovations. You may be one of them. But virtue isn't enough to accelerate the pace of change. As you will see, breaking the hold of the more-is-better myth on your mind means you will change because you want to, not because you have to. You will also gain those status points for being one of the first to adopt what everyone comes to know is the best, smartest, and optimal way to go. You will see clearly that making a dying and having it all are not the only or best ways to make a life—and you will free yourself.

Is More Better?

Many of us are out there making a dying because we've bought into the pervasive consumer myth that more is better. We build our working lives on this myth of more. Our expectation is to make more money as the years go on. We will get greater responsibility and more perks as we move up in our field. Eventually, we hope, we will have more possessions, more prestige, and more respect from our community. We become habituated to expecting ever more of ourselves and ever more from the world, but rather than satisfaction, our experience is that the more we have, the more we want—and the less content we are with the status quo.

In part, the materially expansive frontiersman mentality at the heart of the North American psyche explains our obsession with more; even space on *Star Trek* was called "the final frontier." The West was "won" (or lost, depending on your point of view) through the political sales pitch of Manifest Destiny.

For Americans (and increasingly for consumers in other nations) this "more is better" motto leads us to trade in our car every three years, buy new clothes for every event and every season, get a bigger and better house every time we can afford it, and upgrade everything from our TV to our smartphone simply because a new version has been released. All this stuff isn't just taking a toll on the earth: National Opinion Research Center surveys reveal that the percentage of Americans who describe themselves as "very happy" has been steadily declining since the late 1950s.

"More is better" turns out to be a formula for dissatisfaction. If you live for having it all, what you have is never enough. In an environment of more is better, "enough" is like the horizon—always receding. You lose the ability to identify that point of sufficiency at which you can choose to stop. This is a psychological cul-de-sac, an invisible catch-22 of the consumer myth of more. If more is better, then what I have is not enough. Even when I do get the more I was convinced would make life better, however, I am still operating on the belief that more is better—so the more I now have still isn't enough. But hope springs eternal. If I could only get more, then . . . and on and on we go. We get deeper in debt and often deeper in despair. The more that was supposed to make life better can never be enough.

The Limits to Growth

Our economy's version of "more is better" is "growth is good." Modern economics worships growth. Growth will solve poverty, the theory goes. Growth will increase our standard of living. Growth will reduce unemployment. Growth will keep us apace with inflation. Growth will relieve the boredom of the rich and the misery of the poor. Growth will bolster the GDP, boost the Dow, and beat our global competitors. A rising tide lifts all boats, right?

What we overlook is that all the feedstock for economic growth comes from nature, and even under the best of circumstances, nature is not infinitely abundant. Resources can and do run out.

There are limits in nature. At a physical level, nothing grows forever. Every plant and every animal has a life cycle. Once it reaches an optimal size it stops growing bigger, investing life energy instead in its survival and reproduction. We also know that every population of plants or animals reaches a maximum number, based on the finite resources of energy, food, water, soil, and air, and then begins to stabilize or decrease in size. There always comes a point where the individual or the specific population either collapses or dies off due to lack of resources, or stabilizes at a level that the environment can handle.

By ignoring this fundamental reality of the natural world, we as individuals—and our economy—are now exceeding the earth's capacity to handle our demands, as Earth Overshoot Day vividly demonstrates.

The Cleopatra Explanation

Pam Tillis had it right in her 1993 song with the refrain, "Just call me Cleopatra, everybody, 'cause I'm the Queen of Denial." For so many people, the stronger the evidence of failed strategies, the *deeper* they cling to their ways.

We don't have to change, we say, because we're sure technology will save us. After all, look at the past. Science and technology have eliminated deadly diseases from smallpox to diphtheria. Surely we'll develop the technology to purify our water, genetically engineer seeds that can grow in extreme environments, clean up pollution, and find the key to unlimited cheap energy. And if technology doesn't save us, surely the government will. Look at our social progress as a species. If we lobby for appropriations, the government will develop a program. There are experts who know what's going on and are handling it for us. Anyway, we conclude, it's not my problem. It's a Third World problem. If only "they" would stop having so many babies and burning their forests, we'd survive. It's they who need to change. In any event, it would be silly for us to change because the reports are probably wrong. Scientists and politicians and the media have lied to us before. This environmental problem is a fabrication of some smart lawyers and Nervous Nellie alarmists. And anyway, what can *I* do? After all, I'm in debt, so I can't stop commuting forty miles a day to the widget factory, even if the continuation of life on earth depended on it, which it doesn't . . . does it?

As people and as a planet we suffer from upward mobility and downward nobility. We need to pause and wonder if it's all worth it, if we're getting the fulfillment we're seeking. And if not, why do we persist, like addicts, in habits that are killing us?

The Creation of Consumers

Perhaps we cling to our affluence—even though it isn't working for us or the planet—because of the very nature of our relationship with money. As we shall see, money has become the movie screen on which our lives play out. We project onto money the capacity to fulfill our fantasies, allay our fears, soothe our pain, and send us soaring to new heights. In fact, we now meet most of our needs, wants, and desires through money. We buy everything from hope to happiness. We no longer live life. We consume it.

People in industrialized nations used to be called "citizens." Now we are "consumers"—which means (according to the dictionary definition of "consume") people who "use up," "waste," "destroy," and "squander." Consumerism, however, is just a twentieth-century invention of our industrial society, created at a time when encouraging people to buy more goods was seen as necessary for continued economic growth.

By the early 1920s, once we were starting to win the Industrial Revolution, a curious wrinkle had emerged. The astounding capacity of machinery to fill human needs had been so successful that economic activity was slowing down. Instinctively knowing they had enough, American workers were asking for a shorter workweek and more leisure to enjoy the fruits of their labors. Two sectors of American society were alarmed at this trend. The moralists, who had internalized the Protestant work ethic, believed that "idle hands do the devil's work." Leisure is debasing, they thought, leading at least to sloth, if not to the rest of the seven deadly sins. Industrialists also sounded the alarm. Reduced demand for factory output threatened to halt economic growth. Workers did not seem as instinctively eager to buy new goods and services (like cars, appliances, and entertainment) as they did the old ones (like food, clothing, and shelter).

The alternative to growth, however, was seen not as maturity but as the precursor to the stagnation of civilization and the death of productivity. New markets were needed for the expanding cornucopia of goods that machines could turn out with such speed and precision and for the continued profit of the industrialists. And here's the stroke of genius: These new markets would consist of the same populace, but the people would be educated to want not only what they needed but also new things that they didn't need. Enter the concept of "standard of living." A new art, science, and industry dubbed "marketing" was born to convince Americans that they were working to elevate their standard of living rather than to satisfy basic economic needs. In 1929 Herbert Hoover's Committee on Recent Economic Changes published a progress report on this new (and very welcome, he believed) strategy:

> The survey has proved conclusively what has long been held theoretically to be true, that wants are almost insatiable; that one want satisfied makes way for another. The conclusion is that economically we have a boundless field before us; that there are new wants which will make way endlessly for newer wants, as fast as they are satisfied. . . . Our situation is fortunate, our momentum is remarkable.[7]

Instead of leisure being simply "relaxed activity," it was transformed into an opportunity for increased consumption—even consumption of leisure itself (as in travel and vacations). Henry Ford concurred:

> Where people work less they buy more . . . business is the exchange of goods. Goods are bought only as

they meet needs. Needs are filled only as they are felt. They make themselves felt largely in the leisure hours.[8]

The Hoover Commission agreed. Leisure was not, in fact, an excuse to relax. It was a hole to fill up with more wants (which, in turn, required more work to pay for them). Somehow the consumer solution satisfied both the industrial hedonists hell-bent on achieving a material paradise and the puritans who feared that unoccupied leisure would lead to sin. In fact, the new consumerism promoted all the deadly sins (lust, covetousness, gluttony, pride, envy) except perhaps anger and sloth.

Only temporarily subdued by the Depression, consumerism returned with added vigor in the post–World War II era. In 1955 US retailing analyst Victor Lebow observed:

> Our enormously productive economy . . . demands that we make consumption our way of life, that we convert the buying and use of goods into rituals, that we seek our spiritual satisfaction, our ego satisfaction, in consumption. . . . We need things consumed, burned up, worn out, replaced, and discarded at an ever-increasing rate.[9]

And thus the rat race was born, leading to our excruciating balancing act between working more to buy luxuries and having enough leisure to enjoy them. Today, that has taken on added dimension: With the intrusion of the Internet and smartphones into every waking moment of our lives, we can be consumers wherever and whenever. From desire to delivery, almost anything we want is only a few swipes, taps, or clicks away. What was once a privilege for the few now seems like a right for the masses. In our initial enthusiasm for our new status as consumers, we learned to assert our rights, standing up to unscrupulous business. "Rights," however, have since taken on a different hue.

The Right to Buy

Americans have come to believe, deeply, that it is our right to consume. If we have the money, we can buy whatever we want, whether or not we need it, use it, or even enjoy it. After all, it's a free country. And if we don't have the money . . . heck, what are credit cards for? Born to shop. Whoever dies with the most toys wins. Life, liberty, and the pursuit of material possessions.

Not only have we absorbed the notion that it is right to buy—but we believe consuming is what keeps America strong. If we don't consume, we're told, masses of people will be thrown out of work. Families will lose their homes. Unemployment will rise. Factories will shut down. Whole towns will lose their economic base. We have to buy gadgets to keep America strong. Why else would the Consumer Confidence Index be a benchmark for America's continued dominance?

Part of why our consumers have less money to spend is that saving has clearly become un-American. Even the language of modern economics promotes consumption. What else would we do with "disposable" income besides dispose of it?—we certainly wouldn't want to keep it around, where it would just rot!

So if consuming is the way to keep the economy strong and savers are people willing to put their fellow citizens out of work, an online shopping spree can be considered downright patriotic. The only downside is that our rising expectations have outstripped our incomes, leaving the average consumer-patriot increasingly in debt. This puts us in a bind: The only way for us to exercise our economic patriotism is to go deeper into debt. We are in a no-win situation. You're wrong if you buy and wrong if you don't.

All of this is exacerbated by advertising. The average American child aged two to eleven sees more than twenty-five thousand advertisements a year.[10] Globally, advertising spending is well over $500 billion.[11] These ads influencing our wants and desires used to be confined to TVs, print media, and billboards, but in the digital age, they follow us everywhere. As Americans spend increasing amounts of time on their mobile devices, pop-ups, flashing banners, and sidebar ads are there to greet us—reminding us of past browser searches and online purchases.

Marketing theory says that people are driven by fear, by the promise of exclusivity, by guilt and greed, and by the need for approval. Advertising technology, armed with market research and sophisticated psychology, aims to throw us off balance emotionally—and then promises to resolve our discomfort with a product.

At the same time, television, phone, radio, Internet, and newspaper ads are reporting the bad news about the environment. Product packaging is clogging the landfills. Product manufacturing is contributing to climate change, polluting the groundwater, deforesting the Amazon, fouling the rivers, and lowering the water table. If I wear clothes made from conventionally grown cotton, I'm encouraging massive pesticide use. If I wear synthetic fabrics, I use fossil fuels. If I wear nothing, I'm putting people out of work. It's damned if we do and damned if we don't.

It seems there is no way consumers can be right. Everything we do exacts a cost from the environment. Even new "eco-friendly" or "sustainable" products are only comparatively less stressful to the earth and by no means benign.

Clearly we don't think about this as we're headed to work in the morning. We don't ponder, "To consume or not to consume—that is the question." The notion that it's right to consume daily bumps into the admonition that we're deep in debt personally and playing Russian roulette with the environment to boot.

How in the midst of our busy lives can we become aware of, much less do something about, the enormous problems we're facing? "What can one person do?" we ask, and then change stations on the radio. And so we continue, making a stab at changing one week, bingeing the next, and depending on denial to shield us from the tough choices ahead.

If we continue to rely on making small, token changes, however, we will merely slow our headlong rush toward a diminished and impoverished future. What's needed isn't change; it is transformation. Change seeks different solutions to intractable problems. Transformation asks different questions so that we can see the problems in a new light.

We need to shift from an ethic of growth to an ethic of sustainability, which will certainly require each one of us to transform our relationship with money and the material world. Reevaluating our earning and spending activity could put our lives, our society, and the global commons back on track. We need to learn from our past, determine our present reality, and create a new, reality-based relationship with money, discarding assumptions and myths that don't work. We need a new road map for money and materialism—one that is truly in tune with the times.

THE BEGINNING OF A
NEW ROAD MAP FOR MONEY

What makes consuming so all-consuming? While the advertising industry may have conspired to sell us on materialism, the fact is, we bought it. Why?

Psychologists call money the "last taboo." It is easier to tell our therapist about our sex life than it is to tell our accountant about our finances. Money—not necessarily how much we have, but how we feel about it—governs our lives as much as or more than any other factor. Aside from complaining or gossiping, money as a legitimate and interesting topic just doesn't come up between friends or even between partners. Why not? What do we stand to lose by having an honest talk about money?

Patterns of Belief

To begin to understand this, we need to understand a bit about the human mind. Numerous sources, from modern brain researchers to ancient Eastern philosophers, seem to agree on the basic notion that the mind is a pattern-making and pattern-repeating device. Rather than having a fixed behavioral response for every stimulus, as some animals do, humans tend to create patterns of response. Some come from personal experience, primarily in the first five years of life. Some are genetic. Some are cultural. Some seem to be universal. All of them are there, presumably, to increase our chances of survival. Once a pattern is recorded, once it's been tested and deemed useful for survival, it becomes very hard to change. We salivate to the smell of sautéing onions, step on the brakes at the sight of a red light, and pump adrenaline when someone yells, "Fire!" Clearly we couldn't survive if we didn't have these huge libraries of interpretations coupled with behaviors.

But here's the problem: Not all of these patterns have anything to do with objective reality—yet they persist, governing our behavior. They are so tenacious, in fact, that we will often ignore or deny reality itself in favor of one of our interpretations. Does walking under a ladder or breaking a mirror really bring bad luck? Most of us are beyond such primitive superstitions. But what about other, less suspect beliefs? How do we catch a cold? By going outdoors with a wet head? By being exposed to germs? The former we recognize as an old wives' tale, but the latter? After all, there are people who don't get the cold going around the office. Did the germs skip them? Could the germ theory be just a modern superstition? Which of our beliefs will look quaint to future generations?

What Do Our Actions Say?

Is it possible that some of our financial beliefs are no more reality based than the flat-Earth theory? Could that be true? What does our financial behavior reveal about our superstitions? Are we willing to outgrow these the way we outgrew the conviction that there were monsters under our childhood beds?

For example, while we might vigorously maintain that we know money can't buy happiness and the best things in life are free, honesty requires that we look deeper. Our behavior tells a different story.

What do we do when we are depressed, when we are lonely, when we feel unloved? More often than not we buy something to make us feel better. A new outfit. A drink (or two). A new car. An ice cream cone. A trip to Hawaii. A goldfish. A ticket to the movies. A bag of Oreos (or two).

When we want to celebrate good fortune, we buy something. A round of drinks. A catered wedding. A bouquet of roses. A diamond ring.

When we are bored, we buy something. A magazine. A cruise. A mobile app. A bet on the horses.

When we think there must be more to life, we buy something. A workshop. A self-help book. A house in the country. A condo in the city.

None of this is wrong. It's just what we do. We have learned to seek external solutions to signals from the mind, heart, or soul that something is out of balance. We try to satisfy essentially psychological and spiritual needs with consumption at a physical level. How did this happen?

Here's an illustration.

FIGURE 1-2

The Fulfillment Curve: *Enough*

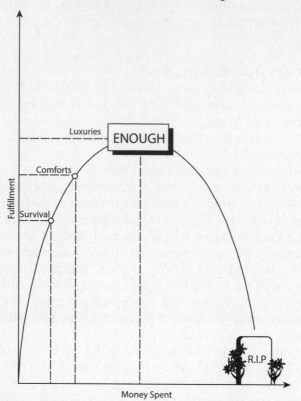

The Fulfillment Curve

The fulfillment curve (see Figure 1-2) shows the relationship between the experience of fulfillment and the amount of money we spend (usually to acquire more possessions). In the beginning of our lives, more possessions did indeed mean more fulfillment. Basic needs were met. We were fed. We were warm. We were sheltered. Most of us don't remember the fear of cold and hunger that was remedied by just a blanket and a breast—but we all went through it. When we were un-comfortable, when we cried, something came from the outside to take care of us. It seemed like magic. Our needs were filled. We survived. Our minds recorded each such incident and remembered: Have a need? Let that mysterious magic need-filling machine know what you need (Cry. Cry louder. Grab. Wave your hands. Ask, if you have words. Whatever works.) and it will deliver it and you will return to happiness. *Need. Look outside yourself. Get stuff. Get fulfillment.*

We then went from bare necessities (food, clothing, shelter) to some niceties (toys, a wardrobe, a bicycle), and the positive relationship between new things and fulfillment became even more deeply embedded. Remember your excitement as a child when you got a toy you'd been dying for? If our parents were being responsible, they soon taught us, "Those things cost money, dear. Money that we go out and earn for you—because we love you." Ahhh. New rule. *Need. Look outside yourself. Get money. Get stuff. Get fulfillment.* We got an allowance to learn the value of money. We could select and purchase happiness ourselves! And so it went, year after year.

Eventually we slipped beyond niceties to outright luxuries—and hardly registered the change. A car, for example, is a luxury that the vast majority of the world's population never enjoys. For us, however, our first car is the beginning of a lifelong love affair with the automobile. Then there's the luxury of our first trip away from home or going away to college. Our first apartment. Notice that while each one was still a thrill, it cost more per thrill and the "high" wore off more quickly.

But by then we believed that money equals fulfillment, so we barely noticed that the curve had started to level out. On we went into life. House. Job. Family responsibilities. More money brought more worry, more time and energy commitments as we rose up the corporate ladder. More time away from the family. More to lose if we were robbed, so more worry about being robbed. More taxes and more tax accountants' fees. More demands from community charities. Remodeling bills. Internet, TV, and phone bills. Just-keeping-the-kids-happy bills.

Until one day we found ourselves sitting, unfulfilled, in our big home on two and a half wooded acres with a three-car garage and expensive exercise equipment in the basement, yearning for the life we had as poor college students who could find joy in a walk in the park. We hit a fulfillment ceiling and never recognized that the formula of *money = fulfillment* not only had stopped working but had started to work against us. No matter how much we bought, the fulfillment curve kept heading down.

Enough: The Peak of the Curve

There's a very interesting place on this graph—it's the peak. Part of the secret to life, it would seem, comes from identifying for yourself that point of maximum fulfillment. There is a name for this peak of the fulfillment curve, and it provides the basis for transforming your relationship with money. It's a word we use every day, yet we are practically incapable of recognizing it when it's staring us in the face. The word is *enough*. At the peak of the fulfillment curve we have enough. Enough necessities for our survival. Enough niceties for our comforts and pleasures. And even enough little "luxuries." We have everything we need; there's nothing extra to weigh us down, distract or distress us, nothing we've bought on credit, have never used, and are slaving to pay off. Enough is a fearless place. A trusting place. An honest and self-observant place. It's appreciating and fully enjoying what money brings into your life and yet never purchasing anything that isn't needed and wanted. Once you have discovered what is enough for you, your fulfillment curve can reverse direction and head straight up. Stay tuned.

Clutter: A Fate Worse Than Dearth

So what's all that stuff beyond enough—beyond the peak, where the fulfillment curve begins to go down? Clutter, that's what! Clutter is anything that is excess—for you. It's whatever you have that doesn't serve you, yet takes up space in your world. To let go of clutter, then, is not dearth (lack); it's lightening up and opening up space for something new to happen. As self-evident as these ideas may be, many people experience a subtle (or not so subtle) resistance to letting them in. This is why downscaling, frugality, and thrift sound like deprivation, lack, and need. On the contrary! Enough is a wide and stable plateau. It is a place of alertness, creativity, and freedom. From this place, being suffocated under a mountain of clutter that must be stored, cleaned, moved, gotten rid of, and paid for on time is a fate worse than dearth.

Stations of the Crass

What creates clutter? The fulfillment curve strongly suggests that most clutter enters our lives through the "more is better" door. It comes from the disease of materialism, of looking for inner fulfillment in outer possessions. It comes from the early programming that discomfort can be alleviated by something external—a baby bottle, a blanket, a bicycle, a BA, a BMW or, eventually, another kind of bottle.

It also comes from unconscious habit. Take gazingus pins. A *gazingus pin* is any item that you just can't pass by without buying. Everybody has them. They run the gamut from earbuds and tiny screwdrivers to shoes, pens, and chocolate kisses. So there you are in the mall or online, a shopping robot on your weekly tour of the stations of the crass. You come to the gazingus pin section and your mind starts cranking out gazingus pin thoughts: Oh, there's a pink one . . . I don't have a pink one. . . . Oh, that one is wireless . . . that would be handy. . . . My, a waterproof one . . . if I don't use it, I can always give it away. . . . Yum, this one has hazelnuts in it . . . and coconut . . . and amaretto . . . never had one of those before. . . . And before you know it, an alien arm (attached to your body) has reached out and picked up (or clicked on) the gazingus pin, and off you go to the checkout, still functioning like a windup zombie. You arrive home with your purchase (or it arrives on your doorstep), you put it in the gazingus pin drawer (where there are already five or ten others), and you forget about gazingus pins until your next shopping trip, at which point you come to the gazingus pin section and . . .

Faces and Functions of Clutter

Just because something is out of sight doesn't mean it isn't clutter. Our various gazingus pin drawers— including our attics, basements, garages, closets, and storage sheds—are havens of clutter, filled with projects we'll never finish and products we'll probably never use. Ignoring them can fill you with shame. Sorting through them can fill you with guilt. Clothing bagged for the thrift store after a few wearings leaves a vague feeling of dissatisfaction and superficiality—not to mention adding to the landfill.

Once you catch on to what clutter is, you'll find it everywhere. Isn't meaningless activity a form of clutter? How many of the power lunches, cocktail parties, social events, and long evenings glued to your screens have been clutter—activities that add nothing positive to your life? What about disorganized days full of busyness with no sense of accomplishment? And what about tasks on your to-do list that never get done? Stumbling over them, week in, week out, on your list is like the frustration of navigating the perennial magazines and kids' toys that litter some people's living rooms.

There are cluttered motives, such as when we are of

many minds about everything from public policy to personal decisions. Unplanned errands are often time clutter—running to the store twice a day for items forgotten on your weekly shopping trip. Hobbies are clutter intensive when the ratio of what you have to what you use climbs—like the photography buffs with suitcases full of lenses and filters who get their best shots with a smartphone. All of that is clutter—elements in your environment that don't serve you yet take up space.

As your awareness of clutter deepens, you'll be inspired to spring-clean your whole life. The urge to purge, in fact, runs deep in the American psyche as well. From the Puritans to Thoreau, the Quakers, and authors like Duane Elgin and Cecile Andrews, simple living has arisen again and again to balance the excesses of our capitalist system. Now it's called minimalism or "tidying up." We call it "enough" because there is no particular, specific thing that is enough, which means it's up to you. It's not "less is more." It's not one perfect daisy in a vase on a spotless dresser with sun pouring through the window. It's not torn jeans or a little black dress. It's not that one perfect chef's knife, alone in a drawer. It's the Goldilocks feeling of just-rightness you recognize as you approach having enough of everything you want and need—but nothing in excess. Everyone's enough looks different—one person's treasure is another person's trash.

As you follow the nine steps outlined in this book, you will develop your own personal definition of clutter and will slowly, painlessly, even joyfully rid yourself of it. The first step will be to ask, "How did it all get here? And what is it worth to me now? Really?" Just as some students learn how much they throw away by having to carry their garbage around in a sack for a week, you will start to look at your relationship with stuff by looking at all you've accumulated, all you've earned, all you've spent, and how much of your life energy you've wasted.

Step 1: Making Peace with the Past

Are you ready to survey your own relationship with money and the things that money can buy? The purpose of this exercise is to increase your awareness, not your arrogance or your shame. It helps you to locate yourself in time and space, to review—without blame—your earning and spending activity in the past.

A caveat before we continue. Stop. Read this. It's important. While this is step 1 of the FI program, you don't have to do it first. And you don't have to stop reading until you do it. You need to do it eventually, but you could start with step 2 and come back to this step later. In fact, we suggest that you read the whole book first, rather than doing each step as it comes up; then come back and get started.

There are two parts to this step:

A. Find out how much money you have earned in your lifetime—the sum total of your gross income, from the first penny you ever earned to your most recent paycheck.

B. Find out your net worth by creating a personal balance sheet of assets and liabilities.

A. HOW MUCH HAVE
YOU EARNED IN YOUR LIFE?

Initially this task may seem impossible. "I haven't kept track!" you may protest. However, a little bit of archaeology pays off. First, dig out your copies of old income-tax returns. Adjust the figures to reflect any cheating you did—tips you didn't report, jobs that paid you under the table, informal consulting, gambling winnings, gifts from relatives that went unreported, any money you've stolen, cash prizes you've won, rent collected from the extra room in your house or the extra house you never use, and all other unreported income. Go down memory lane to those summer jobs you had during high school and college, and all the twists and turns of your own financial meandering through early adulthood and beyond. Spend a few days with whatever financial records you may have stashed away: old bank statements, old paychecks, and abandoned account books. Too young for all that paper? Get your online records from your bank. If you have a résumé, use it as an outline for a year-by-year job history. Tell the truth about those three years you glossed over as "further career training": What odd jobs did you have and how much did you earn picking apples, house-sitting, or lifeguarding?

If you live in the United States and have been a salaried employee your entire working life, the Social Security Administration has also kept a record. Contact your local or state office or the national one and apply for a Social Security Statement, which details your lifetime earnings. If you're having a tough time hunting down the specifics, estimate as best you can. The object is to get as accurate and honest a figure as possible for the total amount of money that has entered your life.

The Value of Step 1

This step is useful in several ways:

1. It clears the fog shrouding your past relationship with money. Most people have no idea how much money has entered their lives, and therefore no idea how much money could enter their lives.

2. It eradicates such myths and false self-concepts as "I can't earn very much money" and even "I don't have to worry; I can always earn lots of money" (often said by individuals being supported by someone else). If you are one of the many who grossly underestimate how much money has entered their lives, this step can be amazingly

powerful. You are worth more than you thought—in dollars and cents and possibly other ways too.

3. It gets you to ground zero, enabling you to begin the financial program with a clear head and confidence in your wage-earning ability.

4. It allows you to see and let go of any skeletons from the past you may have in your closets—any secrets or lies that may be distorting your current relationship with money.

A story about a divorced woman in her midthirties who had attended one of our seminars illustrates the power of this step. She had been a suburban housewife most of her adult life, afflicted with the mental malady that often accompanies this profession: She had an image of herself as dependent, unworldly, and (if the truth be known) unworthy. She "knew" this step didn't apply to her—after all, she had made no financial contribution to her marriage and was, to that day, ashamed of accepting the divorce settlement money—money she felt she hadn't earned. But after digging into her past, she learned that she had earned more than $50,000 from assorted odd jobs during those years of her marriage when she was contributing "nothing." For the first time she saw herself as a competent wage earner. Merely doing this step gave her the confidence to apply for and land a job at twice the salary she had previously assumed she could get.

Similarly, if you're on your first full-time job, you may find confidence in learning how much you've earned from various jobs in the early years of your life. Internships, summer jobs, and freelance work all add up over time.

Useful Attitudes
No shame, no blame. This step may bring feelings of self-criticism—even shame—to the surface. Here's a way to work through those gently, a valuable exercise that

helps people thoroughly "change their minds" and learn to think in new ways. Some people call it by its Sanskrit name, "mantra," but it's really any simple word or phrase that embodies a particular attitude or attribute you want to focus on. A mantra is like a rudder, something that allows you to steer your mind away from danger and toward a clear, open horizon. A useful mantra for following this financial program is "No shame, no blame."

In the choice to change unwanted behavior, there is a difference between recrimination and discrimination. Recrimination is about shame and blame, good and evil, while discrimination sorts out the true from the false. Sinking into blame and shame slows your progress toward financial freedom. Recrimination immobilizes, demoralizes, and distracts you. Discrimination, however, simply shines a bright light on potential pitfalls so that you can skirt them.

You may stumble repeatedly over the desire to blame yourself (or other people) based on what you learn by following this program. At those times, remember discrimination and remember the mantra: No shame, no blame. Your lifetime earnings represent just a number, not your value. It is neither too much nor too little. It does not prove your worth or your unworthiness; it is justification neither for despair because none of the money is left nor for gloating because your friend earned so much less. Any financial mistakes you've made—and the pain they've caused you and others—can melt in the warmth of "no shame, no blame."

Impeccability. Since accuracy and accountability are called for in every step of the program, starting out with these two qualities sets a good example for you to live up to. When you do this step (and the others in this book), set your sights on impeccability—have you really searched your files and your memory banks for all your income? Yes, you could settle for a "close enough" answer—but we suggest you go for full-frontal integrity, since the power of this program increases with every ounce of honesty and integrity you invest in it. Rounding to the dollar takes a lot of soul and paycheck-stub searching. Rounding to the nearest hundred dollars is looser, but over a lifetime that might be plenty accurate. Don't stress over this step; just do the best job you can—it's worth your time.

CHECKLIST

1. Statement of earnings from Social Security
2. Income tax returns
3. Checkbook records
4. Old and current statements
5. Gifts
6. Winnings
7. Loans
8. Capital gains
9. Illegal sources
10. Contract labor not reported to the IRS (tips, baby-sitting, errands)

B. WHAT HAVE YOU GOT TO SHOW FOR IT?

For the years you have been working for wages, a certain amount of money (which you just calculated) has entered your life. The amount that is left in your life now is your net worth.

Be prepared. You will be calculating your net worth (your total assets minus your total liabilities), perhaps for the first time in your life. Brace yourself. You may discover that you are deeply in debt, and until this moment you have been unaware of the awful extent of it. Now is the time to face that truth. On the other hand, you may make the delightful discovery that you are in a position to be financially independent *now*. Many people have made that discovery, simply from doing this step.

There is an implied challenge in the phrasing of this step: "What have you got to show for it?" Say it out loud. Use different intonations. It usually comes out sounding a bit critical—snotty, even. Your commitment to Financial Integrity is stronger than your faintheartedness, however. So on with it: What do you have to show for all those dollars that have entered your life? Let's find out.

Creating a snapshot of your net worth simply means going through your material universe and listing everything you own (assets) and everything you owe (liabilities).

Liquid Assets

Cash, or anything that can easily be converted to cash, belongs in this category. Include the following:

- Cash on hand—include the piggy bank, the change on your dresser, the emergency money hidden in the glove compartment
- Savings accounts. Look for old bankbooks that you may have forgotten about, and that account that you opened with the minimum $100 to get the Free Bonus Digital Doohickey.
- Checking accounts
- Savings certificates or certificates of deposit
- US savings bonds
- Stocks; list at current market value
- Bonds; list at current market value
- Mutual funds; list at current market value
- Money market funds; list at current market value
- Brokerage account credit balance
- Life insurance cash value

Fixed Assets

In listing these, start with the obvious: the market value of your major possessions—for example, your house, your car (or cars). Contact a real estate agent or search online for the current market value of your house. Consult the blue book for the going price on the make, model, and year of your car.

Go through your attic, basement, garage, and storage shed. Itemize everything worth more than a dollar, without subjective evaluations like "That's worthless." Have fortitude. This process alone has been the salvation of several inveterate pack rats, tinkerers, and collectors with garages full of real treasures. If you don't do it now, realize that someone you love will have to do it after you are gone. If your storage area really is piled floor to ceiling with the accumulation of a lifetime, you might want to leave it until last, so you don't get overwhelmed.

Go through every room and inventory everything. Look up at those decorative light fixtures. Look down at that rug. How about the nice walnut shelves you put in a few years ago, and those Native American artifacts? What about that custom-built computer? Confront your clutter squarely. Be thorough, but not irrational—that is, not every knife, spoon, and fork has to be listed individually, but do list separately that expensive rosewood-handled carving set with the mahogany case. And the two sets of dishes that are still in their boxes.

Give an approximate cash value to everything you own. That means current cash value—what you could get for each item at a consignment shop or garage sale, or via online auction or classified ad sites. For help in pricing your possessions, look at online auction or classified listings, or the "For Sale" section in your local newspaper. Get your more valuable personal or household items appraised.

Don't ignore anything. One person's useless junk is another's precious antique. Just because you don't value an item doesn't mean it has no value.

Don't overlook debts owed to you, at least those you can reasonably expect to collect. Include security deposits on utilities, phone, or house or apartment rental.

Any material that can be converted into cash should be listed. You are playing the role of appraiser for your own estate. Let it be an enjoyable exercise. You needn't sell any of it if you don't choose to, so don't let sentimentality deter you from your inventory. In fact, don't allow any emotions to waylay you. Don't let grief dissuade you from assigning a cash value to the power tools your husband left behind. Or the flat-screen TV your roommate left when he or she moved out. Don't let embarrassment about your compulsive spending discourage you from pricing the twenty pairs of shoes sitting unworn in your closet. Don't let guilt keep you from cataloging all the exercise paraphernalia you bought and have never used. Instead, rejoice! You are finally discovering the real value of that stationary bicycle and set of free weights: not the pounds you'll lose but the price they'll command at a garage sale.

While some people can knock this exercise out in a day or two, one woman took three months to do her inventory. She went through every box, looked at every photo, and opened every drawer and cupboard, not only listing the items, but recalling how and why each had come into her life. The process led her into a deep experience of gratitude for what she already had. So much dissatisfaction comes from focusing on what we don't have that the simple exercise of acknowledging and valuing what we do have can transform our outlook. Indeed, some people would say that once we're above the survival level, the difference between prosperity and poverty lies simply in our degree of gratitude.

Liabilities

This category includes all your debts, whether payable in money, goods, or services—everything you owe, from loans to bills outstanding.

If you list as an asset the current market value of your house, include as a liability the balance owed on it. Do the same with the balance on your car payments.

Don't forget to include bank loans or loans from friends, credit card debts, student loans, and unpaid medical and dental bills.

Net Worth

Add the figures for liquid assets and fixed assets, and subtract from that the figure for liabilities. In the most simplified, concrete, material sense, this is your current net worth. That is what you currently have to show for your total lifetime income; the rest is memories and illusions, as far as the reality of balance sheets is concerned.

We do not include your nonmaterial assets: your education, the skills you have acquired, the goodwill you've bought by treating everyone to a free round of drinks, the tax-deductible receipt from United Way, the increased business that comes your way because you belong to the "right" club. Valuable as these may be, they are all intangibles, and as such are impossible to evaluate in the crisp, numeric, objective ways that we are learning to apply to our personal finances.

The net worth exercise might be humbling or heroic. You will confront many hard truths, which can be painful or liberating. Whatever you find, it's important to remember that net worth does not equal self-worth.

WHY DO A BALANCE SHEET?

While it may not initially appear so, this point in the program is very encouraging. So far your financial life has had very little direction or consciousness. Financially speaking, you have been like someone driving around without any destination—burning gas, spinning your wheels, and getting nowhere. You may have many happy memories and other intangibles, but only a few real souvenirs that could be converted into cash. With the power and clear direction that taking the reins of your financial affairs will give you, you will be far more effective in the world.

You now have an overview of your financial status and can objectively choose whether or not to convert some of your fixed assets into cash, thus increasing your savings—or getting a bit further out of debt.

One person, upon completing this step, realized that she could liquidate her excess possessions, invest the proceeds, and have enough interest income to immediately be financially independent in comfort and style. While she didn't choose to do that right away, the awareness itself allowed her to take more risks in the direction of her real love, art.

Another individual realized that he had many possessions that he wasn't using and no longer wanted, but had been hanging on to because he "just might need them someday." His creative solution was to sell these belongings and set aside the proceeds to replace any of them he might need in the future. Meanwhile, his money was earning interest, his life became simpler, and someone who really needed those items was getting use out of them.

And remember: No shame, no blame. In creating your balance sheet, many feelings associated with your material universe may arise: sadness, grief, nostalgia, hope, guilt, shame, embarrassment, anger. A dispassionate and compassionate attitude can go a long way toward making this step truly enlightening—that is, able to lighten the physical and emotional loads you've been toting around for so many years.

SUMMARY OF STEP 1

A. Find out how much money you have earned in your lifetime.

B. Create a balance sheet of your assets and liabilities. What do you have to show for the money you've earned?

MONEY TALK QUESTIONS

It can be surprising, exciting, and even a bit disturbing to discover that you have a *relationship* with money made up of beliefs, assumptions, experiences, admonitions, and perhaps reactions to your parents or culture. Money Talks are a perfect way to learn about how others were shaped by their past, and what unconscious rules and stories guide us to this day. The "no-shame, no-blame" spirit lets you peer behind the curtain of money and see what's going on.

Using the suggestions in the epilogue for how to have a Money Talk, raise these questions in your daily reflections, with your partner, or in social groups. Remember, adding "Why?" to the end of any question will take it deeper. Adding "How has society shaped my answer?" to any question will take it wider. There are no right answers.

- Who gave you your first lessons about money? What did you learn?
- What messages did you get about money growing up? Where did you get them from? Parents, teachers, ads, or . . . ?
- Talk about an early memory of money and how it affects you now.
- Talk about a money mistake. What would you do differently?
- What does "enough" mean to you?
- What do you have (in storage or closets) that you'd be better off without? Why do you keep it?

2

Money Ain't What It Used to Be—and Never Was

It wasn't too difficult for **Ondrea and Kyle W.** *to do step 1. Kyle, a twenty-two-year-old idealist, had been "allergic" to money for many years. He grew his hair long, rented a small room in a house in a rural area, and considered deep conversation the best entertainment money could buy. Even though (or because?) he had "avoided" money, he had accumulated a $15,000 debt that he planned to pay off "someday." When he met Ondrea, he was attracted to the thoughtful and dedicated person inside her, not to her lifestyle. It was only after falling in love that he discovered she was well over $40,000 in debt. Like so many young people, Ondrea had equated being on her own with accumulating possessions, furnishing an apartment and going into debt. Debt was a way of life for her, as it is for so many people, and she was in no rush to pay it off. Play now, pay later, which for her meant working part-time as an administrative assistant to cover immediate expenses and pursuing personal growth. Even when Ondrea and Kyle moved in together, she was as leery of Kyle's austerity as he was of her penchant for shopping. Then they came to our financial seminar, and Ondrea saw the disparity between her desire to become more conscious spiritually and her desire to stay unconscious about her mounting debt. She made a commitment to examine and question her attachment to having nice things. Kyle, in turn, agreed not to push her, to let her* *discover what was right for her rather than pressure her to comply with his value system. They decided to get married, and Kyle said, "I do," not only to his beloved, but to nearly quadrupling his debt. Doing step 1 forced them to face the fact that they had a net worth of minus $55,000—and a new way of life was born for both of them.*

Once you've done step 1 for yourself, you too will know how much you are worth. Or will you? Like Ondrea and Kyle, you have a dollar figure (we hope a positive one), but what, if anything, does that mean? Our task now is to unravel the mystery of money. What *is* money, anyway? This is an important task because we can't have an effective working relationship with anything (or anyone) when we don't know what (or who) it is—or worse, when we identify it as something it is not. Without a universally and consistently true definition of money, our handling of this substance is anywhere from inept to insane, and almost always counter to getting us what we think we want.

What *is* money?

We are awash in financial transactions every day, money flowing in as salary and investment returns, money flowing out through cash and credit card purchases and recurring payments and interest on debt and taxes. Your phone plan, your Internet plan, your car payments, your insurance, your energy consumption in your car and house, your rent or HOA dues or property taxes, service people to fix your car, clean your house, or soothe your soul, your tickets to concerts and conferences and vacations, your walking-around-hungry grazing from vendors and restaurants, your clothes and groceries and pet food. Every moment a pinch of money moves in or out, much of it out of sight and mind as electronic blips. It's easy for us to identify money in our lives, but what is it really? What does it represent?

Joe Dominguez, the practical genius behind these tools, posed this question to thousands of people attending his 1980s seminars. He'd come onstage in his best Wall Street costuming and pace the front of the stage looking silently and piercingly at the audience. He'd then focus on the biggest, toughest-looking guy (Joe was barely five feet seven) and bark the question "How big is yours?"

Silence. Tittering.

"I said"—his voice booming—"how big is yours?"

Titter. Silence.

"What are you all thinking? I'm just asking him how big his paycheck is. Isn't that really the most personal question you can ask a man?"

Before anyone can learn anything new, they need to have their cage of certainty rattled. This opener certainly got people off balance, and set Joe up for asking, "What is money?" It's a question we never ask because we think we know. But do we?

"You use the stuff every day. You die for it. You'd kill for it. Surely you know what it is!"

Then he'd take out a hundred-dollar bill.

"Hmmm. It's paper."

He'd pull on it, twist it, and say, "Pretty strong paper."

Then he'd take out a lighter and say, "Let's test it. See if it burns."

Gasp—the room would lurch forward. He'd snap shut the lighter short of putting flame to paper.

"What was that reaction? Why would burning this piece of paper make you react? Clearly money is more than pieces of paper or metal [or these days plastic or ones and zeros]. So what is this stuff?"

A brave Economics 101 student might say: Money is a means of exchange.

"Good. I can give you this hundred dollars and buy your wife, right?"

No! Sometimes at this point he'd tell the George Bernard Shaw story about Shaw's leaning over to a dinner party partner and saying, "Madam, I'd wager you'd go to bed with me for a hundred dollars." She of course was shocked and insulted. Then Shaw said, "How about a thousand?" and she paused, giving him an opening to say that clearly it's not the act, it's the price.

Joe's point was that money is a means of exchange only if the trading partners agree it has value.

"Imagine your boat capsized and you swim to an island in a piranha-infested part of the Amazon River. You think you're done for but then you notice that you have your wallet and it's stocked with money. Saved! You later see two men in a canoe (cannibals, I might add) paddle by and you raise a fistful of dollars, yelling, 'Help! Help!' But they don't recognize your money. They recognize you as dinner."

Money is a means of exchange only when both parties agree on its value. It is a fiat currency. It's not even worth the paper it is printed on.

"What can you say that is always true about this stuff?" he'd demand loudly, waving the hundred-dollar bill.

Economics 101 would brave another answer: "It's a store of value," meaning you can save it up to spend another day. You can turn a forest (natural value) into lumber (economic value), sell it, and bank the money to pay for future needs.

Indeed, this is a major function of money, an abstraction that has allowed us to transform from hunter-gatherer tribes sharing daily harvests into cogs in some industrial wheel who "make money" by selling our time and talents in the workplace—probably an hour's commute away.

"Yes, of course it's a 'store of value,' but consider what happens when bubbles burst and governments fail and hyperinflation sets in and the money that would buy a cow yesterday won't buy a quart of milk today. Money's value can disappear overnight." Had Joe lived long enough, he might have referred to the pensions of Enron employees when the company tanked in 2001 or the Great Recession of 2008 or the Madoff Ponzi scheme that came crashing down in 2009.

He might have used the comedian Stephen Colbert's term *truthiness*—"store of value" is truthy, but not true. Oh, you could almost hear the audience think together. The trick is that it isn't the *stuff*. It's what the stuff *means*.

"Money is status," another participant would offer. Yes, Joe would say, but not always. Other qualities, like appearance or intellect or family reputation, might confer more status than ostentatious wealth on display in the winter watering holes of the nouveau riche.

It's power, another would try. You can make people do things with money. You can buy favors. You can influence. Look at lobbyists. Look at dark money in politics. Look at arms deals. Yes, yes, Joe would say, but you have to admit there are other forms of power that may win the day. Think of Gandhi and the British leaving India. Think of Martin Luther King Jr. Think of all the myths and stories and movies about the little guy with integrity beating out the evil giants. Money is no guarantee of power, though it is often used to wield power.

OK, now we get it, they'd cry. Money is evil. It's the root of all evil. A student of the Bible, Joe would counter, "No, the love of money is the root of all evil, not money itself."

It's a tool of repression.

It's not fair.

It's a mystery.

It's not important.

It's abundant.

It's how we keep score.

One guess after another, each one with a bit more lightness because the audience would realize there was a trick somewhere they couldn't see. No definition would stick. All are true—sometimes. None are true always. You could practically hear a collective decision to unload all known definitions for Joe to shoot down one by one and finally get to the punch line. And as merciless as Joe seemed, swatting guesses like annoying flies, people could feel the love underneath it all. Especially because they knew he was not standing up there—flapping his arms, giving voice to our fears and half-truths—for fame or fortune. We'd formed a charitable foundation, the New Road Map Foundation, to give all the proceeds away. Every penny from every seminar. (We weren't rich—we each lived on less than $800 a month!—but we had enough and loved using these seminars to raise money for other organizations.)

Finally, he'd agree to share the secret.

"Here's the only thing you can say that is always true for you, one hundred percent of the time: Money is something you trade your life energy for. You sell your time for money. It doesn't matter that Ned over there sells his time for a hundred dollars and you sell yours for twenty dollars an hour. Ned's money is irrelevant to you. The only real asset you have is your time. The hours of your life.

"You're born. You have about eighty-eight hundred hours in a year. Maybe six hundred and fifty thousand hours before you die. You'll easily spend half of them sleeping and keeping your body fed, clothed, and reasonably comfortable. Maybe you're already halfway through your life, meaning you're down to a hundred and fifty thousand hours left to spend. This is your treasure. This is all you have for everything that matters to you—the love of your family, your contribution to society, your enjoyment of the great outdoors, your rising to challenges, your search for meaning, your legacy, your ecstasies [in church or in bed], your *life*. And you sell some of those precious hours for this [waving the hundred-dollar bill]—this has no meaning; your time is where all meaning and value lie.

"Knowing that money is simply your life energy puts you in the driver's seat of your money life. How much of my life am I willing to sell to have money in my pocket? Looking around at your accumulation of stuff you can ask, 'How many hours of my life did I invest to have this . . . chair . . . car . . . matched set of cookware . . .

diploma on the wall?' See what this does to your next purchase."

This program does not promise more or less money or stuff. It only promises to transform your relationship with money.

"Did you ever think about that?" Joe would ask. "That you have a relationship with money?" He'd get on his knees, begging money to love him. He'd exhibit mock terror, shrinking from the evil hundred-dollar bill. He'd hold it out like a carrot and run around after it, reaching but never grasping it.

"This is what your relationship with money looks like! Think about it. If you were money, would you hang out with you?"

A Simple Summary of What Money Is—and Is Not

Joe's antics took audiences rapidly though four levels of misunderstanding about what money is—and isn't.

Material. The pieces of paper and metal and plastic. The daily transactions of earning and spending, of banking and investing. This mundane level is what most people most of the time think of as money.

Psychological. Your fears and longings. Your personality—are you modest or flamboyant, the last of the big spenders or a tightwad? Who influenced your feelings and thoughts about money?

Cultural. The beliefs embedded in our laws and customs. More is better, growth is good, winners and losers, private property, rewards and punishments. Do you recognize these as the warp onto which you've woven your money life?

Life energy. Something you trade the hours of your life for.

The first three layers are real and important—but not always. In fact, simply getting up-to-date with the material level of money can bring immense peace of mind.

Understanding how your money psychology affects the money choices of your daily life brings an even greater level of freedom. Seeing how you are unwittingly living some of the beliefs of our culture can further liberate you from unconscious habits. Is more *really* better? Is growth *really* good? The last is the big one: Knowing that money is your life energy transforms your relationship with money, shining a bright light on all your false notions.

This program promises to clear out the fog, the confusion, the myths and mistaken notions we have in our relationship with money. It promises we will be at peace with our choices. The key to transforming our relationship with money is this utter clarity that money is not all the meanings we project on it, nor is it the dark realities of the financial systems. It is something we choose to trade our life energy for.

While the insight "Money is life energy" comes in an instant, living that truth is a lifelong path of discovery. It isn't a magic wand, vaporizing the consequences of your past money mistakes. You still grew up in a family where your parents battled over money or hid problems or used it like a carrot or stick. You still came of age in circumstances in which money came hard or easy, in which hard knocks or golden opportunities made a big difference. You still have your debt; you still have your disagreements with your partner.

Even once you change your relationship with money, it will still make concrete demands on you. It is like a hard-edged, many-faceted diamond, and your obligations are real. Checks bounce. Products break. Salaries are negotiated. Doctor bills come due. Mortgages get paid or not and your fortunes change. Knowing money is life energy doesn't change the requirement that you treat your obligations with utmost integrity.

Money is also like water—it flows, and as it flows, it nourishes life. We feel happy when it flows our way, distressed when it doesn't. We buy gifts of love and brighten others' days. We turn a bonus into a trip to Hawaii with the family and make memories. Knowing money is life energy doesn't flatten our emotional responses as it flows through our lives. Examining its role in our lives can actually make our experience richer. Rather than thinking that buying a new car will make us happy, we can wonder what does make us happy, and whether happy could come from a day at the beach rather than three years of monthly car payments. Money is like a mirror that allows us to see ourselves. Notice what happens when you get a check in the mail. A bill. When your partner says, "Honey, we have to talk about our finances." Notice how you feel when you tip well. Tip poorly. When someone notices you have an expensive watch.

The more we clarify this watery-feeling aspect of money, the better equipped we are to deal with those hard daily transactions. Fewer overdrafts and late fees. More control over spending. Better timeliness with taxes and bill paying. The clearer our feelings, the cleaner our transactions.

Money is a game and we have to play by the rules. Like it or not, we are all in the money game. By playing by the game rules, we can sell our services and products locally and globally, we can buy products with components mined in Africa and Venezuela, assembled in China, branded in Los Angeles, packaged in the Philippines, and sold at Walmarts everywhere. Our credit card purchases are reconciled daily by some vast set of computers whirring away—and we take home groceries and buy tickets for concerts. We live and move and have our being in this money game—and we understand one another through the language of these transactions. Everyone needs money. Everyone hustles to get it. Few of us could live for a day of our lives without touching something that money has touched. Because of that, our minds resist looking squarely at how dependent and embedded we are. Money may be life energy, but daily life grinds to a halt without it.

Knowing this shared-game aspect of money, though,

gives us a way to make conscious choices about when we play the game using money and when we play the game using other currencies—like love or skills or knowledge or the work of our hands. We can see how the money game plays us as well, how malls and department stores and websites are all designed to grab our attention and our money, playing on our insecurities and our longings. Resisting consumerism becomes easy: Is that bathing suit or car worthy of my life energy?

Many of our assumptions about money are really part of the game design. "Whoever dies with the most toys wins" is part of the design to keep us all in the system and playing. Upgrading your technology is part of the game design. Planned or manufactured obsolescence. Fashion is part of the game. "Starter" homes. Advertisements show beautiful women and muscular men decorated with products for you to purchase. On a grander scale, the interstate highway and cathedrals are part of the money game. Most of us decide to ignore the bad and try to use money for good. Look, it's all part of the game, we tell ourselves, the only game in town. The game feeds on players being involved. If players lose interest, the game collapses—which horrifies us. We depend on money for just about everything. Buy something. Feed the economy. Everyone wins if we all play.

This game comes complete with bad guys, the bogeymen of personal finances that keep us in line and playing: inflation, cost of living, recession and depression. We are encouraged to take economic indicators personally. If the economist-gods announce the economy is in a recession, we might decide not to go on vacation this year, just to be safe—even if we have plenty of money and a secure job. If the economist-gods tell us the cost of living is up, we automatically feel poorer, even though what's now included in the consumer price index was a luxury item just a few decades ago, something we all did without and never missed—like our cell phones and other technological doodads.

Some would call this design aspect of money the Matrix—a simulated reality created by sentient machines to subdue the human population and harvest their energy. In the film, Morpheus, a leader of the liberated humans, tells Neo, the hero, "The Matrix is everywhere. It is all around us. Even now, in this very room. You can see it when you look out your window or when you turn on your television. You can feel it when you go to work . . . when you go to church . . . when you pay your taxes. It is the world that has been pulled over your eyes to blind you from the truth." Morpheus offers Neo a choice, now famous in pop culture, "You take the blue pill, the story ends. You wake up in your bed and believe whatever you want to believe. You take the red pill, you stay in Wonderland . . ."

Knowing that money is life energy is like taking the red pill. You see your choices, make them, see the consequences, and learn. Winning isn't having the most toys. It's having precisely what you need and nothing in excess and being able to stop playing the game at will.

Knowing money is life energy allows you to maximize and optimize your most precious resource: your time; your life.

Your Life Energy

What does "money = life energy" mean to you? After all, money is something you consider valuable enough to devote easily a quarter of your allotted time on earth getting, spending, worrying about, fantasizing about, or in some other way reacting to. Yes, there are many social conventions regarding money that are worth learning and abiding by, but ultimately you are the one who determines what money is worth to you. It is your life energy. You "pay" for money with your time. You choose how to spend it.

This definition of money gives us significant information. Our life energy is more real in our actual

FIGURE 2-1

Age and Average Remaining Life Expectancy[1]

Age	Average Remaining Life Expectancy	
	Years	Hours
20	59.6	522,096
25	54.8	480,048
30	50.1	438,876
35	45.4	397,704
40	40.7	356,532
45	36.1	316,236
50	31.6	276,816
55	27.3	239,148
60	23.3	204,108
65	19.3	169,068
70	15.6	136,656
75	12.2	106,872
80	9.1	79,716

Source: US National Center for Health Statistics

experience than money. While money has no intrinsic reality, our life energy does—at least to us. It's tangible, and it's finite. Life energy is all we have. It is precious because it is limited and irretrievable and because our choices about how we use it express the meaning and purpose of our time here on earth.

If you are forty years old, you can expect to have approximately 356,500 hours (40.7 years) of life energy left before you die. (See Figure 2-1 for life expectancy at various ages.) Assuming about half of your time is spent on necessary body maintenance—sleeping, eating, eliminating, washing, and exercising—you have 178,000 hours of life energy remaining for such discretionary uses as:

◆ your relationship to yourself
◆ your relationship to others
◆ your creative expression
◆ your contribution to your community
◆ your contribution to the world
◆ achieving inner peace and . . .
◆ holding down a job

Now that you know that money is something you trade life energy for, you have the opportunity to set new priorities for your use of that valuable commodity. After all, is there any "thing" more vital to you than your life energy?

A FIRST LOOK AT FINANCIAL INDEPENDENCE

As we said in the introduction, one purpose of this book is to increase your Financial Independence. By following the steps, you will move inexorably toward Financial Integrity and Financial Intelligence and will one day (we hope before you die) arrive at Financial Independence. In showing you how this is possible, however, we must first show you what Financial Independence isn't.

Let's begin by exploring what images the phrase "Financial Independence" conjures up for you. Making a killing? Inheriting a fortune? Winning the lottery? Cruises, tropical islands, world travel? Jewels, Porsches, designer clothes? Most of us picture Financial Independence as an unreachable fantasy of inexhaustible riches.

This is Financial Independence at a material level. While it simply requires that we be rich, there's a caveat: What is "rich"? Rich exists only in comparison to something or someone else. Rich is a helluva lot more than I have now. Rich is way more than most other people have. But we know the fallacy of the myth of more. More is like a mirage. We can never reach it because it isn't real. John Stuart Mill once said, "Men do not desire to be rich, only to be richer than other men." In other words, as soon as rich becomes available to the likes of us, it will no longer be rich.

Only when we take personal responsibility for our relationship with money does the first definition of true Financial Independence appear. Our definition of Financial Independence cuts through the Gordian knot of not knowing what rich is. Financial Independence has nothing to do with rich. It is the experience of having enough—and then some. Enough, you will remember, is found at the peak of the fulfillment curve. It is quantifiable, and you will define it for yourself as you work with the steps of this program. The old notion of Financial Independence as being rich forever is not achievable. Enough is. Enough for you may be different from enough for your neighbor—but it will be a figure that is real for you and within your reach.

Financial and Psychological Freedom

Your first step toward the experience of having enough—and then some—is liberating your mind from its preexisting attitudes toward money. Until you do so, no amount of money will free you. Once you have, you are free from unconsciously held assumptions about money, and free of the guilt, resentment, envy, frustration, and despair you may have felt about money issues. You may have these feelings, but you have them the way you have an article of clothing—you can try it on, but you are free at any time to take it off. You are no longer compelled by the parental and social messages you received as a child—messages about how we should relate to money in order to be successful, respected, virtuous, secure, and happy. You are free of the confusion you had about money. You are no longer intimidated by the financial professionals you hire to do your taxes or invest your money. You never buy things you don't want or need, and you are immune to the seductiveness of malls, markets, and the media. Your emotional fortunes are no longer tied to your economic fortunes; your moods don't swing with the Dow Jones Band. The broken record in your mind stops, the one that calculates hours till quitting time, days till payday, paydays till you have a down payment for a motorcycle, costs for the next home improvement project, and years till retirement. The silence, at first, is thundering. Days and even weeks can go by without you thinking about money, without you mentally reaching for your wallet to handle life's challenges and opportunities.

When you are financially independent, the way money functions in your life is determined by you, not by your circumstances. In this way money isn't something that happens to you, it's something you include in your life in a purposeful way. From this point of view, the normal drama of "nine to five till you're sixty-five," of making a dying, of getting ahead, of being rich and famous—all these brass rings we automatically reach for—can be seen as just one series of choices among many. Financial Independence is freedom from the fog, fear, and fanaticism so many of us feel about money.

If this sounds like peace of mind, it is. Fiscal bliss. And if this sounds as unattainable as being rich, it isn't. It's been the experience of tens of thousands of people who have followed the approach to money described in this book, who have done the practical steps recommended.

Step 2: Being in the Present—Tracking Your Life Energy

How does this great truth—money = life energy—manifest itself in your life? When you thought money was just something to deal with, or that it was security, power, or a tool of the devil, or the grand prize in your life, you could rationalize your behavior in terms of shoulds and oughts. But now you know that money = life energy—*your* life energy—and you have a rising interest in knowing just how much of the stuff is actually passing through your hands. Step 2 on the road to financial freedom is where you satisfy this curiosity.

There are two parts to step 2:

A. **Establish the actual costs in time and money required to maintain your job(s), and compute your real hourly wage.**
B. **Keep track of every cent that comes into or goes out of your life.**

A. HOW MUCH ARE YOU TRADING YOUR LIFE ENERGY FOR?

We have established that money is simply something you trade life energy for. Now let's look at how much life energy (in hours) you are currently trading for how much money (in dollars)—that is, how much money are you making for the amount of time you work?

Most people look at this life-energy-to-earnings ratio in an unrealistic and inadequate way: "I earn a thousand dollars a week, I work forty hours a week, so I trade one hour of my life energy for twenty-five dollars." It's not likely to be that simple. Think of all the ways you use your life energy that are directly related to your money-earning employment. Think of all the monetary expenses that are directly associated with the job. In other words, if you didn't need that money-earning job, what time expenditures and monetary expenses would disappear from your life?

Be prepared to be surprised. Some people resent their work—the hours of drudgery, the boredom, the office politics, the time away from what they really want to be doing, the personality conflicts with their boss or co-workers. Feeling powerless, they indulge instead in some retail therapy. Be prepared to discover how much you spend with "I hate my job" as the underlying reason.

Be prepared, too, to discover how much you spend on expensive alternatives to cooking, cleaning, repairs, and other things you would do yourself if you didn't have to work.

Be prepared to discover the many costs of ambition, all the things you "must" have in order to continue up the ranks. The right car. The right clothes. The right house in the right neighborhood in the right city. The right private schools for your kids.

Using the following discussion as a stimulus, discover for yourself the real trade-offs in time and energy associated with keeping your nine-to-five job. Not all of the categories will necessarily apply to you, and you may think of others relevant to you that are not mentioned here.

For freelancers, this might be extra complicated, but the value will be even greater. You'll subject each gig to the same analysis. You may be surprised that you are undervaluing some of your jobs and overvaluing others!

In the following examples we will assign arbitrary numeric values to these time and money trade-offs simply to generate a hypothetical tabulation. At the end of the discussion we will tabulate these calculations and come up with an actual exchange rate of life energy for money. When you do your own calculations you will be using your actual figures and will determine your own personal hourly wage.

Commuting
Getting to and from work incurs an expenditure of time or money, or both, whether you drive a car you

own, grab a cab, rideshare, bicycle, walk, or take public transportation. For our purposes here, let's assume you commute by car. Don't forget to include parking fees and tolls for bridges or turnpikes, as well as wear and tear on your car. Let's say that you commute 1.5 hours a day or 7.5 hours a week at a cost, in gas and maintenance, of $100 a week. (If you use mass transit, your figures will be somewhat different.)

7.5 hours/week, $100/week

Costuming

Are the clothes you wear at work the same ones you wear on your days off or on vacations—or do you need a special wardrobe to be appropriately attired for your job? This includes not just the obvious costumes like nurses' uniforms, construction workers' steel-toed boots, and chefs' aprons, but also the tailored suits and the high-heeled shoes, the neckties and panty hose that are the norm in offices. Look at those clothes. Would you wear a noose around your neck or walk around on three-inch heels every day if it weren't expected for the job? Consider too the time and money spent on personal grooming, from aftershave to exotic cosmetics.

Quantify all your costuming activities, from shopping to putting on mascara, shaving and tying your tie. Let's say you spend 1.5 hours a week on this at an average cost of $25 a week (i.e., annual clothing expense divided by 52 weeks, plus cost of cosmetics).

1.5 hours/week, $25/week

Meals

Extra costs, in time and money, for meals affected by your job take many forms—for example, money for morning and afternoon coffee, time spent in line in the employees' cafeteria, and meals ordered in or eaten out because you are too tired or busy to cook dinner.

Let's say you spend a total of 5 hours a week out to lunch or stopping for a morning coffee. Your lunches at the local deli cost about $30 a week more than if you made lunch at home, and the latte breaks you treat yourself to as a reward for working come to $20 a week. Total spent: $50.

5 hours/week, $50/week

Daily Decompression

Do you come home from your job zestful and full of life, joyously launching into personal or planetary projects or into intimate sharing with your family or other loved ones? Or are you tired and drained, taciturnly lurching into the soft chair in front of the television set or computer screen, beer or martini in hand, because "It's been such a day"? If it takes a while for you to "decompress" from the pressures of the job, that "while" is a job-related expense. Include in this calculation the time you spend ranting about your job and your coworkers to whoever will listen. A wild guess would put this at 5 hours a week and $30 a week in recreational substances.

5 hours/week, $30/week

Escape Entertainment

Notice that common phrase "escape entertainment." Escape from what? What is the prison or restrictive circumstance from which you must flee? If your experience of life was consistently fulfilling and exciting, from what would you escape? Would you devote so many hours to screen time? Take a look at scenarios like "It's been such a heavy week at work, let's have a night on the town to blow it off!" or "Let's get away from it all this weekend and go to Vegas!" Would these be necessary? What are the costs in life energy and money? How much of your weekend entertainment do you consider your just reward for sticking it out at a boring job? Of course some consumption of the arts deliciously disturbs, sublimely inspires, and deeply nourishes; life energy spent here makes life worth living and so is worth every second. This absorption into art is not about escape. It's about elevation—and as such it isn't a job-related expense. Let's assign escape entertainment 5 hours and $40 a week.

5 hours/week, $40/week

Vacations

Time in nature and travel to other cultures and places can be, like art, the best experiences of your life. But if "vacationing" is more like time-out in a corner to recover so you can get back into the fight, then it is a job-related expense. For example, if you are too tired to even plan a special trip and decide to just take the whole family to a resort in the Bahamas, where you collapse in a lounge chair rather than the La-Z-Boy at home, this might be a job-related expense. However, if you sell off everything from your storage unit to volunteer for a week with a research team in the Bahamas measuring the health of coral reefs, that might count as diving into life—literally. Only you know which is which.

What else? How about the vacation home, boat, or recreational vehicle that you use only a few weeks each year just to "get away"? String this all out, divide by 52, and you might have 5 hours and $30 a week for absenting yourself from the daily grind.

5 hours/week, $30/week

Job-Related Illness

What percentage of illness is job-related—induced by stress, by physical work conditions, by the desire to have a "legitimate" reason to take time off from work, or by conflict with employers or fellow employees? The Greater Good Science Center, an organization promoting science-based practices for a meaningful life, gathered research about health and happiness. They found evidence that happiness increases heart health, strengthens the immune system, combats stress, reduces aches and pains, reduces chronic illness, and lengthens our lives.[2] In our own experience over the years we have seen considerably less illness and illness-caused absenteeism in volunteers than in paid employees. Stated simply, happy, fulfilled people are healthier.

For this category a more subjective "inner sensing" is the only way to evaluate what percentage of medical costs (time and money) is attributable to your job. Let's guesstimate $25/week to out-of-pocket expenses (co-pays, medications) for all job-related illness expenses and add 50 hours a year for visits to the doctor, trips to the drugstore, and sniffling under the covers.

1 hour/week, $25/week

Other Job-Related Expenses

Examine your balance sheet of assets and liabilities (step 1). Are items listed there that you wouldn't have bought had they not been directly related to your job? Look at what you pay "the help": Would you need a housekeeper, gardener, handyman, or nanny if you didn't have a job? Day-care expenses for single parents or two-income families take a big chunk out of your salary and wouldn't be necessary if you didn't have a job. Do a time log for a typical week. How many hours accounted for are strictly job related? Things like perusing online job listings or social evenings to network for business. Are the hours of taking your frustrations about work out on your partner a job-related activity? As you progress through the other steps in this program, make special note of such hidden job-related expenses.

Don't overlook job-enhancement expenses, such as educational programs, books, tools and conferences. Remember, your situation is unique, but the basic ideas will apply. Discover your own categories of job-related time and money expenses.

Your *Real* Hourly Wage

Now compile these figures and create a table, adding the approximate extra job-related hours to your normal workweek and subtracting the job-related expenses from your usual pay. On longer-term items like vacations or illness, simply prorate over 50 weeks (1 year minus 2 weeks for your vacation—presuming you have a job that gives you a vacation at all). A $1,500 vacation that you wouldn't have taken if you enjoyed your job would be computed as $1,500 divided by 50 weeks equals $30 a week . . . and so on.

The specific entries will be approximations, of course, but with diligence you can come up with fairly accurate figures.

Figure 2-2 illustrates this process of calculating your real hourly wage—as well as a corollary figure: the number of hours or minutes of your life that every dollar you spend represents. Remember, the numbers here are arbitrary. Your figures will probably be considerably different from these, as might your categories.

Note: If you get benefits from your workplace (like health insurance and matching retirement investments), by all means add those to your nominal hourly wage, but since not everybody does, we don't include them in these calculations.

FIGURE 2-2

Life Energy vs. Earnings: What Is Your *Real* Hourly Wage?

	Hours/Week	Dollars/Week	Dollars/Hour
Basic Job (before adjustments)	40	1,000	25
Adjustments			
Commuting	+ 7.5	– 100	
Costuming	+ 1.5	– 25	
Meals	+ 5	– 50	
Decompression	+ 5	– 30	
Escape entertainment	+ 5	– 40	
Vacation	+ 5	– 30	
Job-related illness	+ 1	– 25	
Time and money spent on maintaining Job (total adjustments)	+ 30	– 300	
Job, with adjustments (actual total)	70	– 700	10

Every dollar spent represents 6 minutes of life energy.

The Bottom Line: Figure 2-2 clearly shows that you are actually selling an hour of your life energy for $10, not the apparent $25. Your real hourly wage is $10—before taxes, even! A good question to ask at this point is: Are you willing to accept a job that pays this hourly wage? (You should make this calculation every time you change your job—or change your job-related habits.)

The corollary figure is also interesting. In this example, every dollar you spend represents 6 minutes of your life. Think of that figure next time you're shelling out your money for yet another $20 gazingus pin. Ask: Is this item worth 120 minutes of my life energy? Is it worth the two hours of sitting in traffic, driving to work, or hunting down future clients?

Notice that our calculations have ignored such intangibles as time spent on planning strategies for moving up the corporate ladder, time handling deteriorating family life due to job demands, and time and expenses incurred in maintaining a lifestyle in line with the job. The costs of a job radiate throughout your life in countless ways.

*When **Mark H.** did the first part of step 2, his life turned upside down. He had been working as a project manager in the construction industry for ten years. "I was unhappy with what I did for a living," he wrote, "but income equaled expenses, so I went on with the attitude of 'Well, that's life in the big city.'" Then Mark did step 2 and calculated his real hourly wage. "After I analyzed our spending patterns, it became clear that nearly half of what I made was spent on the job; that is, spent on gas, oil, repairs, lunches, a little here, a little there, and most of it unrecoverable. In short, I could stay home, work part-time where I live, and actually save money by making half of what I formerly made." It was then, when he realized he could give up this job and pursue his real desires and goals, that everything changed. Affairs in his financial life that he'd procrastinated handling for years got handled—everything from paying off credit cards to eliminating restaurant lunches to having long-overdue money discussions with his wife without the old arguments. As he rearranged his financial world, he and his wife recognized that they could survive quite well on her paycheck from a job she loved (teaching kids with special needs), and he could go back to school to train for the career he'd always wanted as a counselor and therapist. "We're actually feeling less stress because we're focused on healing our crazy relationship with money, not just [focused on] the bucks."*

Why Do This Step?

Why is this exercise essential to a transformed relationship with money?

1. This exercise puts paid employment into real perspective and points out how much you are actually getting paid, which is the bottom line. ·

2. It allows you to assess current and future employment realistically, in terms of actual earnings. It is useful to apply the information gathered in this step to prospective jobs: A job that requires a longer commute or has more costuming expectations might be less remunerative in reality than one with a lower salary. Compare job offers from the true perspective of how much you are really selling your life energy for.

3. Knowing the financial bottom line for your job will help to clarify further your motives for working and for selecting one job over another. Mark H.'s story is not an anomaly. Many, many people spend all of their income and then some on maintaining their job—and consider themselves fortunate. Another FIer said that doing this step increased his consciousness of unnecessary job-related expenses to such an extent that his net earnings per hour doubled. Once he recognized how many of his expenses were due to his job, he was able to reduce or even eliminate many of them. For example, he began bringing his own lunch instead of sending out to the deli, switched from driving to using mass transit (doubling the benefit of this choice by using the time for decompression on the way home), reevaluated the supposed need for so many changes of stylish clothes, and even began exercising by taking a daily walk with his wife (improving their relationship as well as their health). Someone else used the results of this step as a criterion for accepting or rejecting jobs. When she could figure out just what hourly wage she'd be getting, she could see very clearly whether the job was worth it to her. Indeed, there are some jobs that she might have applied for previously that she now doesn't even consider.

No Shame, No Blame

And remember, this is where your feelings about your work/job/identity will most strongly bubble to the surface. Compassionate self-awareness is the key. Just notice each feeling as it presents itself, without criticizing it—and without criticizing your job, your boss, yourself, or this book. So what if you've been paying to work? So what if you've been blowing every paycheck on "rewarding" yourself for surviving another week? So what if you've been leading a fast-track lifestyle on a $10-an-hour paycheck? That's all in the past. It's what you thought you needed to do before you knew that money = your life energy.

CHECKLIST: LIFE ENERGY VS. SALARY

	Time hours/week more	Money $/week less
Commuting:		
wear and tear for commute miles		
gas and oil		
public transportation		
parking fees		
tolls		
maintenance		
walking or bicycling		
Cabs/Ridesharing		
Insurance		
Costuming:		
clothes bought for work		
makeup bought for work		
impressive briefcase		
shaving for work		
Meals:		
coffee breaks		
lunches		
entertaining for work		
food rewards for unpleasant Job		
convenience food		

	Time hours/week more	Money $/week less

Daily decompression:
    time until kids are allowed to yell again
    additional time till civil
    additional time till able to do anything
    recreational substance
Escape entertainment:
    movies
    bars
    cable TV
    online subscriptions
    game systems
Vacations, "toys" (if to compensate for job):
    exercise equipment
    sports equipment
    boat
    summer home
Job-related illness:
    colds, flu, etc.
    massages to relieve aching back
    hospitalizations for stress-related illness
Other job-related expenses
    hired help to
        clean house
        mow lawn
        babysit
    day care for kids
    educational programs
    professional or trade magazines
    conferences
    life coach

B. KEEP TRACK OF EVERY CENT THAT COMES INTO OR GOES OUT OF YOUR LIFE

So far we have established that money equals life energy, and we have learned to compute just how many hours of life energy we exchange for each dollar. Now we need to become conscious of the movement of that form of life energy called money in every moment of our lives—we need to keep track of our income and expenses on a daily basis. The second part of step 2 is simple, but not necessarily easy. From now on, keep track of every cent that comes into or goes out of your life.

Many people intentionally remain aloof regarding money. Their mythology puts "money" and "love-truth-beauty-spirituality" in two separate boxes. Plenty of people will show all to a lover but never show that same person their paycheck. Plenty of families fall deeper and deeper into debt because it seems unloving to call each other out on unconscious spending. Community service groups burn out because they are reluctant to ask for money to pay at least one person to manage the day-to-day tasks of running an organization. Friends never get back the money or things they lend others because keeping track seems somehow nasty and insisting on payback even nastier. This happens between parents and children often. Tracking money somehow seems to cheapen transactions that should be based solely in love. All of these situations stem from the same root thought: Money is money and love is love and never the twain shall meet. Look at your own attitudes. Do you excuse financial unconsciousness with high-minded philosophical or spiritual ideals?

A Spiritual Discipline

Religions, ancient and modern, all have techniques for training the mind to be here now, "in the moment."

These practices take many forms and include such seemingly diverse techniques as watching the breath as it goes in and out; repeating a phrase over and over in order to focus the wandering mind; concentrating on an object without entertaining past memories or future fantasies about it—just being with it right now; practicing various martial arts (such as aikido or karate); developing an inner "witness" to simply observe what you are doing now.

To this list we add another discipline designed to sharpen awareness—one that is indispensable to the financial program and perhaps more easily accepted by our grounded, materialistic Western mentality than some of the more esoteric practices: Instead of watching your breath, you watch your money.

This practice is simple: Keep track of every cent that comes into or goes out of your life.

The rule for this highly developed tool of transformation technology is: Keep track of every cent that comes into or goes out of your life.

The methodology for this marvel of monetary metaphysics is: Keep track of every cent that comes into or goes out of your life.

There are no specifications for how to track every cent that goes into or out of your life. There is no official notebook to buy ("only $49.95 with indices, quick-reference charts, and a solar calculator"). For many people, a pocket-size memo book is the perfect constant companion in which to note every cent that enters or leaves their lives, along with the occasion of its entering or leaving. Others, more enamored of time than money, log their expenses and income in a special section of their appointment book. And some track their money—along with their appointments, tasks, addresses, and more—on their phones and computers, linking their bank accounts with online tools and only using debit cards (or credit cards paid off monthly) so they have an up-to-date record literally at hand. Computers and smartphones are making this easier than ever, but there's no right way to do it—whatever works best for you is the best method.

Some people stumble here. They don't want to track their money. Too hard. Too anal. Too much time. Too confronting. Every penny? How about every dollar? Or every ten? Or kinda more or less . . .

Carolyn H. is a natural tracker—but her husband is not. He says that the emphasis on "every penny" is not helpful. Most people just don't want to live like that. "Years ago," she said, "as part of my method of bringing him on board with tracking, I streamlined our tracking to better suit him and it's been a success. We use round numbers. We track cash as best we can but don't make a fetish of it. We allow for a minimum amount of unaccounted-for cash—and added a category for that. Sometimes there's almost nothing there, sometimes after a complicated month there might be as much as two hundred dollars there—which used to drive me crazy, but now doesn't. Here's why—interestingly, my husband has begun to watch that number and really try to get it down to a trivial or at least reasonable amount. Seeing a large number there has gotten his attention about being more aware of his spending far more effectively than all the talk, argument, FI reading, etc., ever did. I'm pleased."

Mike L. led voluntary simplicity groups for years and encouraged everyone to "do the steps" religiously—the way he and his wife had, with stunning results. He was an "every penny" stickler. When he and his wife moved to a fixer-upper house in a new community, though, Mike finally developed some understanding of his group members' feelings of being overwhelmed with step 2. He decided to be his own contractor—and builder. His number of daily financial transactions shot up, as did the time he spent each day uncrumpling receipts and logging expenses. He decided to be satisfied with using a debit card and having his bank send his data to his financial program, simplifying his life this way until his spending settled down.

One person noted that the Financial Ninja types mentioned in the introduction to this book find tracking as natural as breathing and need no convincing, while for right-brained people (known for their creativity and intuitive thinking), it's like writing with their nondominant hand. Karen E. wrote, "I love tracking, still do it after all fourteen years, can't imagine not. It's enabled us to figure out how to live half time in Europe (on a houseboat in France) and half time in the States, to volunteer as we wish, and to travel as well." She's a natural.

Minimalists and creative types have adopted strategies like Mike L.'s—pay for everything with a debit card—and get a surprising amount of peace from gaining control of something that had been an utter mystery. When they link tracking with time to create, meditate, or travel, they are willing to develop the habit.

Once **Don S.**, *a young fan of Mr. Money Mustache's blog about personal finance and early retirement, started tracking, a clearer view of where his income was going led him to swap restaurant lunches for packing a lunch to bring to work and doing more home cooking. He says, "For me, it wasn't about limiting my spending in some authoritarian way to try and be more 'responsible.' It was about understanding how I was currently spending my money in a guilt-free way. I was able to cut this [food] expense category by nearly fifty percent, saving hundreds of dollars a month. My awareness of how I was spending my money allowed me to rein in wasteful spending in a way that felt instinctual, and then put that money towards the things that were more important to me and my overall happiness. Those few hundred dollars of savings each month quickly added up to cover a three-week* *trip to Europe! Being more efficient with my money meant I was happier overall, saving more money for the future, and less stressed about spending money on things that bring me joy."*

Whatever system you choose, do it (the program works only if you do it!)—and be accurate. Let it become a habit to record any and all movements of money, the exact amount, and the reason for the exchange. Every time you spend or receive money, make it second nature to note it instantly.

In *The Millionaire Next Door*, the authors, Thomas J. Stanley and William D. Danko, note that people who have achieved a high net worth relative to income know how much they are spending on clothes, travel, housing, transportation, and so on, and those who don't achieve high net worth relative to income have no idea how much they spend. It's a stark contrast.

Figure 2-3 is a fictional example of two days' entries. Note the degree of detail given for each expenditure. Notice how expenditures at work are specifically labeled as such. Observe the differentiation of the expenditures at the convenience store between snacks ("chips, dip, soda") and batteries. Similar differentiations of spending categories are made in Saturday's grocery store and department store trips. The subcategories or "breakouts" within the total are rounded approximations (though you are certainly encouraged to be close in your approximations, it would be time consuming to calculate the exact cost of toilet paper, wine, etc.), but the total must be accurate to the penny.

Every Cent? . . . But Why?

Remember that the purpose of this procedure is simply to keep track of every cent that comes into or goes out of your life.

"Why," you may ask, "do I need to go to such great

FIGURE 2-3
Sample Daily Record

Friday, August 24	In	Out
Bridge toll to work		1.50
Coffee and Danish at work		5.50
[Found in restroom]	0.25	
Lunch at work		7.84
Tip for lunch		1.50
[Repaid by Jack for Monday's lunch]	7.00	
Coffee break at work		3.25
Office contribution (Di's shower)		10.00
Soda from machine at work		1.25
Candy bar from machine at work		0.75
Gas: 10 gal at $3.50/gal		35.00
Convenience store: chips, dip, soda		5.39
Convenience store: 8-pack AA batteries		7.59
[Paycheck, net for week]	760.31	
(see stub for deduction)		
Saturday, August 25	In	Out
Grocery shopping		121.55
Breakout: approx.		
motor oil	6.00	
greeting card	3.50	
magazines	4.50	
household	17.75	

Saturday, August 25 *(cont)*		In	Out
toiletries	15.50		
wine	10.00		
approx. subtotal	57.25		
groceries	64.30		
TOTAL	121.55		
Department store			75.92
Breakout: approx.			
household	12.00		
shirt, for work	27.00		
candy	4.50		
photos	16.00		
hardware	6.00		
auto accessories	10.42		
TOTAL	75.92		
Lunch, sandwich shop			7.88
Dinner with friend, China Star			23.94
Tip for dinner			4.50
Concert with a friend			24.00

lengths?" Because it's the best way to become conscious of how money actually comes and goes in your life as opposed to how you think it comes and goes. Up to now most of us have had a rather cavalier attitude toward our small, daily monetary transactions. In practice we often reverse the old adage of "penny wise, pound foolish." We might search our souls and discuss with our partner the advisability of spending $75 for a new four-color left-handed veeblefitzer, yet over the course of a month an even larger amount often goes out of our wallets in small, "insignificant" purchases.

"But must I keep track of every cent?" you may ask.

Yes, every cent!

Why every cent, rather than just rounding off to the nearest dollar, or using approximate figures? Because this helps to establish important lifelong habits. After all, how big is a "fudge factor"? How close is "close enough"?

Granted, in practice many FIers settle into rounding to the dollar, but that's as far as they slip. Human nature being what it is, if you start cheating, even "just a little bit," that little bit tends to get bigger and soon you'll find yourself thinking, "Well, I don't have to write everything down, just the major expenses"; and then, "Well, I've done this for a month now, so I think I'll start rounding it off to the nearest thousand." (It's like dieting: If you break your diet on Tuesday morning by having a buttered English muffin instead of dry toast, the tendency is to cheat even more, and by evening you're gobbling down a carton of ice cream and a pound cake.) If you want this to be a worthwhile undertaking, it's worth your while to do it right. If you rebel against every penny, try every dime or dollar (or euro or yen), but more than that is a little like eating ten slivers of cake as though it were nothing rather than face the big fat slice you're actually consuming.

Since the original writing of this book, credit cards have become second nature in consumer culture. Now getting a credit card is almost a rite of passage into adulthood. While credit cards bring many efficiencies, they enable you to you spend much more carelessly and unconsciously. If you're having trouble tracking your money, we encourage you to go "plastic-free" for a month. Withdraw cash from your bank and keep track of how much you spend throughout the month. Not only will you gain a greater awareness of spending, you'll most likely find it more motivating to save. Many diligent savers find this exercise brings them back to earth about their spending habits.

Since money has a direct correlation to your life energy, why not respect that precious commodity, your life energy, enough to become conscious of how it is spent?

You may have some initial resistance to doing this impeccably, but ultimately this step must be embraced, regardless of feelings, for it is a vital section of the royal road to money mastery:

Keep track of every cent that comes into or goes out of your life.

Useful Attitudes

No leeway. A telescope with one lens just a wee bit out of alignment still doesn't allow you to see the stars. The same holds true for a human life. A little bit of fudging cuts down the amount of light that can shine through. This is where you get to be ruthless, tough-minded, and absolute.

Your commitment to clearing up your relationship with money is really tested here. One of the keys to your success in this program (and in life) is a shift in attitude from one of laxity and leeway to one of accuracy, precision, and impeccability. (By the way, such integrity might work miracles in other aspects of your life. People have lost weight, kept their desks cleared, and patched up broken relationships—all through doing this step. Integrity is integrity is integrity.)

No judgment—lots of discernment. Judgment (blaming ourselves and others) is labeling things in terms of good and bad. On the road to transforming your relationship with money and achieving Financial Independence, you will find that judgment and blame do not serve. Discernment, on the other hand, is an essential skill. Discernment is sorting out the true from the false, separating the wheat from the chaff. In the process of writing down every cent that comes into or goes out of your life, you will begin to discern which expenses are fitting and fulfilling and which are unnecessary, extravagant, or even downright embarrassing. Discernment has to do with that higher faculty we all have—the one that knows the truth, that sees a bigger picture and recognizes that what we really want is to make a difference before we die. This faculty will be increasingly on duty as you work with the financial program. Aligning your spending with this faculty is the key to Financial Integrity. Through writing down every cent that comes into and goes out of your life, you are awakening this latent superpower and inviting it increasingly to direct your life.

SUMMARY OF STEP 2

1. Establish (accurately and honestly) how much money you are trading your life energy for, and discover your *real* hourly wage.

2. Learn about your money behavior by keeping track of every cent that comes into and goes out of your life.

MONEY TALK QUESTIONS

If you engage in Money Talks, you'll be surprised at what you discover for yourself. You make the insights your own. You go from agreeing with what we say to knowing the truth for yourself.

Using the suggestions in the epilogue for how to have a Money Talk, raise these questions in your daily reflections, with your partner, or in social groups. Remember, adding "Why?" to the end of any question will take it deeper. Adding "How has society shaped my answer?" to any question will take it wider. There are no right answers.

- ◆ What is money?
- ◆ Describe your relationship with money in five words or less. Why those words?
- ◆ Do you experience more stress when you have money, or when you don't have it?
- ◆ Finish the sentence "If I had more money, then I'd be . . ." Elaborate!
- ◆ Are you earning what you're worth?
- ◆ What belief about money keeps you from being, doing, or having what you want?

3

Where Is It All Going?

Congratulations! You've made it into the present. Knowing how much money has come into and gone out of your life—today, last week, last month, and since your first allowance—is a monumental feat, a giant step toward Financial Intelligence. In terms of where this program will take you, however, you've just begun. The insights you've had, as vivid as they may have been, are just a taste of what's in store.

To do steps 1 and 2 you only needed to take the word of some apparent experts (the authors and all the others who have successfully used this program) that this kind of obsessive counting is necessary to break the hold that money has over your life. You've only needed to name and number such tangible items as your income, expenses, bank balances, and possessions. With step 3, however, you'll need to call on more of yourself to make it work. Here you'll begin the process of evaluating the information you've collected.

DO YOU NEED A BUDGET?

This approach to money is actually the opposite of a budget.

Mind you, a budget can be an amazing tool to lasso

your wild spending and get it to behave. Based on your income, a budget helps you plan your spending so that everything is covered every month and you don't impulsively blow the rent money on a pretty dress or your utilities money on a late-night online shopping spree. But budgeting is a planning tool, while this program is an "awareness of your enough point" tool. It's about your uniqueness rather than standard budgeting categories with conventional wisdom advice like Housing should be 25 percent to 35 percent of your total or Food 20 percent or Health Care 5 percent to 10 percent. Or saving only 5 percent of your income and crossing your fingers for Social Security. Applying these norms to your life might well lead you down the normal path of nine to five until you're sixty-five.

Maybe you're like **Justin**, though, who is trading ten hours a week of household work for a room in an older woman's home. No place for that in a budget. Justin is saving to buy a camper. Where would he put that in a budget? He plans to live in it and travel the United States, contacting couch-surfing hosts for a driveway to park it in. A budget vacation? But he plans to blog about it and invite sponsors to support him. Is that now an income? He wants to learn to forage and possibly hunt. Does that go under Food? Entertainment?

These categories go to show that not everyone can get their squiggly lives into the straight lines of a spreadsheet. Unlike a budget, step 3 in this program gives you the freedom of getting clear about money without cutting off a lot of individuality and creativity.

Rather than using standard categories and standard percentages and making a spending plan, with this approach you will discover your patterns from observing how you actually spend your life energy, and revealing your own unique relationship with money. Guaranteed, this awareness will change you not because of an arbitrary financial goal, but because you want nothing more than to spend your life well.

Think of it like the difference between dieting and mindful eating. With "a diet" you apply a formula to your eating to achieve a result—weight loss. There is a confusing array of diets out there, often utterly contradictory, and people dissatisfied with themselves migrate from one to the next seeking salvation from excess pounds. It's imposing change from the outside in.

With mindful eating you slow down, pay attention to what you are actually hungry for. Without such self-awareness, we might eat when we are tired or thirsty or in need of a walk in the sunshine. With mindful eating, you taste your food. Taste is one way the body senses whether what is being eaten is good for us. You pause often enough to see if your body has had enough, and if so, you stop. It's an inside-out job, guided by the well-being of the body, not conforming to a standard.

In a book called *Diets Don't Work!* Bob Schwartz offers four rules for getting off the diet-go-round:

1. Eat when you're hungry.
2. Eat exactly what your body wants.
3. Eat each bite consciously.
4. Stop when your body has had enough.[1]

Very simple. All you have to do is be conscious. Being conscious means you become aware of what you are thinking and feeling as you think and feel it. It's cultivating an inner witness that simply observes what's going on with warm awareness, not judging, not evaluating, just curious. And when you find yourself in your old habits—eating when you are bored, alone in the kitchen, between tasks, wanting a treat for a job well done, blue with depression, green with envy, or red with fury—you return to being conscious, skipping the guilt step and just returning to observing hunger, satiation, and motivation. Simple—but not always easy. It takes discovering and exercising some mental muscles that may have atrophied from misuse. You have to identify what "hungry" is, what "full" is, what you truly want as opposed to what you crave out of feeling perpetually deprived, and what you are actually eating while you are eating it. This financial program points you in the same direction as mindful eating:

1. You need to identify and follow internal signals, not external admonishments or habitual desires.
2. You need to observe and adjust your patterns of spending over the long term, not what you spend over the short term.

This is not about following our (or anyone else's) budgets, with standardized categories and a suggested percentage of income that should go toward each category. This is not about swearing at the beginning of each month that you'll do better. This is not about guilt. It's about identifying, for yourself, what you need as opposed to what you crave, what purchases or types of purchases actually bring you fulfillment, what represents "enough" to you, and what you actually spend money on. This program is based on your reality, not a set of external norms. Consequently, its success rests on your honesty and integrity.

And here is where this program is different from the tens or hundreds of other recipes for fiscal health. It is based on consciousness, fulfillment, and choice, not on budgeting or deprivation.

Step 3 is where you begin to exercise these awareness muscles. If you're out of shape you may feel some pain, but in reality there is nothing painful about doing this step. In fact, it's fun!

NO SHAME, NO BLAME

Remember the mantra: No shame, no blame. What you are confronting is just the truth about the choices you've been making in your life. No shame, no blame. How fortunate to be able to do this yourself, instead of being audited by the IRS. How lucky you are to be doing this now and not in your last hours on earth. No shame, no blame. Remember to use the mantra at those moments when you want to hide under the bed, go on a spending spree till you've forgotten what was bothering you, or decide that this program doesn't work and give up. No shame, no blame.

> **Anita C.** *needed something like that mantra to help her survey her closet with this new spotlight of consciousness. No doubt about what her addiction was: clothes and costume jewelry. She had been a shopaholic. Anytime she was out in her car she had a compulsion to stop at the mall just to see what was on sale. Somehow this ritual of shopping and spending helped her feel OK about herself. But there it all was—the result of years of addiction, sitting in her closet. It would have been nice if she'd had a conversion experience right then, but she didn't. She continued to shop until the balance tipped and it no longer felt good to her to have so much and not wear it. As an interim measure, she justified her excess by giving it away as presents. It was fun to place things she'd never worn with just the right friend or relative. Slowly the desire to shop weakened. Then one day she found herself at one of her favorite department stores, surveying the new colors in sweaters. Consciousness struck. "Is this going to be what I do with my life? Is this what it's all going to be about? What am I doing? I have enough already!" She left the store empty-handed. Sometime after that experience, Anita discovered that she had lost her desire to shop.*

If Anita had been working with the standard budget and spending plan strategy, she might not have recognized her shopping as a compulsion. She would have remained a "social shopper," denying any kind of underlying problem. By steadily applying consciousness and compassion to her shopping habit, she was able, eventually, to have the profound insight that she already had enough. She is now so allergic to shopping that she's lost a few old friends whose central social ritual is browsing through the mall. But she's gained a lot more.

So, having set the context, let's get on with step 3, creating your Monthly Tabulation.

Step 3: Monthly Tabulation

After a month of keeping track of your income and expenses (step 2), you will have a wealth of specific information on the flow of money in your life—down to the penny. **In this step you will establish spending categories that reflect the uniqueness of your life** (as opposed to the oversimplified budget-book categories like Food, Shelter, Clothing, Transportation, and Health).

While you still might choose to have such basic categories, within each major category you will find and separate out numerous important subcategories that will give you a vastly more accurate picture of your spending. The fun—and challenge—of this step will come in discovering your own unique spending categories and subcategories. These subcategories will be like an encyclopedia of your unique spending habits. They will be perhaps your most accurate description to date of your lifestyle, including all your peculiarities and peccadilloes.

This detailed portrait of your life is your true bottom line. Forget the mythology of your life. Forget the story you tell yourself and others. Forget your résumé and the list of associations you belong to. When you do step 3, you will have a clear, tangible mirror of your actual life—your income and expenses over time. In this mirror you will see exactly what you are getting for the time you invest in making money.

ESTABLISHING CATEGORIES

In establishing your categories, you will want to be honest and precise, without becoming overly fussy.

Food

Unless you are very different from other humans, you will have a broad category called Food. As you look at your food expenses for the month, however, you may observe that there are actually several different types of food buying that you can usefully track. There is the food you eat at home with your family. There is also the food you eat at home when you have friends or extended family over for dinner. So you might have two categories: "Just Us" and "Guests." But don't get fanatic. Don't hover over your dinner guests, recording in your little notebook how much and what they eat. "Would you like seconds, Uncle Hal?" could take on a whole new meaning. It is sufficient to estimate, within the exact total of your grocery bill, what proportion went to guests. For example, if four extra people are around your dinner table and you normally shop for just you and your partner, approximately two-thirds of that grocery bill should be attributed to Guests. The totals are accurate to the penny, but the breakouts from the totals are estimates.

Then there is the Restaurants category, from grab-and-go lunches at work to dinners out. You could parse that further into "Too Tired to Cook" and "Special Occasions" if eating out is no longer a special occasion and you have a serious and expensive restaurant habit. In our busy lives with maybe twelve hours between leaving for work and coming home, this can seem the only option if you want a clean kitchen and eight hours of sleep. You might also want to see what snacking is costing you. What do those coffee breaks actually cost a month? What about TV food—the chips and popcorn and candy and soft drinks that so often go hand in hand (or hand in mouth) with TV watching? You may break it down further to healthy food and junk food if you are curious about where your allegiances really lie and whether you could go organic without going broke.

All such spending patterns will show up if you establish categories that reflect your actual behavior rather than just writing everything in the budget-book column called Food. This precision is not for the purpose of a more exact confession to your financial adviser. It's so that when you throw your hands up in disgust, crying, "Where does it all go? I hardly buy anything!" you can answer yourself in a firm and steady tone, "It goes to the candy machine on the third floor of my office building."

Housing

Your housing category might include mortgage (or rent) with subcategories of utilities, mortgage deduction (if applicable), as well as recording income from renting the family room to tourists.

On the other end of the scale, perhaps you have multiple homes—one in the suburbs, one at the beach, and a small apartment in the city. Having a category for each one can help you see whether renting when needed would be a better bet than owning.

Fifty years ago the budgeting rule of thumb was to allow 25 percent of your income for housing. Now when people tally up all their costs in this category, they often discover that housing eats up 40 percent or more of their income. Motivated by seeing their numbers in black and white, they are finding clever ways to reduce what they spend on a roof over their heads, sometimes down to zero. One couple whose tech jobs let them live anywhere halved this category by spending summers in a lively, costly city in the northern hemisphere and wintering for next to nothing on out-of-the-way beaches in the southern hemisphere in winter. A single woman paid off her mortgage in a tourist area by living in her camper on a friend's land in the summer months while she rented out her house with a view. A retired older woman knew from past homeowner experience what a time and money sink ownership can be; she gained a reputation for meticulous caretaking and now is an in-demand house sitter, getting paid while having some of the most elegant roofs in her region over her head. Of course, there are now matchmaking websites for house sitters who are willing to travel. See why the standard budget book categories don't work anymore?

Clothing

When it comes to clothing, you may find that you aren't getting enough information about your unique spending patterns by simply having one category called Clothing. You may need to distinguish between utility and fashion (the desire never to appear in the office in the same outfit twice in a row, for example, or one-upmanship in elegant attire at social gatherings). In other words, be specific. Make appropriate distinctions. To get an accurate map of your spending patterns, you may need several subcategories. There is the clothing you wear in your everyday home life, the clothing you believe is appropriate attire for the workplace, and whatever specialized apparel you think you need for recreational activities. One doctor, who followed this program to get a handle on how a consistently unaccounted-for 20 percent of his income disappeared, discovered that he had a real penchant for buying shoes. He had golf shoes, tennis shoes, running shoes, boating shoes, walking shoes, hiking shoes, and climbing shoes, as well as cross-country-ski shoes, downhill-ski boots, and after-ski boots. Just having a category for shoes helped him find some of that missing income and face the fact that he rarely wore anything but comfortable around-the-house slip-ons. He wasn't alone in his shoe fetish. As of 2015 the US footwear industry exceeded $64 billion in sales.[2]

A nationwide survey of American women conducted that same year by Consumer Reports National Research Center revealed that the average woman owns nineteen pairs of shoes—only four of which she wears regularly.[3]

This isn't just accounting—this is a process of self-discovery. It may even be the only process of self-discovery that promises to leave you in better shape financially than when you embarked on it. You may also choose categories that reflect your feelings, not your occasions: clothes to cheer you up, clothes to impress a boss or a date, clothes to fit in. They say clothes make the man—or woman—so it's good to see who you are trying to be by what clothes you buy, and what that ambition is costing you.

Transportation

By using appropriate subcategories for Transportation, you may gain insights that save you many hundreds of dollars a year. If you own a car, doing your tallies is a great opportunity to reflect on why you own one at all instead of relying on public transportation. Convenience, status, necessity, fitting in, a sense of freedom . . . ? Could you make up for the lack of a car with ridesharing and short-term rentals or the many car-sharing options now available thanks to hailing services through your phone? In some cities you can rent your car via a sharing app. And your RV!

What percentage of your transportation costs come from wrong location, location, location? Many people fail to think about walkability; they buy or rent homes in areas with no public transit options or bike paths. A farmer in Kansas might not be able to survive without a truck, but if you moved from the burbs to a few blocks from work, school, and shopping, your transportation expenses might zero out. It is also a good time to review your auto insurance: What portion of your insurance is necessary and how much is habit, convention, and buying into your agent's scare tactics? While you're at it, look at anything else overinsured, from your home to antiques. And what category would your second car go under: Transportation, Hobby, or Ostentation? If you don't have a car, are you overspending on pricey cab fares when you could be using public transit or other options?

Your Technology

Staying informed and connected is a crucial part of modern-day society, and a growing expense over the past decade has been the cost of accessing and sending data. Cell phones, Internet, cable access, tablets, and smart watches are rapidly becoming a substantial spending category. If you just have a category called Phone, you may miss numerous options for saving. Many people give up their landlines once they see how much staying connected costs. Or they change their cell service to one that doesn't have a two-year contract—and buy their phones through Craigslist. With categories called Landline, Cell Phone, and Equipment, you can see your patterns more clearly. Think also about what technology you need for work versus leisure or personal development.

Entertainment

Going to the movies used to be the only way to consume this type of entertainment, but now the movies come to us through home entertainment systems, phones, tablets, computers, and more. It could be revelatory to have an Entertainment category in which you break out streaming services (as one item or, even more specific, your multiple subscriptions). Do you need them all? What about streaming services for music? And your home entertainment center—is that a site of consumption with upgrading your tech and then having to upgrade your furniture to house your tech and then having to repaint your family room and . . . ? Do you go clubbing? Do you rent entertainers for your kids' parties—and adult parties as well? If you have children, what portion of the services and gadgets you buy them are under Entertainment? Or maybe they fit under Babysitting? Should you have a category called Children, which might lead you to find less expensive ways to distract them as well as introduce them to the old kind of fun, like going outdoors?

Refining Your Categories

What makes this sort of ruthless honesty bearable is that you can confront your little sins and indiscretions in the privacy of your own account book, rather than when you "get caught." So don't skimp on being truthful if you find yourself face-to-face with some of your faults and frailties while innocently doing your Monthly Tabulation. What better way to face the music? If you remember that doing this exercise will lead not to the punishment of a budget but rather to the freedom of self-acceptance, you will press on regardless. For example, into what category do you put the part of the food money that you use to play the slots or buy lottery tickets? Yet another moment of truth may come as you vacillate over where to record liquor. Is it food? Is it entertainment? Or is it a drug?

It is also important to distinguish between job-related expenses and other expenses. For example, under Transportation you would list separately the cost of commuting and other (non-reimbursed) work-related transportation expenses. If the same vehicle is used for both commuting and pleasure, then split costs according to mileage in each category. Similarly, if you use your cell phone for work-related as well as personal calls, those costs should be listed separately.

Within your Medical category you may find several subcategories: sickness, wellness (i.e., what you purchase to keep yourself vital and alive, like vitamins, membership in a health club, annual checkup), health insurance (even though, really, let's be honest: Health care is what you do for yourself; access to the medical system is sickness care), prescription drugs; nonprescription drugs, and so on. You can see why this process has allowed people to transform more than just their relationship with money.

A further refinement will come as you decide how you want to account for large, "unusual" expenses like annual insurance premiums, capital expenses like a new refrigerator, the money you put into IRAs, or a balloon payment on your house. As far as we are concerned, there is no "right" way to do this. For us, after a year of hearing ourselves make the same excuse every month about all the extraordinary expenses ("This was an unusual month because the X, Y, or Z Thingamabob had to be paid"), we realized that every month is an unusual month and that these extraordinary expenses are a continuing part of life.

You may perfect your categories over time. The exercise should be easy and a lot of fun. It will draw on a blend of honesty and creativity, stimulate your imagination, and challenge your morality—all at the same time. It's better than most video games, TV shows, and board games all rolled into one.

Over time as you do this step, not only will you refine your categories, you'll find each one settles into a predictable range. You will get clarity about your spending patterns and have an internally generated (rather than externally imposed) picture that is unique, deeply satisfying, and fluid as you grow and change and learn—a far cry from the old budget book categories.

Remember, you are also recording all the money that flows into your life; you may want to establish subcategories for income also. It is important to distinguish between wages/salaries/tips and interest/dividend income; your primary income versus your "side hustle." Where will you record the dimes you find on the sidewalk, the quarters you retrieve from vending machines, and your gambling winnings? If you are an independent contractor, you likely have a separate line for each client on your business accounts, but when you pay yourself you might just have subcategories for each type of work: dog walking, handyman, coaching, substitute teaching, renting your guest room to travelers. As you go along in this program, you might have an income category called Selling Off My Clutter and subcategories called eBay, Yard Sales, and Antiques. You will also have a growing category called Investment Income (more on that later). You may also have unusual income months, like when you get an advance for writing a book or finally receive the $70,000 from Uncle Harry's estate. These income categories are not as revelatory as your spending ones. You already have the wake-up tool to analyze each income stream: your real hourly wage.

After you have examined the month's itemized entries from your tracking tool and created categories that accurately depict your spending patterns, devise a way to record expenses under each category in a way that works for you. Figure 3-1 will give you an idea of how such a tabulation might be set up. You will notice that there are a few blank columns. We will talk later about what these columns are for, but for now just include them.

TOTALING IT ALL UP

A word of warning: Yes, there are a variety of computer programs and apps that can be useful here, but the meat of this step is categorizing your expenses, and even the best software can't distinguish how to categorize golf—is it Recreation or is it a job-related expense because the golf course is where you transact your business? Make sure you aren't assuming you just can't do this step because you don't have the right program. Many do-it-yourselfers enjoy crafting a personalized spreadsheet complete with automatic calculations and color-coded cells. We've met others who simply jot down cryptic codes on a note card in their purse. Others may use monthly bank statement charts and graphs as a

FIGURE 3-1

Sample Monthly Tabulation Form

Month: _____   Actual Hourly Wages: _____

Expenses	Total Dollars	Life Energy			
FOOD					
At Home					
Restaurants					
Entertaining					
SHELTER					
Principal/Rent					
Interest					
Hotels					
UTILITIES					
Electricity					
Cell Phone					
Water					
CLOTHING					
Necessary					
Work					
Special					
HEALTH					
Prescription Drugs					
Nonprescription Drugs					
Doctor					
RECREATION					
TV/Internet/Gaming					
Online Streaming					
Hobbies					
Alcohol					

Expenses	Total Dollars	Life Energy			
TRANSPORTATION					
Gas/Oil					
Maintenance					
Public Transportation					
Tolls/Parking					
OTHER					

Income		
PAYCHECK		
BONUSES/TIPS		
INTEREST		
LOANS		

(A) Total Spent This Month _____

(B) Total Income This Month _____

(B – A) Total Saved This Month _____

starting point for their own financial journal. While some online platforms allow you to link bank and credit card accounts for a one-stop summary, it's important you take the time to filter common transactions. These tools are incredibly useful, but the key is finding a system that works for you. Both of the authors did it the old-fashioned way, with paper and pencil and adding up columns of figures by hand. Yes, these steps worked brilliantly even before calculators!

Whether by hand or machine, here's the simple process. At the end of the month you will transfer each entry from your tracking system into the appropriate column on your Monthly Tabulation. Add up your income columns to get your total monthly income. Add up the expenditures in each column and enter the total of each subcategory at the bottom of that column. Then add the totals for all expenditure categories—this sum is your total monthly expenses.

THE BALANCING ACT

Next, count the cash in your wallet and piggy bank and note the balance of your checking and savings accounts. Now you have enough information to see how closely you have kept track of the money flowing into and out of your life over the past month. If you have kept accurate records (and haven't physically lost any money), the money you actually have at the end of the month (in cash and bank accounts) will be equal to the money you had at the beginning of the month plus your total monthly income minus your total monthly expenses. If you haven't kept accurate records (or have physically lost some money), you will have lost or gained cash that you can't account for. The difference between your total monthly income and total monthly expenses (plus or minus your monthly error) is the money you have saved this month. When your monthly error is consistently zero, you will know you have mastered step 2 (keeping track of every penny). Congratulations! You have achieved a minor miracle.

Figure 3-2 shows a sample set of monthly figures, but please use it only as a model. The fun and empowerment come from creating a balancing system that works for your particular situation.

MAKING MONEY REAL

Now comes one of the magic keys to this program. What you have in front of you, as accurate and balanced as it may be, does not yet have the power to transform your relationship with money. It is simply the by-product of a month of successfully tracking little pieces of paper and bits of metal. You may have had emotional reactions

FIGURE 3-2

Sample End-of-Month Balancing

Part I			
Equation:			
$ at START of month + $ IN during month – $ OUT during month = $ at END of month			
$ at START:		Cash on hand	103.13
	+	Checking account balance	+	383.60
	+	Savings account balance	+	1,444.61
			1,931.34
+ $ IN:	+	Total monthly income		
		(from Monthly Tabulation)	+	2,622.23
			4,553.57
– $ OUT:	–	Total monthly expenses		
		(from Monthly Tabulation)	–	1,996.86
= $ at END:	=	$ you should have	2,556.71	(A)
		at end of month		
Part II			
ACTUAL $ AT END OF MONTH:		Cash on hand	173.24
	+	Checking account balance	+	597.36
	+	Savings account balance	+	1,784.69
	=	$ you actually have at end of month	2,555.29	(B)
Part III			
MONTHLY ERROR:		$ you should have (A)	2,556.71	(A)
	–	$ you actually have (B)	–	2,555.29	(B)
	=	$ lost or improperly recorded	1.42

Part IV			
SAVINGS:		Total monthly income	2,622.23
	−	Total monthly expenses	− 1,996.86
	±	Monthly error	− 1.42
	=	$ Saved this month	623.95

to this accounting, but they will be forgotten as soon as you embark on your next trip to the gazingus pin store. The fact that you may spend, let's say, eighty pieces of paper (dollars) on magazines a month does not have any direct relevance to your experience of life. However, remembering that money is something you trade your life energy for, you can now translate that $80 into something that is real for you: your life energy. Use the following formula:

$$\frac{\text{Money spent on magazines}}{\text{Real hourly wage}} = \text{Hours of life energy}$$

In chapter 2 we did a sample calculation that showed how a theoretical $25-an-hour salary could end up being, in reality, $10 an hour. Obviously your real hourly wage will end up being a different figure, but for the sake of this example, let's use $10 an hour. So, in the case of this magazine habit, you can divide that $80 by your real hourly wage ($10) and find out that you spent 8 hours of your life for this particular pleasure:

$$\frac{\$80}{\$10} = 8 \text{ Hours of life energy}$$

Now you can measure your growing pile of all the wonderful (yet unread) magazines on your bedside table against something real—eight unredeemable hours on your one-way journey from cradle to grave. That's a whole day of work! Those magazines drain your energy three times over: once in earning the money to buy them, again in staying up late to read them, and finally in feeling guilty when you haven't finished them by the time the next issue arrives (to say nothing of having to store or dispose of them). Could those eight hours have been better spent? How about taking Friday off? Is it still true that you have no time to spend with your family? What does this do to habitual procrastination? You've been wanting to catch up on your sleep—did you just find a way to do that? Or were those magazines worth every hour spent to acquire them? Did they give you eight hours of pleasure or valuable education, and then some? Don't answer these questions yet. Just notice that translating dollars into hours of your life reveals the real trade-offs you are making for your style of living. In chapter 4 we'll analyze these findings further.

Let's look at another example: your rent or mortgage payment. Let's say you pay $1,500 a month for the privilege of living in your house or apartment. Applying the awareness that your real hourly wage is $10, divide that $1,500 by $10. Here's the reality: It costs you 150 hours a month to put this particular roof over your head. If you're putting in the standard 40 hours a week, you'll soon realize that your housing costs eat up almost every hour you put in on your job. Every working hour is going to pay for a house that you get to enjoy perhaps two or three hours a day. Is it worth it? Sure, you can shave off some hours to account for your mortgage deduction or the benefit of your mother-in-law rental, but excuses like "I live in an expensive city" let you off the hook too easily. Be grateful for the starkness of this awareness. It will do wonders for your personal bottom line. No shame, no blame—but no wheedling and whining either.

Now take the total of each row of your Monthly Tabulation and convert the dollars spent in each subcategory into hours of life energy spent (you may round off to the nearest half hour). Your Monthly Tabulation form will now have the "[Total Hours of] Life Energy" column, as seen in Figure 3-1.

SOME PICTURES ARE
WORTH A THOUSAND WORDS

Let's look at real-life examples of how some FIers put this step to work for themselves.

Take a look at how **Rosemary I.** *set up her categories in Figure 3-3. Don't you feel as if you know a little about her unique personality just from looking at her tabulation for January? She obviously puts a high value on beauty, since she has two categories that refer to it (Beauty and Aesthetics). She obviously takes care of her body and is willing to spend money on maintaining her health. It is telling that she has wellness categories like Health Products and Health Services, rather than sickness categories like Drugs and Doctors. The Donations category says that she contributes to causes enough to have a separate category, rather than lumping donations under Miscellaneous. The Personal Growth category is one you wouldn't find in a standard budget book. This is aware-ness, as opposed to strict budgeting.*

The very process of creating this form provided Rosemary with valuable information about her priorities and gave her a tangible way to track how much of her life energy she was devoting to the things that mattered to her. The monthly ritual of filling in the numbers has the quality of an exciting game: How did she do in each category? Is it up or down from last month? How does it compare to last year's average for the same category? Are trends up or down?

Now let's look at how one couple has gone about creating categories and a Monthly Tabulation form for tracking them.

FIGURE 3-3

Rosemary's Monthly Tabulation with Hours of Life Energy

Month: January   Actual Hourly Wage: $12.14

Expenses	Total Dollars	Hours of Life Energy	Income	
Rent	560.00	46.1	Salary	2,085.00
Natural gas			Mileage reimbursement	37.00
Electricity	21.70	1.8	Other	23.25
Combined utilities				
Cell phone	5.72	0.5		
Household	29.39	2.4		
Groceries	85.25	7.0		
Treats	3.44	0.3		
Eating out	6.03	0.5		
Alcohol	6.57	0.5		
Gasoline/oil	37.88	3.1		
Car repair/maintenance				
Car insurance/ registration	248.47	20.5		
Parking	2.00	0.2		
Bus/ferry				
Health insurance	55.89	4.6		
Health products				
Health services	7.75	0.6		
Hygiene				
Beauty	13.18	1.1		

Expenses	Total Dollars	Hours of Life Energy	Income	
Clothing, necessary	10.74	0.9		
Clothing, unnecessary	25.45	2.1		
Entertainment				
Aesthetics				
Gifts/cards	18.60	1.5		
Subscriptions	25.11	2.1		
Personal growth				
Postage	3.15	0.3		
Office supplies				
Copies				
Donations				
Bank fees				
Miscellaneous	0.62	0.1		
Loan payments	78.00	6.4		
TOTAL	1,244.94		TOTAL	2,145.25

Maddy and Tom C. *live in rural Maine. Professionally they are quite different—he drives a truck and she's an accountant. Personally, though, they are best buddies and are enjoying the awareness and communication that come from combining their incomes and expenses. When they computed their real hourly wage, they combined their totals to come out with a single figure for the two of them: $10.23 an hour. As you can see in Figure 3-4, Maddy's total adjusted hours were 77.5 and Tom's were 67.5, or 145 hours combined. Maddy's total income was $1,080.31 and Tom's was $402.50, making a grand total of $1,482.81. Dividing combined income by* *combined hours is how they established that figure of $10.23 per hour. Dividing sixty minutes by that real hourly wage tells us that every dollar spent represented nearly 6 minutes of life energy.*

Combining their income and expenses works for Maddy and Tom. Other couples have found that separating their income and expenses was the only way to get an accurate reflection of their unique patterns.

FIGURE 3-4

Maddy and Tom's Calculation of *Real* Hourly Wage

Life Energy vs. Earnings		Hours/ week	Dollars/ week	Dollars/ hour
Maddy's basic job, after taxes				
(before adjustments)		50.0	1,207.50	24.15
Maddy's adjustments (list):		Add hours	Subtract costs	
Commuting		3.0	11.27	
At-work food		5.0	24.15	
Getting ready		0.5	3.22	
Entertainment/eating out		7.0	48.30	
Vacation		12.0	40.25	
Maddy's total adjustments		+ 27.5	– 127.19	
Job with adjustments:	Maddy	77.5	1,080.31	
	Tom	67.5	402.50	
	Total	145.0	1,482.81	10.23

How does it compare to last year's average for the same category? Are trends up or down?

You'd think that because **Mary and Don M.** *shared the same passion (music) and the same profession (computer programming), it would be natural for them to track their income and expenses together. But while they were outwardly a matched pair, their personalities and styles were at opposite ends of the spectrum. Don was near the rational, conservative, and deliberate end. Mary was more toward the emotional, experimental, and disorganized end. Their gazingus pins were different. Their shopping habits were different. Their hobbies (besides music) were different. Doing their Monthly Tabulations together wasn't giving either one of them much good information. Not only that, but soon after starting on the program, Mary left her programming job and started teaching piano full-time out of their home. Her hours and pay became irregular, so they decided that she would offset her smaller contribution to the household kitty by doing the housekeeping chores. This nonmonetary arrangement didn't show up to their satisfaction in the Monthly Tabulations. The more they struggled to make it work, the more tension arose. In order to maintain a friendly marriage and stay on the program, they decided to separate their finances. To Don it was sensible. To Mary it was threatening— but she agreed to give it a try. To her amazement Mary found that having her own accounts gave her a wonderful feeling of autonomy. She discovered that she'd become dependent in many subtle ways during the years of her marriage, and she reconnected with the strength and independence she'd felt when she was single.*

Let's look now at how another Her did her end-of-the-month balance sheet.

Elaine H., *from chapter 1, applied her computer programmer's logical mind to the task of setting up a balance sheet for herself. Her Monthly Tabulation categories are enough like Rosemary's that we don't need to reproduce them, but her balance sheet has a precision and elegance that are instructive (see Figure 3-5). Setting up this form for herself made the*

FIGURE 3-5

Elaine's Balance Sheet

August			
Assets	Beginning	Ending	Change
Savings Account	609.03	609.08	0.05
CDs	5,949.26	2,477.53	–3,471.73
Bonds	104,650.00	112,700.00	8,050.00
Checking account	700.40	2,159.99	1,459.59
Cash on hand	151.73	111.80	–39.93
Tracked income	6,878.56	Change in net worth	= 5,997.98
Tracked expenses	–865.18	Tracked change	6,013.38
Tracked change	6,013.38	Amount out of balance	= –15.40

end-of-the-month balancing process easy and accurate. Her capital is the combination of what she has in savings, a money market account, and bonds. This is all money that is earning interest, which she likes to keep separate from the money in her checking account. During the month of August, her net worth increased by nearly $6,000, and she mistracked $15.40.

The point of these stories is not to provide you with a standard to follow but to inspire you to create a Monthly Tabulation form that works for you. Remember, this is not a budget book or a spending plan. This is not trying to fit your square (or octagonal) peg into society's round hole. Creating your form will be a process of self-discovery. You aren't learning "the right way"; you are creating your own way. There is no right way to do it other than to do it.

This step is crucial to the whole rest of the program, which is why those people who proudly report that they are on the program but are guesstimating rather than tracking are off base. This step provides insight and empowerment and will be worth every minute you invest in setting it up to work for you.

SUMMARY OF STEP 3

1. Discern your unique spending and income categories and subcategories from your month of tracking income and expenses.

2. Set up your Monthly Tabulation.

3. Enter all money transactions in the appropriate category.

4. Total your money spent in each subcategory.

5. Add up total monthly income and total monthly expenses. Total your cash on hand and balance all bank accounts. Apply equation (total monthly income minus total monthly expenses plus or minus monthly error). The money you actually have at the end of the month should equal what you had at the beginning plus your monthly income minus your monthly expenses.

6. Convert the dollars spent in each subcategory into hours of life energy, using the real hourly wage that you computed in step 2.

MONEY TALK QUESTIONS

Two, three, four, or more minds are better than one. Sometimes seeing how others do the steps helps, and just the tangible work will raise so many interesting questions.

Using the suggestions in the epilogue for how to have a Money Talk, raise the following questions in your daily reflections, with your partner, or in social groups. Remember, adding "Why?" to the end of any question will take it deeper. Adding "How has society shaped my answer?" to any question will take it wider. There are no right answers.

- How do you stay conscious with your money?
- What do you insure—and why?
- What question would you most like to ask a friend about money? An expert? A relative?
- How do you feel when you spend money?
- What are some of your best experiences with tipping, tithing, or giving?
- What are your top priorities and how does your spending support them—or not?

4

How Much Is Enough? The Quest for Happiness

In saving my life she conferred a value on it. It is a currency I do not know how to spend.   —*Sherlock*, TV series

What will you do with your one wild and precious Life?
                                        —Mary Oliver, poet

Don't ask yourself what the world needs, ask yourself what makes you come alive, and then go do it. Because what the world needs is people who have come alive.
—Howard Thurman, philosopher and theologian

What makes you come alive? What will you do with this life you have been given?

Ashleigh Brilliant, the master of the under-seventeen-word quip, once drew a cartoon of a forlorn boy saying, "I don't know how to be happy. They didn't teach it in school."

If the pursuit of happiness is our birthright, written into the Declaration of Independence, and yet our aptitude for happiness was all but squeezed out of us in school, we need to look now at what fills us with happiness—or fulfillment. Fulfillment is our compass and our rudder for transforming our relationship with money.

Whether in the sense of accomplishing a goal or letting go into a moment of real contentment, fulfillment is that experience of deep satisfaction when you can say, "Aaahh . . . that was [a delicious meal, a job well done, a purchase worth the money . . .]." You have an aspiration or an expectation and you recognize—and celebrate— that the very thing you wanted has arrived. To find such fulfillment and be mindful of it, then, you need to know what you are looking for. It's fairly easy to know what fulfillment is in terms of food or other temporary plea- sures, but to have fulfillment in the larger sense, to have a fulfilled life, you need to have a sense of purpose, a dream of what a good life might be.

For many of us, however, growing up has meant out- growing our dreams—or having them shrink in the face of harsh circumstances or people. Debt for many has been the great dream destroyer, acquired to fund a dream of an education or a home or a wedding and then standing by the door of every future dream, arms crossed, saying, "Pay up! Or you can't go further." Some of us just accept debt as a part of adult life and trod on, shackled by consequences we don't fully understand. Whether to the debt collectors, your bills, hard luck, poor choices, or your own insecurities, if you have sacri- ficed your dreams on the altar of the almighty dollar, you need to reclaim them, as they are the fuel for this journey.

Did you dream of writing a great book, but now write marketing copy for money? That book is still there. Did you dream of being a healer, but now work for an HMO, with back-to-back fifteen-minute appointments? That dream of selfless service is still in there. It might take radical change to reclaim it, but it's not gone. Were you inspired by your faith to inspire others in their search for God, but now spend most of your time in congregation politics and fund-raising? That dream is not gone, just deferred. Between the life you dreamed of and the life you have, what happened—and has it diminished your courage to dream big again? Has the constant buzz of daily tasks slowly narrowed your vision to the plodding steps ahead? Have you been told, "Don't worry, those dreams will go away in time," as if dreams themselves are childish affairs? Do we really just need to "grow up"?

We cannot let our lives be "dreams deferred," as Langston Hughes wrote in his famous poem, "Harlem." It's time to let your dreams speak—even as you still have to put food on the table and pay off debts. Dreaming once again does not mean absolving ourselves of financial responsibilities. It means reviving our dreams as juice for the journey.

Wherever you are, take a few moments now to reflect upon your dreams. Can you remember what you wanted before you were told to grow up and fit your round peg in a square cubicle? Use these questions to trigger memories and stimulate thoughts:

- What did you want to be when you grew up?
- What have you always wanted to do that you haven't yet done?
- What have you done in your life that you are really proud of?
- If you knew you were going to die within a year, how would you spend that year?
- What brings you the most fulfillment—and how is that related to money?
- If you didn't have to work for a living, what would you do with your time?

These are potent questions. You may have looked at some before, but without a bridge between your present reality and your aspirations. This program is your bridge, so no dream is too large. Take your time. Use your journal. Dig. Keep asking the same question until you run out of answers before going on to the next one. Talk to your friends. Invite them to dig with you. Revisit your answers frequently to see what has changed.

A few years after graduating from college, **Grant Sabatier** had his wake-up call when he discovered he hadn't enough money to buy a burrito. He was living with his parents, a classic failure-to-launch millennial. That was when he decided that he was going to make $1 million by age thirty. He says the first thing he needed to do was change his mind-set to one of saving—which he refers to as paying yourself first. He took a screenshot of his measly bank balance, set the goal of having $1 million in assets in five years, and immediately started educating himself.

He's now a successful blogger (*Millennial Money*) and digital strategist who offers six steps to wealth, which include side jobs, stock market investment, lifestyle changes, and daily saving goals.

He hit his goal, took another screenshot when his total assets passed $1 million—and then realized his dreams were actually far bigger than $1 million, as motivating as that number had been. As a graduate in philosophy from the University of Chicago, he knows that life is about asking big questions. What is empathy? Fulfillment? Happiness? Peace? He sees his FI as a chance to think, write, and speak about these fundamental questions—and go where his answers take him.

Amy and Jim D., inspirations for an earlier generation's shift to thrift through their financial magazine, *The Tightwad Gazette*, had a simple dream. They wanted to raise a family in a big farmhouse in a rural area. When they got married they had, between the two of them, logged more than twenty years in the workaday world—Jim as a career navy man and Amy as a graphic artist—yet they had only $1,500 in savings to show for it. They recognized that they valued family and community above the fast lane of life in which they had both been living, and they decided to raise their children and realize their dream on only one income—Jim's salary from the navy.

To realize their dream, they called upon all the frugality training they'd gotten from their thrifty parents and devised scads of new strategies for saving money. Neither had any sense of deprivation. They thrived on this challenge to their creativity, and their relationship thrived on their shared purpose. In seven years they had four children and saved enough to make a down payment on a rural farmhouse in Maine, pay off all debts, and buy a new car, furniture, and appliances. Two years after that, Amy decided to put her graphic skills to work and create a forum where frugal ideas could be exchanged. In June 1990 she published the premier issue of *The Tightwad Gazette*, an eight-page newsletter full of practical tips about living the good life on a shoestring. A year later they had twins— and were still able to live within their means. Their story is testimony to the fact that common dreams, like having a house in the country and staying home to raise a family, are truly within reach.

Wes L.*'s passion is nature—both being in it and preserving it. For him the FI program is a way to do what he's always wanted to do: contribute to humanity's understanding of and respect for the natural world—full-time. He's aligning as many parts of his life as possible with this dream. His paid employment is as a chemist measuring air quality. He's moved within walking distance of work so he won't contribute as much to the air pollution he's measuring. On vacations he kayaks through unspoiled wilderness areas, and on weekends he teaches kayaking to help others experience nature safely and respectfully. And with his "disposable" income he builds up his savings and supports major conservation organizations. The compass of his life is the natural world, and every aspect of his life points in that direction.*

Kathy and Langdon L. *had dreams not just for themselves but for making the world a better place, as corny as they knew that sounded. Langdon was a physician and the* *medical director of a migrant worker clinic. Kathy was a former teacher active in the programs of a number of nonprofit organizations who also held down the fort for her family. They loved their lives but looked forward to an empty nest so that they too could fly the coop. The financial program gave them a way to retire from their paid employment at the same time they retired from being full-time parents. They moved to a small town and bought land that became the heart of an eco-village—an intentional community committed to sustainability on every level possible. At first it was a village of two, but over time others joined in, building their own small and unique houses and building a rich communal life together. At one point, the outgoing, energetic Langdon became the mayor of the town, while Kathy was drawn to her painting studio.*

What dreams are calling you? Step 4 of this financial program is your chance to make your dreams come true by aligning your earning and spending with your values, aspirations, purpose, and happiness. It will turn making a dying into making a living!

Step 4: Three Questions That Will Transform Your Life

In this step you evaluate your spending by asking three questions about the total money spent in each of your subcategories:

1. **Did I receive fulfillment, satisfaction, and value in proportion to life energy spent?**
2. **Is this expenditure of life energy in alignment with my values and life purpose?**
3. **How might this expenditure change if I didn't have to work for money?**

Each of these questions points to a facet of your dreams. The first asks if your spending is bringing you the kind of happiness you feel when you are living your dream. The second asks if this spending is taking you in the direction of your dream. The third asks you to imagine how this spending would change if you no longer had to make money to support your lifestyle.

To do this step, go back to your Monthly Tabulation form (see figure 3-1) and notice the three blank columns you should have included next to your expenses. This is where you will write the answers to our three questions. You have already converted dollars to hours of life energy; now you can take a look at how you want to spend that precious commodity. These three questions, applied to each spending subcategory on your Monthly Tabulation, will give you a basis for evaluating the way you spend your money.

QUESTION 1: DID I RECEIVE FULFILLMENT, SATISFACTION, AND VALUE IN PROPORTION TO LIFE ENERGY SPENT?

This question provides a way to evaluate your expenditures. Take a look at each subcategory with this question in mind. If you received so much fulfillment from this expenditure of life energy that you'd even like to increase spending in this subcategory, place a + (or an up arrow) in the first box. If you received little or no fulfillment from it, put a − (or a down arrow) in that box. If the expense feels OK just as it is, mark the box with a 0.

This simple exercise will show you where your spending is so automatic, or even addictive, that your life energy flows in that direction while fulfillment lies in the opposite. You might even find your "shopping weaknesses"—your gazingus pins. At first you might angrily defend one or another of your gazingus pin habits. "I like having lots of shoes. Every pair has a function.

Anyway, it's my money." "I like books and so what if I stop at the bookstore every day on the way home—and so what if I don't read them? Someday I'm sure I will." "I like quilting and so what if I collect fabric for my quilting projects even if I'm not making a quilt now? OK, I haven't made one in a decade, but . . . you can never have enough variety of fabric." "So what if I have . . . ?" And on and on we defend our gazingus pin buying habit. But no one is trying to take your gazingus pins away from you. In fact, no one is even listening, since the honesty required by this exercise emerges most readily in solitude. Over time, seeing the number of hours of your life you spent in order to reward yourself with yet another gazingus pin might make it less of a treasure and more of a booby prize.

On the other hand, you might find you've been too much of a penny-pincher in categories in which you get a lot of fulfillment. Make sure you note these areas of supreme satisfaction and put your + (or up arrow) in the columns in which you are actually underspending.

The trick to doing this evaluation is to do it objectively, without rationalizing to yourself why the expenditure was so high or low and without condemning yourself by agonizing about how you spent so much in that category. The key phrase to remember is "No shame, no blame." Couples have also found this step a valuable way to discuss differences in their spending habits with equanimity and objectivity.

Martha and Ted P. *discovered that this question provided a gentle way to evaluate each other's spending patterns without getting defensive or adversarial. Rather than directly challenging one of Ted's purchases, Martha can just calmly ask whether he really got fulfillment, satisfaction, and value in proportion to the amount of life energy spent. They find that they are able to observe—and even comment on—each other's gazingus pins with a lot more compassion. Being able* *to discuss financial choices without subtle bickering has been invaluable for them and has actually helped their marriage.*

Cheap Thrills and Deep Thrills

A grandfather with a love for simple living had tried to instill his values in his young grandson. One day the boy excitedly announced a brand-new discovery.

"Grandpa, I know what happiness is."

"What?" the old man asked, sure he would hear a gem worth sharing.

"It's that feeling you get right after you buy something."

Cheap thrills are like that little feeling you get when you buy something. It's the ka-ching of the pinball machine. The happiness rarely lasts. It has a half-life of the distance from cash register to car.

Deeper thrills come when you've achieved a dream bigger than your ego's aspirations.

"This is the true joy in life," George Bernard Shaw wrote in his preface to *Man and Superman*, "the being used for a purpose recognized by yourself as a mighty one; the being thoroughly worn out before you are thrown on the scrap heap; the being a force of Nature instead of a feverish selfish little clod of ailments and grievances complaining that the world will not devote itself to making you happy."[1]

Cheap thrills come from external rewards. Deep thrills come from "being used for a purpose recognized by yourself as a mighty one." Cheap thrills are passing. Deep thrills are lasting. Your internal yardstick for fulfillment measures deep thrills.

Developing an Internal Yardstick for Fulfillment

The primary tool for developing this internal yardstick is awareness. Answering question 1 helps you develop an internal yardstick for fulfillment and kick any unhealthy spending habits in the process.

Most of us use external yardsticks for fulfillment. In fact, Ashleigh Brilliant, they did teach that in school. We measure our fulfillment by:

- Pleasing others
- Getting an A
- Proving ourselves to the bully from third grade who still lives in our minds
- Beating out the competition
- Making it onto whatever top-ten list you worship
- Winning
- Not winning but getting a trophy anyway
- Scoring big—in romance or sales records

These are external yardsticks for fulfillment. You look elsewhere to see how you are doing—the gleam in your mother's or partner's eye, the tally of votes, best-seller lists.

This feeling, though, isn't true fulfillment. There is a difference between the jolt of energy you get from a temporary win and the long-term satisfaction you get from achieving a dream. Guaranteed, if you think your dream is getting an A on a test or beating your opponent, you will chase after external rewards your whole life.

Enough—the Deepest Thrill

The affluence that surrounds us has been called the American Dream, and with good reason: We've been asleep. We wake up by questioning the dream. Asking yourself, month in, month out, whether you actually got fulfillment in proportion to life energy spent in each subcategory awakens that natural sense of knowing when enough is enough.

You come to differentiate between a passing fancy and real fulfillment. Recall the fulfillment curve from chapter 1, that point of enoughness where desires disappear because they have been completely met. Any less would be not enough. Any more would be too much. A fulfilling meal is one in which all the flavors, smells, and textures blend perfectly and your appetite is satisfied without even a trace of the discomfort of having overeaten. In the same way, a fulfilling car is one that meets your transportation needs perfectly, is pleasing enough to the eye, that you will enjoy owning for many thousands of miles, that doesn't insult your wallet or your values, and that, with good maintenance, will be both reliable and a pleasure to drive. (Unless, of course, buying and driving a classic 1957 big-tail-fin, gas-guzzling convertible has been a lifelong dream—then it's worth every hour you'll have to work for it.) Your internal yardstick dismisses superficial desires—to impress others or relieve the boredom—as good reasons to upgrade your ride and tack three more years of work onto your making-a-dying work life.

One test of whether you're using an internal rather than external yardstick is this: The purchase or experience leaves you satisfied, content, at peace. You stop craving the very thing you just consumed because you've actually scratched the right itch in the right way.

Financial Integrity

Having an internal yardstick for fulfillment is actually one part of what we call Financial Integrity. You learn to make your financial choices independent of what advertising and industry have decided would be good for their business. You are free of the humiliation of being manipulated into spending your life energy on things that don't bring you happiness. **Nina N.**, whose story we'll be hearing in chapter 7, reported that before doing this evaluation she felt powerless over the money in her wallet. "I'd walk into a store and my money would fly out of my wallet. Not literally, but that's how it felt. I couldn't stop it." It is a form of Financial Independence to be able to "just say no" to unconscious spending. By putting your up and down arrows and zeros in month in and month out, perhaps just from a gut sense, perhaps from careful, conscious thought, you will build this financial "muscle" of stopping at enough. Sometimes you'll see old habits creeping back in, get angry with yourself, and want to quit. That's when "no shame, no blame" comes in handy.

QUESTION 2: IS THIS EXPENDITURE OF LIFE ENERGY IN ALIGNMENT WITH MY VALUES AND LIFE PURPOSE?

This question is illuminating. It gives you a concrete way of looking at whether you're practicing what you preach. As you did with the first question, ask of each spending subcategory, "Was this expenditure of life energy in alignment with my values and my life purpose?" If your answer is a strong yes, put a + (or an up arrow) in the second box in that row. If it's a no, just put a – (or a down arrow). If it's fine as it is, put a 0.

People like Amy and Jim D. had a clear set of values and a strong sense of purpose when they undertook their tightwad campaign. So did Wes L. and Kathy and Langdon L. Measuring their financial choices against question 2 helped them to align their finances with their dreams. On the other hand, many people living otherwise well-off lives are suffering from a poverty of ideals. Many heirs and heiresses are among the lost and confused—all dressed up financially and nowhere to go. And lots of ordinary people who've achieved the American Dream are also wondering whether there isn't more to life than . . . this.

What about you? Are your values and life purpose clear, or are they out of focus, buried under the weight of a lifestyle that doesn't seem to fit?

Part One: What Are Values?

Our values are those principles and qualities that matter to us. Truth is a principle, and honesty is a quality of how we live truth. Living our values gives us peace of mind. Not doing so disturbs our conscience and, if we aren't aware of what's going on, disables that inner gyroscope that orients us. Values are like an ethical DNA, made up of our sense of right and wrong, that structures our choices. So our values reflect our beliefs. But since how we act reflects our real motivations, our values are revealed by our behaviors. (Parents sometimes try to sidestep this fact with the phrase "Do as I say, not as I do!") When we choose to provide food, shelter, and clothing for our children, we are making that choice on the basis of values—being a good parent, expressing a natural feeling of love. Whether we spend our day off walking in the park or going back to the office, our choice is based on values. "But I had to go to the office!" you say. "That's not a values decision; that's pure necessity!" Yet you value the paycheck, so you choose to do the job. Or you value being responsible to your family. Or you value the good opinion of your boss. Our behavior is a concrete representation of our values. How we spend our time and money speaks volumes about who we are and what we stand for.

This book deals with one of the chief social manifestations of our values: how we handle money in our lives. Looking at your Monthly Tabulations, what does the $250 (or 25 hours of life energy, at the $10 per hour we calculated in our example in chapter 2) spent on eating out reveal in terms of values? It could indicate any number of things: that you value convenience, that you like good food, or that you want social time with friends. What about the 12 hours donated to a charity? The 15 hours for the cell phone bill?

You may find that you are comfortable with many of these expenditures. And some you may question. Twenty-five hours of life energy spent on eating out may seem fine—until you realize upon reflection that you devoted only eight hours this month to one of your children. Or that those hours spent eating out dwarf what you've spent on concerts and museums, though you claim to get your life's pleasure from the arts. For many people, the values expressed in their expenditures are not the values they really want to be living. Your totals in some of your categories may reveal that habit, peer pressure, or even boredom has gotten the best of you.

Go back to the questions at the beginning of the chapter. If you didn't have to work for a living, what would you do with your time? What have you done with your life that you are really proud of? How would you spend the next year if you knew it was the last year of your life? Your answers to these questions will tell you a lot about what you truly value.

Your Monthly Tabulations are like a mirror. As you ask the question "Is this expenditure in alignment with my values?" month in and month out, you will find that you are looking ever more deeply into yourself. Simply as a result of asking and answering this question, you will make changes, large and small, that bring you closer to Financial Integrity, in which all aspects of your financial life are in harmony with your true values.

Samuel D. *had the traditional makings of a very nice life, but was angry and frustrated with the system that had led him to believe that if he had the right stuff (i.e., house, cars, job, etc.), he'd feel fulfilled. He didn't. As he did his monthly evaluation, the problem became clear. He realized that his predominant desire was to contribute something toward solving some of the world's problems instead of just being one of the decent yet sleeping millions. He took a risk, and a cut in pay, by leaving the school system to develop a private counseling firm. Eventually he went into partnership with an associate, holding training sessions and seminars to help people get in touch with their values and worth, and with their* *responsibility to themselves and the larger community. His insides now match his outside, and he's finally happy.*

Part Two: What Is Purpose?

The second part of this question calls on you to evaluate your expenditures in light of your "life purpose." Purpose is the overarching goal that embodies our values and our dreams. But what does that really mean? Purpose implies direction and time—you do something now to have something later that you value. It's a concerted intention to do something meaningful for both yourself and the world at large. For some people, like Amy and Jim D., doing work they enjoy and raising a loving family defines their purpose. For others the sense of purpose might be elusive, not quite in focus—their actions don't reflect their deepest desires. Some individuals, waking up to the emptiness of a purposeless life, spend years looking for some purpose to give life meaning. Others, like Wes L., seem to have it identified from the moment of birth. What is this thing called purpose in life?

Purpose can be as straightforward as your goal (I am doing this in order to get that). It can be revealed in the answer you give when someone asks, "Why are you doing what you're doing?"—your motivation. It can be the deeper meaning you ascribe to the events of your life (the real purpose of my job was to meet my wife).

"Life purpose," however, implies something beyond "reason." It isn't simply achieving a goal or acquiring some longed-for possession. It is a chosen dedication of your life energy to something you believe is more important than your individual little existence. It is your commitment. It becomes your identity as surely as your name, your body, or your story to date—and can become more important than life itself.

You can see these different kinds of purpose—goal,

meaning, and dedication—in this story about three stonecutters, each chipping away at a large block. A passerby approaches the first stonecutter and asks, "Excuse me, what are you doing?" The stonecutter replies rather gruffly, "Can't you see? I'm chipping away at this big hunk of stone." Approaching the second craftsman, our curious person asks the same question. This stonecutter looks up with a mixture of pride and resignation and says, "Why, I'm earning a living to take care of my wife and children." Moving to the third worker, our questioner asks, "And what are you doing?" The third stonecutter looks up, his face shining, and says with reverence, "I'm building a cathedral!" (dedication to a higher purpose).

How Do We Find Our Purpose?

Joanna Macy, an educator, ecologist, and author, has suggested three directions in which to look for your own purpose.[2]

1. Work with your passion, on projects you care deeply about. What was your dream before you stopped dreaming? What's the work you would do even if you weren't paid to do it? You're not looking for those superficial preferences depicted on bumper stickers, like "I'd rather be surfing." You're looking for something you'd give your life to, not something you use to get away from your life.

2. Work with your pain, with people whose pain touches your heart. Have you "been there so you know how it feels"—in grief, sorrow, despair, hunger, terror? Can you offer others the wisdom and compassion you gained from this experience? Is there an aspect of suffering in the world that calls you to action? If you are in such pain that you've lost touch with your ability to help others, then now is the perfect time to extend your hand to others in pain. It's healing.

3. Work with what is at hand, with the opportunities that arise daily for responding to the simple needs of others. Finding your purpose has often been equated with discovering the perfect job or service project that will galvanize you to be as saintly as Mother Teresa. This suggestion to work with what's at hand is a reminder that in an interconnected world all acts of service contribute to the good of the whole. If you remember that there is no single act of greatness, just a series of small acts done with great passion or great love, then in doing what you see needs to be done—taking dinner to a sick neighbor, helping a child learn to read, writing a letter to the editor of your newspaper, being an advocate for the homeless in your city—you will discover a life filled with the experience of having a purpose worth living for.

Passion, pain, what's at hand—these are doorways to finding a purpose beyond material acquisition.

Measuring Our Movement Toward Purpose

Take a few minutes right now to write down your purpose in life. It may have nothing to do with how you now spend your time. It may or may not seem significant to others. It may not even be very clear to you yet. Just do the best you can. Use this stated purpose to measure your actions. If over time you see your purpose changing, that's fine; simply write what life purpose now means to you and use this new statement of purpose as your measuring stick.

However you define your purpose, you'll need a way to measure your results, some feedback to tell you if you are on track. Often we measure how we are doing in fulfilling our purpose by material success, or by professional or community recognition. Another way to measure whether you are living your purpose—one that goes beyond material success, rewards, and recognition—is your answer to question 2: "Is this expenditure of life energy in alignment with my values and life purpose?" Asking this question faithfully—every month, for every category—will nudge you toward clarifying your values, living in alignment with your stated purpose, and further defining your true purpose in life.

Viktor Frankl, author of *Man's Search for Meaning* and a survivor of the Nazi death camps, observed that there was a factor beyond intellect or psychology that allowed some people to retain their humanity in inhumane circumstances. This factor, he concluded, was meaning. The will to have meaning and purpose in life, he said, is superior to the will to have power or the will to find pleasure. He observed that "being human means relating and being directed to something or someone other than oneself."[3] Going through the questionnaire in Figure 4-1 which is based on Frankl's profound work, will assist you in your own movement toward meaning in your life.[4]

To tally your score, add the numbers you've circled. If you are below 92, you probably lack meaning and purpose in life; if you scored 92 to 112, you are indecisive or hazy regarding your sense of purpose; and if your score is greater than 112, you have a clear purpose. How did you do? Remember that asking the question "Is this expenditure in alignment with my purpose?" will help you connect with your sense of purpose.

Your Monthly Tabulation maps your spending patterns onto your quest for meaning. To return to integrity (alignment of your actions with your values), you can either adjust your spending or adjust your purpose.

FIGURE 4-1

Purpose in Life Test

For each of the following statements, circle the number that would be most true for you. Note that the numbers always extend from one extreme feeling to its opposite. "Neutral" implies no judgment either way; try to use this rating as little as possible.

		1	2	3	4	5	6	7
1.	I am usually:	completely bored			(neutral)			exuberant, enthusiastic
2.	Life to me seems:	7 always exciting	6	5	4 (neutral)	3	2	1 completely routine
3.	In life I have:	1 no goals or aims at all	2	3	4 (neutral)	5	6	7 very clear goals and aims
4.	My personal existence is:	1 utterly meaningless, without purpose	2	3	4 (neutral)	5	6	7 very purposeful and meaningful
5.	Every day is:	7 constantly new	6	5	4 (neutral)	3	2	1 exactly the same
6.	If I could choose, I would:	1 prefer never to have been born	2	3	4 (neutral)	5	6	7 like nine more lives just like this one
7.	After retiring, I would:	7 do some of the exciting things I have always wanted to do	6	5	4 (neutral)	3	2	1 loaf completely the rest of my life
8.	In achieving life goals, I have:	1 made no progress whatsoever	2	3	4 (neutral)	5	6	7 progressed to complete fulfillment
9.	My life is:	1 empty, filled only with despair	2	3	4 (neutral)	5	6	7 running over with exciting good things
10.	If I should die today, I would feel that my life has been:	7 very worthwhile	6	5	4 (neutral)	3	2	1 completely worthless
11.	In thinking of my life, I:	1 often wonder why I exist	2	3	4 (neutral)	5	6	7 always see a reason for my being here
12.	As I view the world in relation to my life, the world:	1 completely confuses me	2	3	4 (neutral)	5	6	7 fits meaningfully with my life
13.	I am a:	1 very irresponsible person	2	3	4 (neutral)	5	6	7 very responsible person

14. Concerning man's freedom to make his own choices, I believe man is:

14.	7	6	5	4	3	2	1
	absolutely free to make all life choices			(neutral)			completely bound by limitations of heredity and environment

15. With regard to death, I am:

15.	7	6	5	4	3	2	1
	prepared and unafraid			(neutral)			unprepared and frightened

16. With regard to suicide, I have:

16.	1	2	3	4	5	6	7
	thought of it seriously as a way out			(neutral)			never given it a thought

17. I regard my ability to find meaning, purpose, or mission in life as:

17.	7	6	5	4	3	2	1
	very great			(neutral)			practically none

18. My life is:

18.	7	6	5	4	3	2	1
	in my hands and I am in control of it			(neutral)			out of my hands and controlled by external factors

19. Facing my daily tasks is:

19.	7	6	5	4	3	2	1
	a source of pleasure and satisfaction			(neutral)			a painful and boring experience

20. I have discovered:

20.	1	2	3	4	5	6	7
	no mission or purpose in life			(neutral)			clear-cut goals and a satisfying life purpose

QUESTION 3: HOW MIGHT THIS EXPENDITURE CHANGE IF I DIDN'T HAVE TO WORK FOR MONEY?

So far, we've seen how well our purchases fulfill us and align with our values. But question 3 evaluates how much your job costs you and focuses more clearly on your life apart from work. Ask yourself, "Which expenses would decrease or disappear altogether if I didn't work for money?" In the third column next to your expense categories mark a − (or down arrow) if you think this expense would decrease, a + (or up arrow) if it would increase, or a 0 if it would probably remain unchanged. If you can come up with an estimated dollar figure, write it in a separate line on the Monthly Tabulation.

This question opens the possibility of a lifestyle in which you don't have to report to your job week in and week out. What would your life be like if you didn't work for money forty or more hours a week? What expenses might disappear? If you didn't have to work for money, would you buy more clothes? Fewer clothes? Burn more gas? Less gas? Sell your car entirely? Move to a cheaper house farther from a center of commerce? Would you have higher or lower medical bills (insurance costs might go up, but illnesses down)? Would you still take weekend getaways in hotels? Would your travel expenses go up or down? Would you no longer reward your hard work with brand-new gazingus pins? What do you now spend to simply compensate for doing a job that claims the majority of your waking hours?

You don't have to know precisely what you would do if you didn't have to work for money. You don't even have to want to do anything other than your job. You just need to ask the question of each expense category: How would expenditures in this category change if I didn't have to work for a living? Remember: No shame, no blame. You aren't violating your commitment to your profession by asking that question. Nor are you expressing disloyalty to your boss or dissatisfaction with your job by considering how you might spend your money if you were doing something else. If you love your job, the simple monthly exercise of asking this question will only increase your job satisfaction because you will increase your certainty that you are there by choice.

By asking question 3, you may find yourself coming to a startling conclusion. If you weren't spending most of your time making money, life could be a whole lot cheaper! Because your days are consumed by your job, you need money to handle every other aspect of your life—from day care to home repair, from entertainment to being listened to with compassion. You will discover that Financial Independence has this "independence from needing money to meet my needs" component—quite the opposite of Financial Independence as being rich enough to pay a multitude of minions to do everything for me.

ASSESSING THE THREE QUESTIONS

Now take a look at your tabulation sheet. Find all of your – marks (or down arrows). Note which subcategories didn't meet your criterion for question 1—you did not receive fulfillment in proportion to the amount of life energy spent. Which ones didn't measure up on question 2—this expenditure was not in alignment with your values and life purpose? And which ones are expenses that would change significantly if you didn't have to make a dying? Do you see any patterns? What have you learned about yourself? Don't punish yourself and don't resolve to "do better next month." (Remember, this is not a budget!) Simply use this information and any insights you've gained to assist in clarifying your values and purpose. Remember: No shame, no blame.

Step 4 is truly the heart of this program. Don't worry if your life purpose or your internal yardstick are not crystal clear. For some individuals this program has been the process by which they defined their values and purpose. Trust that asking and answering the three questions month by month, year by year will clarify and deepen your understanding of fulfillment and purpose. The steps of this program work synergistically, building upon and enhancing one another. So just relax and do the steps. All of them. With integrity. And remember: No shame, no blame.

This is simply an information-gathering process. It is the first step toward reprogramming yourself. Any unconscious, addictive patterns of spending will be exposed and identified when you bring them into the light of honest evaluation and clear, numeric expression. The point is not to drive yourself to change through guilt or self-criticism. The point is to adjust your spending until you have zeros or pluses for all your categories.

Here are a few reminders about working with step 4 to maximize your benefits.

Getting to Enough

In chapter 1 we talked about the fulfillment curve and that interesting place at its peak called "enough." You have enough for your survival, enough for your comforts, and even some special luxuries, with no excess to burden you unnecessarily. Enough is a powerful and free place. A confident and flexible place. And it's a place that you will define for yourself numerically as you follow this program. Asking the three questions is the primary tool for defining, experientially, how much is enough for you. You will do it each month, but you may find them coming to mind with each purchase you consider making.

Our own experience is that "enough" has four components, four common qualities:

1. Accountability—knowing how much money is flowing into and out of your life—is basic Financial Intelligence. Clearly, if you never know how much you have or where it's all going, you can never have enough.

2. An internal yardstick for fulfillment. As we pointed out earlier, you can never have enough if you are measuring by what others have or think. It's like trying to go up a down escalator. Other people's opinions are fickle. Other people's stuff is ever changing, and just when you have the stuff you think achieves that coveted parity with the Joneses, along comes the craze of tidying up and the Joneses are now minimalists. Self-awareness is key.

3. A purpose in life higher than satisfying your own wants and desires, because you can never have enough if every desire becomes a need that must be filled. What

is a purpose higher than getting what we want? The opposite of getting is giving—and therein lies a secret to fulfillment. Beyond the point of enough, we achieve happiness by expressing our natural desire to offer our gifts and talents to others.

4. Responsibility, living for more than just "me, myself, and I." If we don't give a hoot about anyone but ourselves, we can never have enough until we have it all. Responsibility, then, is good for you—it gets you off the more-is-better treadmill—as well as being good for others. Break down responsibility and you get "response" and "ability" You go from blindness to the ripples of your actions to being able—and willing—to respond to the needs of others. The first place to take responsibility is for yourself. You stop the blame game, tell the truth, and align your actions with your professed values. You define enough for you. Ultimately, you live your life in "widening circles," as Albert Einstein said in 1950:

> A human being is part of a whole, called by us "Universe," a part limited in time and space. He experiences himself, his thoughts and feelings, as something separated from the rest—a kind of optical delusion of his consciousness. This delusion is a kind of prison for us, restricting us to our personal desires and to affection for a few persons nearest us. Our task must be to free ourselves from this prison by widening our circles of compassion to embrace all living creatures and the whole of nature in its beauty.

Buckminster Fuller, another twentieth-century dreamer of possible worlds, had a similar insight. Some hold him as a near-saint of sustainability, yet in his twenties—after the death of his son and a business failure—he felt worthless and considered ending it all. In that moment of extreme pain, he had an epiphany. "It"—as in his life—did not belong to him. It belonged to the world. He dedicated the rest of his life to seeking ways to optimize life for everyone. His game became "Make the world work, for 100% of humanity, in the shortest possible time, through spontaneous cooperation, without ecological offense or the disadvantage of anyone."[5] Eventually hundreds of thousands of people joined him in this quest, taking on as a personal goal a world that works for everyone with nothing and no one left out.

Imagine that there is enough, as Fuller believed, for everyone—enough food, enough energy, enough resources. Imagine, as Einstein told us, that we could widen our circles of compassion to embrace all living creatures. No two creatures' "enough" bundles have to match, but everyone's sense of enough has to be fulfilled. What an exquisite design problem to solve! What a great dream this could be for all of us who discover our personal enough through doing these simple steps consistently over time and then dedicate our liberated life energy to service.

If this speaks to you, craft a fourth question for your evaluation along these lines:

What would expenditures in this category look like in a just and compassionate world where everyone had everything they needed for a life they loved, now and in the future?

Rephrase that however you like. A brief reformulation would be "What if everybody did this?" Just as the fulfillment and alignment questions guide your choices to make life better for you and the people you love, this question guides your choices with Einstein's "wider circles of compassion" in mind. You'll never know everybody, but you can imagine them in a "do unto others as you would have others do unto you" way.

Looking at your tallies, you could ask, "What if everybody . . . ate at restaurants, bought used clothes, planted fruit trees in the yard, bought this vacation package, picked this car for their daily commute . . . ?" Remember, no shame, no blame, just widening those circles of compassion.

Some people focus on the environment for this responsibility question: Is this good for (the planet/the climate/the environment)? These particular ways of phrasing the responsibility question may not square with your understanding of life and the future—but you can craft it differently. "What would Jesus do?" is used by many Christians to make ethical decisions. "What does the scientific consensus say?" could work for people who are not religious. Some might find answers in silence or in nature. You could call this the *Financial Interdependence* question.

Is this fourth question necessary for transforming your relationship with money? No. However, following the steps of this program, doing your tracking and Monthly Tabulation, and asking yourself the three questions will become so simple, so second nature, you might find yourself wondering what would happen if everyone did it. If so, you are right where Joe and I arrived in 1990 that lead us to writing this book.

SUMMARY OF STEP 4

1. Of each spending subcategory in your Monthly Tabulation ask question 1: "Did I receive fulfillment, satisfaction, and value in proportion to life energy spent?" Mark your answer with a + (or an up arrow), a – (or a down arrow), or a 0.

2. Of each spending subcategory in your Monthly Tabulation ask question 2: "Is this expenditure of life energy in alignment with my values and life purpose?" Mark your answer with a + (or an up arrow), a – (or a down arrow), or a 0.

3. Of each spending subcategory in your Monthly Tabulation ask question 3: "How might this expenditure change if I didn't have to work for money?" Mark your answer with a + (or an up arrow), a – (or a down arrow),

or a 0 and write the estimated change on the Monthly Tabulation.

4. Review and make a list of all categories with the – symbol (or down arrow).

MONEY TALK QUESTIONS

Your dreams, values, memories, and stories make for endlessly interesting conversations. If you hear a dream or goal you like from someone else, steal it! Together we can build compelling visions for a really good life.

Using the suggestions in the epilogue for how to have a Money Talk, raise these questions in your daily reflections, with your partner, or in social groups. Remember, adding "Why?" to the end of any question will take it deeper. Adding "How has society shaped my answer?" to any question will take it wider. There are no right answers.

- What did you want to be when you grew up? What about now?
- What's on your "bucket list," those things you want to do before you die?
- What is your calling, the work of your heart and soul?
- Talk about one of your happiest memories. What made you happy?
- What could happen out of the blue that would be like a dream come true?
- What do you want for your children/loved ones that money can buy?

5

Getting It Out in the Open

Step 5: Making Life Energy Visible

   In step 5 you make visible the results of the previous steps, plotting them on a graph that gives you a clear, simple picture of your financial situation, now and over time, and the transformation in your relationship with money (life energy).

Your first month of tracking and evaluating your expenses will be revelatory as you realize how much money has flown your financial coop for no good reason. Confronting the reality of why and how you are slipping further and further into debt may be so uncomfortable you are tempted to stop. "Fine little exercise," you think, "but I've had all the insights I really need."

   If you persist, though, tracking for another month, you may find dramatic reductions in your spending. A bit of consciousness goes a long way. If you wince at anything, no one is watching. Apply "no shame, no blame" and keep going. Gold star.

   During month three, big changes may happen again—in either direction. You might save more. You might slack off because in month two you proved you could do it. Whether you give yourself a pat on the back or want to shut your eyes in the face of glaring truth, it might take some willpower to stay the course.

How do you motivate yourself to keep going?

Anyone who has undertaken any behavior change knows three keys:

1. Make it a habit rather than a choice. You do it whether you want to or not. You have a system and you follow the system and it drops into the background of daily life—like brushing your teeth.

2. Be accountable to someone else. Make a commitment to one or more people that you will write down everything you spend and do your monthly accounting with your up and down arrows and zeros. You may meet your accountability partner monthly to share your results and have a Money Talk. You may text or call one another daily. You may give your accountability partner(s) your password for your tracking app so they can check on you randomly, and you do that for them as well. Nosiness can be interesting—and effective.

3. Chart. Checking off a daily to-do list, or weighing yourself daily and posting your weight above the scale, does wonders for your commitment to keep going. The same goes for money. Keeping track does wonders for quelling the urge to splurge.

In step 5 you will make a chart where you will post your income and expenses. You will also decide how to use it to keep yourself accountable, and we'll offer some suggestions for intensifying and therefore speeding up your journey to Financial Integrity.

Fasten your seat belts.

MAKING YOUR WALL CHART

Step 5 entails setting up a graph of your income and your expenses, one that is large enough to accommodate three to five years of data. This graph will be simple to create, simple to maintain, and simple to interpret. All the information you need is already on your Monthly Tabulation. You don't need a computer or app to do step 5. You just need to do it! If you have an app, online service, or accounting program you use for managing your money, graphs and charts will be built in and always up-to-date—but there is a second part of step 5 that the computer won't do for you.

To do it by hand, get a large sheet of graph paper (an 18 × 12-inch or 24 × 36-inch sheet with 10 squares per inch will do nicely) from a business supply store or college bookstore. If you can't find one, never fear. You can use any large piece of paper and rule it yourself. The left-hand, vertical axis represents money. On it you will chart both your income and your expenses. Mark it in increments of dollars. Start with 0 at the bottom, leaving plenty of room on the upper part of the chart. As outrageous as this may sound at the moment, you should probably allow enough space at the top for your income to double. More than one FIer has sheepishly shown us a chart with extra graph paper taped at the top to account for a level of earnings he or she never thought possible. Set up your scale so that the larger of the two figures (income or expenses) for this month falls about halfway up the scale. The lower, horizontal scale represents time in increments of months. Allow five to ten years on this axis. That's enough to see large-scale trends—and maybe enough to see you through to Financial Independence! For those interested in doing this electronically, Excel or other spreadsheet software works well. If you know how to do this, it can open up a whole world of analyzing your finances, but it may not replace the shock or satisfaction of charting by hand.

At the end of each month you will plot the figures for your total monthly income and total monthly expenses. It is helpful to use one color for your income and another for your expenses. Connect each point with a line to the previous month's entry.

That's all there is to it. When you do this step the first

month, you have a snapshot—a very revealing one—of your habits around money. But the real learning—and the real fun—comes as you plot your figures month by month, year by year. Your Wall Chart will take the static snapshot of Monthly Tabulations and add the dynamic dimension of time, making vivid your movement toward the goal and your progress over time. Your graph will also move you—renewing your commitment to keep going.

THE INITIAL PURGE AND SPLURGE CYCLE

In the first month of recording your figures you might confront one of our national foibles. Your income entry may well be lower than your expenses entry. You may have spent more than you earned. (It is, after all, the American way.) Seeing this reality might come as a bit of a shock. Chances are you'll want things to change— and change now. Accustomed to budgets, diets, and New Year's resolutions, you swear on a stack of bank statements and credit cards that next month will be better.

This is when people often go on a "wallet fast" with overeager zeal. They scrimp. They save. They deprive themselves and their families, putting everyone on beans, rice, and oatmeal rations. They concentrate daily on that expenses line, determined to cut it in half in one short month. Amazingly enough, many do. Entering the expense figure the second month, they proudly note a steep decline.

This kind of austerity, however, isn't sustainable. By the third month expenses often rebound with a vengeance, making up for the second-month deprivation.

Now what? In the old way of thinking, you might be tempted to take up the burden of budgeting again . . . or to quit. But take heart. There is a better way, and it works.

Elaine H., the computer programmer we met in chapter 1 who hated her job but couldn't find a way out, had no trouble setting up her Wall Chart. Numbers and tracking were her business. While she had acquired many "trophies" to prove her success, her Wall Chart looked no different from those of many other American Dreamers: Her expenses were higher than her income.

"What I saw truly shocked me. I had no idea I spent more than I earned. But there it was: income $4,400 for that month and expenses $4,770." She felt challenged. If the odds were against spending less than you earn, she wanted to beat the odds. She decided to experiment on ways to lower her expenses. Rather than going out to lunch with her coworkers or even ordering less expensive meals, she brought her lunch from home. For a month she bought no new clothes or dinners out—after all, you can endure anything for a month. Lo and behold, by month two her expenses had dropped way below her income. She'd proved she could do it.

"I was elated! The next month I paid less attention, returning to my old shopping habits and wiping out much of the financial gain of the previous month. My Wall Chart looked bad." And she realized that instead of trying to change the chart, she would need to change herself.

How did this change in spending happen? Elaine explains that as she followed the steps of the program and noted her successes, her self-esteem rose. She saw that she could do it—and her dissatisfaction turned into a drive to do the best job she could. This spirit transformed her experience of working—surprising her as much as it surprised her supervisors.

"Within four months I was debt-free and my expenses were down to $1,640. I had cut my grocery bill from $359 a month to $203 without even trying. Perhaps part of it was that I was happier on my job, so I needed fewer treats. My restaurant bill dropped to $77 a month from $232, just by eating out only when I really wanted to. I moved to a house for less rent that was closer to work, so my gas bill was 60 percent lower. My medical costs were also cut in half, most likely for the same reason my food bill went down. I was enjoying my job more and had no need to get sick. None of this felt like deprivation. I wasn't struggling to spend less. It didn't even feel like I was doing anything in particular. It all happened gradually."

Through the years, she'd spent thousands of dollars on seminars that were designed to change everything from her self-esteem to her effectiveness on the job, but the change never lasted. So what was different this time? A major component was the Wall Chart. The Wall Chart seemed to be a challenge to the way she was living her whole life. It drew a picture of her spending habits, graphically showing her why there was not enough money at the end of the month. (See Figure 5-1)

The Wall Chart reminds us that transforming our relationship with money doesn't happen in a blaze of insight. You need to do the steps—faithfully—and that takes time and patience. Impatience, denial, and greed are actually part of what is being transformed. It takes time to reflect on our lives and see if we still want to go where we're headed. Reading this book may take only a few days, but transforming your relationship with money will happen over time. By observing your reactions to your Wall Chart instead of getting upset about it, you will be clearing away the attitudes and beliefs that got you where you are today.

There are two keys to making this process work for you:

1. Start.
2. Keep going.

FIGURE 5-1

Elaine's Wall Chart—with Expenses

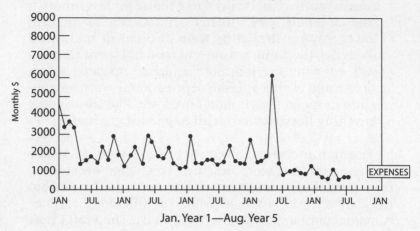

Jan. Year 1—Aug. Year 5

We often hear that the journey of a thousand miles begins with a single step. What we don't hear as often is that you arrive at your destination by hundreds of thousands of additional small steps forward. Keep taking those steps. Eventually you'll begin to experience the magic of this process. Without even trying you'll find your expense line heading down. How?

HOW THE THREE
QUESTIONS CAN SAVE YOU MONEY

Remember those three questions in step 4? You will be finding out the profound effect these questions have on your consciousness about money—and consequently on your Wall Chart.

Automatic Lowering of Expenses

Question 1 is: "Did I receive fulfillment, satisfaction, and value in proportion to life energy spent?" Asking this question every month about each of your spending categories increases your consciousness about your choices and thus results in an automatic reduction in your total monthly expenses, giving you the pleasure of seeing the expenses line on your chart go down. As we saw in chapter 4, greater consciousness about which expenditures actually bring us happiness and which do not activates our "survival mechanism." In fact, you are reprogramming yourself. Each of your "–" marks are an affront to your survival instinct, that automatic movement toward pleasure and away from pain. This powerful mechanism becomes an ally as you become aware that some expenditures that you thought brought pleasure, or that you simply incurred out of habit, are actually not fulfilling or pleasurable at all.

Remember our gazingus pins? You will soon know what yours are. Those blinding moments of awareness as you catch yourself about to spend your life energy on yet another gazingus pin will all add up to lower expenses. Let's see how this works.

In the past, when you tried to change your habits and thus increase your experience of satisfaction, you didn't have an accurate overview of your spending patterns. Rather than identifying gazingus pin purchases as a source of dissatisfaction, you continued to think it was the one thing to hang on to. Sometimes you might have tried to give up gazingus pins as a painful penance for your spendthrift ways . . . only to find yourself once again at the gazingus pin counter thinking, "Just this once. Just this once." But now you have identified those dead ends and are looking down from above the money maze. You have seen the light: "I am not getting fulfillment, in reality, from this expenditure of life energy." You will feel as if you are waking up.

"Wait," you blurt, eyes wide open now, "I haven't read half the books in my library or made a quilt in a decade. Enough!" That little moment of awareness makes a big difference. Now that you've solidified the link between how you spend your money and how much fulfillment you get, your gazingus pins no longer retain their old grip on you. Now you can be in line with yourself—you're neither fighting yourself nor trying to buy happiness and satisfaction. On the contrary, you're now getting fulfillment from other uses of your life energy; you are valuing your life energy and thus yourself. From this perspective, it is easy to change direction.

Ivy U. had grown up poor, the daughter of Mexican American parents. There was never enough money, but rather than acknowledge and talk about the pain of poverty, her parents gave her platitudes. "We are blessed," her Catholic father would say, "because only the poor can enter the kingdom of heaven." Religion, poverty, and frustration at counting pennies got all tangled up, leaving Ivy confused and resentful. She resolved that when she grew up she'd have enough money so that she'd never have to worry about watching her spending and would be able to buy whatever she wanted.

Ivy easily identified her gazingus pin: clothes. In doing her inventory in step 1 she breezed through her home, satisfied with her simplicity, until she came to her closet. Where did all these clothes come from? Of course, they came from a variety of stores—most of them expensive department stores. But why? Her determination to never again be poor had turned into the need to always be perfectly dressed. She could measure her distance from poverty by the number of daily compliments on her attire.

Yes, as a career professional she did need to look her best. But for Ivy that had been translated into several new outfits every month. If she even wore last month's blouse with this month's new suit she felt shabby.

In doing her Monthly Tabulations she quickly saw that she did not get fulfillment commensurate with the hours of life energy she put into keeping several department stores in the black. With no struggle, denial, or deprivation, she stopped buying clothes she didn't need. To her amazement, the number of compliments she received per day didn't decrease at all.

Hal N., an activist turned financial planner, found that his unconscious spending categories weren't just gazingus pins. You would have to call them mega–gazingus pins—or simply major spending blind spots. The FI course for him was more like cataract surgery than simply getting a new pair of glasses.

When he asked himself the questions about fulfillment and alignment, he realized how bored and tired he'd been for the past eight years. He also saw clearly what had gotten him into trouble. First of all, to play the role of financial planner he had assumed he needed an expensive office. But when he looked at the amount of life energy his office was costing him—$2,900 per month—he questioned whether he was really getting value. In fact, he wasn't. He did most of his business on the phone, through the mail, or in clients' homes. Nobody ever saw him in his office. So he moved his office to his home. Total current office cost: $750 per month.

The second-biggest blind spot for Hal had been his kids. They lived with their mother, but he provided well for their support. That was no problem. The problem was that he gave his kids extra money every time they asked because he felt guilty about not being with them. He has nine children, so that added up. No matter how much he gave, they always wanted more. Having had his street smarts sharpened by this process of honest evaluation, Hal recognized that his kids had become addicted, and he was the enabler. He decided to change, and even though the children are now going through a form of withdrawal, Hal is satisfied with his choice to stop paying guilt money for being an absent father. With a few other minor adjustments, asking the three questions cut 50 percent off Hal's expenses—and he is a lot happier for it.

Not everyone has the amount of "padding" that Hal did, but after looking at hundreds of FIers' Wall Charts, we can say that those who get past the three-month hump will find their expenses drop naturally—and painlessly—by about 20 percent. These people report no feelings of deprivation, no struggling to keep to a budget—just a natural decline. Knowing that you are not getting satisfaction proportional to the expenditure of life energy in a given subcategory of spending generates an automatic, self-protective reversal of your spending habits. Over time, you actually find yourself feeling better by not spending; not buying a gazingus pin now becomes a source of fulfillment because you yourself have determined that gazingus pins don't bring you fulfillment.

Alignment and Personal Integration

There is still more to look forward to as you work with your Wall Chart. Watch that expense line go down simply by asking question 2 each month: "Is this expenditure of life energy in alignment with my values and life purpose?"

This is a feedback system for integrity. Your statement of your values and life purpose reflects your highest vision, what you truly want for yourself. Thus you will want to act in your day-to-day life in a way consistent with your values and purpose. Unfortunately, however, it is sometimes all too easy to overlook the reality of what you're actually doing. It is possible to behave in ways that are not only unsupportive of but contradictory to your highest vision and intention—and to be unaware of it. Worse yet, sometimes conflicts between whims and higher purpose are resolved by swiftly silencing the voice of conscience. The Bible, Romans 7:19, puts a sharp point on this all-too-human habit: "I want to do what is good, but I don't. I don't want to do what is wrong, but I do it anyway." The data on how you spend your life energy provides a nitty-gritty, tangible measure of that integrity, which is an invaluable support in keeping your material life in line with your ideals and goals. When your spending and your goals are in alignment, you have an experience of wholeness and integrity; you feel good about yourself. When they are not aligned—when the answer to the question "Does this expenditure support my values and life purpose?" is a resounding no—then the experience is more likely to be one of disappointment or self-criticism.

Often expenses will go down with this question because so many unconscious expenses are simply emotional or cultural programs playing themselves out through your wallet. But not always. With a focus on that Goldilocks "just-rightness" for each category, you may find you've been stingy with yourself and need to spend more. Perhaps you once dreamed of being an opera singer. Where are singing lessons—if anywhere—in your categories? Do you need to move to Italy to study with the best? Perhaps you choose to pour *more* money into training your voice while developing a long-term plan for how that training may pay off in income. On the other hand, you may decide that you can join the volunteer light opera company in your city, get coaching for free from the director, and be happier staying home among friends.

The subtle but effective process of reinforcement (spend money on X = feel good; spend money on Y = feel bad) actually works; it serves to break robotic spending patterns. The simple recognition that you're not experiencing alignment from a given spending category acts to realign your responses to the stimuli in that category. You will automatically begin to spend less on those things that don't support your values and life purpose, and you will feel better about yourself, knowing that increasingly you are putting your money where your life purpose is, integrating your material life with your inner awareness. This integration is at the heart of Financial Integrity.

As far as she could tell, **Elaine H.** didn't have a purpose in life. She just wanted to make it through, seeking pleasure and avoiding pain as best she could. Thinking back on her childhood, she remembered that her only happiness had been wandering off in the woods when her family took trips to the country.

When she started the FI program, she was the only one of her siblings who had "gotten ahead." One was a recluse living on welfare, another had committed suicide, and the third lived on the streets. Having a high-paying job, a sports car, and a nice house made her look like a winner—to herself and to her family.

The question about aligning her spending with her values shook her complacency. Having always measured herself by externals, Elaine started covertly checking out her friends and coworkers. Did they have a higher purpose? One of the people in her office was one of those "save the world" types. Intrigued by someone who didn't measure her own net worth by material possessions, Elaine cultivated a friendship with her. Soon both of them were attending meetings of a local peace group. The people Elaine met there were all questioning how they could better live their values, and what actions they could take in the world to express their sense of purpose.

These meetings became her chief form of entertainment. Instead of expensive workshops or outings to all the latest movies, she attended lectures and participated in fund-raising phone-a-thons. She found a large park near her home and spent hours on weekends wandering in the woods. And at charting time her expense line kept going down. From a monthly outlay of more than $4,500, her cost of living dropped to a steady $900 to $1,200 per month. Looking for her purpose in life turned out to be a key component in the change she was undergoing.

Asking the third question, "How might this expenditure change if I didn't have to work for money?" can further affect your expense line. Since people often find that more expenses go down post–Financial Independence, they sometimes draw a faint line that floats below the current expense line as an estimation of their post-job lifestyle. Maybe the mortgage or rent is gone because you live in a motor home or travel in less-expensive countries. Maybe restaurant meals disappear. This question also whets your appetite for that free life, and you want to speed the process up so you can get there sooner. So you consciously save more.

If you've chosen to ask the fourth question, "What would this expense look like in a just and compassionate world?" there's no telling what will happen.

WHAT ABOUT "UNUSUAL" MONTHS?

Yes, there will be "unusual" months, months when your expenses line takes an alarming leap upward. The insurance payment is due. You have an unexpected repair expense. April comes and goes, with the annual bloodletting known as taxes. How do you handle these? For one thing, you may recognize that every month is an unusual month. You learn to take "unusual" expenses in stride and to pay for them with cash instead of hiding them under a blanket of plastic. One month's tax payment is another month's insurance payment is another month's doctor bill.

Another strategy would be to prorate annual expenses over the whole twelve months. For example, if your auto insurance bill is $841 per year,[1] you might (in addition to questioning whether a car is worth it) choose to divide that by twelve and make it a monthly expense. Ditto with health insurance, income tax payments, property taxes, and so on.

There is no right way to do the accounting. You need to choose the way that gives you the information you need so that as you glance at your Wall Chart you know where you are and where you're going.

GETTING YOUR FINANCES OUT IN THE OPEN

Now that charting has become a habit, even a pleasurable one as you see your progress, you can add the element of Accountability. How?

Open the subject with friends via a Money Talk. By raising "the M-word" you're letting your friends know you are a safe listening ear for them to risk talking about money. You aren't setting yourself up as an adviser, coach, or expert. You're signaling that you are open and interested and on your own transformational journey. At the same time, you are inviting others to hold you accountable simply because you're the friend who's getting his or her money act together . . . which will really make you want to get your money act together. Hundreds of people have started blogs about their journeys to Financial Independence in which they dialogue with their readers. Many post their monthly accounting and tax returns.

Posting your monthly accounting on a blog? Yes, this is another accountability technique. In Joe Dominguez's seminars—and in earlier editions of this book—we suggested hanging your Wall Chart in a prominent place where you will see it every day. To do you the most good, the chart must be visible so that it can inspire you—often—to stay on track.

Some people start out with their chart in the closet—literally. They hang their chart on the inside of their closet door. It keeps their financial affairs private while still providing a reminder every day as they dress for work that they want to be conscious in their handling of money. For those opting for Financial Independence, it reinforces the awareness that work is no longer about "another day, another dollar," but is rather about drawing one day closer to their goal of freedom from financial fears and fiscal failures. It's a boost, as good as a cup of coffee or a hug.

Ivy U., who never wanted to be poor, met her Prince Charming. And so, as they say in fairy tales, it came to pass that she had a successful life—husband, two sons, built-to-order dream house with three decks, two patios, and furniture selected by an interior designer—and no need to balance her checkbook. Then reality intervened. The fantasies on which she'd built her life weren't strong enough to maintain her marriage—or her sanity. So she said good-bye to her husband, her house, her furniture, and her high-stress job, packed a few select possessions into a U-Haul, and headed west with her sons.

Seven years later, through the FI course, she found a path to even greater freedom. She and her friend **Margaret P.** invited a group of twenty friends to take the course so that they could support one another in following the program. They met every month, sharing insights, successes, and roadblocks—and the intimate details of their financial lives.

When Ivy did her chart she challenged herself to bring it to the group, and some of her ancient fears reappeared. Her first thought was "My parents would think I'm crazy. You don't show people how much you earn and spend. It's—it's—it's not in good taste. It's . . ." What was that reluctance? Why was she afraid of exposing her finances? The reason, she realized, was a fear that it would allow people to judge her and decide whether she was a person of worth. They could sum her up with a few numbers and discard her if she fell short. With the same resolve that had helped her to leave her marriage, she took her chart to the group. The fear melted, and something inside her relaxed about money. What she spent was just . . . what she spent. Her income was just her income. She could tell it to someone as easily as she could tell someone the color of her living room couch. It was no big deal.

Over time you may find that your feelings about your chart change as a reflection of changes in your relationship with money. The chart becomes a representation of how well you are living your values, something that reflects the care you are taking with every decision about your material world. It becomes a source of pride—not arrogance, but that kind of deep satisfaction that comes with integrity. Once this happens, many people find that they feel so good about their progress that they bring their chart out of the closet and hang it on a wall.

Stop a minute and reflect on your own feelings about your current relationship with money. How would you feel about hanging this graphic representation of your financial affairs on your living room wall, right out where everyone who comes into your house could see it? Would you feel at ease—or uneasy? The degree of your discomfort is a measure of the degree of your financial disease. Don't worry. That uneasiness will disappear as you follow the steps of this program.

FINANCIAL INDEPENDENCE AS A BY-PRODUCT OF DOING THE STEPS

People who put the steps of this program into practice report that the process of transforming their relationship with money becomes both challenging and fascinating. Recording every penny becomes an enjoyable ritual at the checkout counter—and it also sparks some interesting Money Talks with people who want to know what you're up to—in a grocery line or around a table somewhere. Monthly Tabulation time is a highlight. Asking the three questions provides a quick yet penetrating check-in with your values and life purpose. Entering income and expenses on the Wall Chart becomes a time to reflect on the truth of your consciousness around money. After a few months or a year of following these steps you will begin to notice a stunningly satisfying by-product of the process: As you consistently earn more than you spend, you eventually get out of debt and accumulate savings.

Does some of this seem impossible, considering your particular financial situation? It's not the conditions of your life but how you interact with them that will allow you to move forward. Followers of this program include people who were deeply in debt and out of work, who didn't have a college education and had huge gaps in their résumés, who had families to support and who lived in depressed parts of the country. They didn't have "the wind at their backs." They just made skillful use of the winds they encountered and sailed with them.

In the strictest sense, Financial Independence, as we have defined it, means having a choice of what you do with your time because you have an income sufficient for your basic needs and comforts from a source other than paid employment. But there are other aspects of FI, such as getting out of debt and accumulating savings.

Financial Independence Is Getting Out of Debt

For many people, debt is a heavy millstone and getting out of debt is a tremendous milestone. Often they don't even realize what a burden debt is until it disappears.

What about you? Are you in debt? Do you know how much you owe and to whom? Do you know how much it's costing you to be in debt? Or do you just make payments on your mortgage, your car(s), and your credit cards till death do you part?

Many students march out of college with an expensive piece of paper and tens of thousands of dollars in student loans. For those lucky enough to land a job offer, they feel like they've made it! Soon comes a brand-new car to showcase their long-awaited graduation, and with it—another pile of debt. But hey, what's another $20,000 when I have a full-time job? Little do they realize how much further this pushes them back from the starting line.

People who see debt as endless and just pay down as little as possible are, in effect, lowering their income. They don't see that using a high-interest credit card to buy a new stereo to celebrate a raise can wipe out the gain in salary—and then some. A car financed with a multiyear loan will ultimately cost quite a bit more than the original sticker price. A house with a thirty-year mortgage will cost—depending on the interest rate— two or even three times the purchase price by the time the final payment is made.

Numerous studies suggest that people spend more when they use credit cards instead of cash.[2] Dave Ramsey, famous for helping people get out of debt, is a major advocate of eliminating credit cards from your life altogether. The rise of easy credit makes it far easier to opt for instant gratification, especially with online shopping. Every transaction we make is simply represented as pixels on a screen. We are no longer limited to what we can afford based on what we have already earned— we can now buy based on what we hope to earn in the future! Debt has become the American way, making it hard to see that it is debt that chains us to our jobs. It's debt that keeps us with our noses to the grindstone, making a dying to pay off pleasures we've long forgotten and luxuries we scarcely have time to enjoy.

Tanya N. used to subtitle her life "Bombs by Day— Peace by Night." She worked for money as a graphic designer for a high-tech company with major defense contracts and worked for love on a variety of church-sponsored service projects. Thanks to her $26,000 debt, there seemed to be no alternative. And because she had been told repeatedly that there was no other way, her conscience had stopped bothering her.

The FI program provided a merciless mirror—but it freed her. On her chart she placed a small sign that read ON MY WAY TO DEBT-FREE. Below it she put a series of Velcro patches with numbers and kept track of the exact amount she owed. "It was as if I were melting a candle or losing a hundred pounds," she told us. Without a raise and without any feeling of deprivation, she was debt-free in two years.

When she looked for what was really fulfilling in her life, she saw that her greatest joy came from short-term work trips she'd participated in, helping with construction jobs in places like Costa Rica and Kenya. Upon returning from her first trip to Kenya, she had become extremely depressed. Yes, she'd helped build an addition to a rural hospital in a remote mountain village, but now what? She was still rich, while they were poor. So she started collecting medical supplies that would otherwise be discarded and packed them off to Kenya with safari-bound tourists.

By the time she was debt-free Tanya knew just what her next step would be. She had discovered that people in Kenya were dying from untreated tooth abscesses. She quit her job, rented out her town house, leased her car, and left for Kenya for a year to help establish a dental clinic. With no debts and with the rent on her house and car providing all the cash she needed to live in rural Kenya, Tanya was financially liberated. Being debt-free, she now had a choice—and she chose to follow her heart.

Getting out of debt, then, is one form of Financial Independence. Retiring your debt returns to you the freedom to choose. Whatever the economic climate, being able to say "I don't owe anything to anyone" is a statement of sanity, dignity, and freedom.

Once you're out of debt, you have choices. It's very empowering to realize that every dollar of every paycheck is your own. You might choose, as Tanya did, to follow your heart to distant lands or different pursuits. Then again, you might continue to enjoy the process of transforming your relationship with money right where you are. As you continue to spend less than you earn (while savoring life to the fullest), an ever-larger gap will develop on your Wall Chart between your income line and your expenses line. This gap has a name, one that has fallen into disuse in recent years. It's called savings (see Figure 5-2). Savings are another form of Financial Independence.

FIGURE 5-2

Wall Chart with Expenses, Income, and Savings

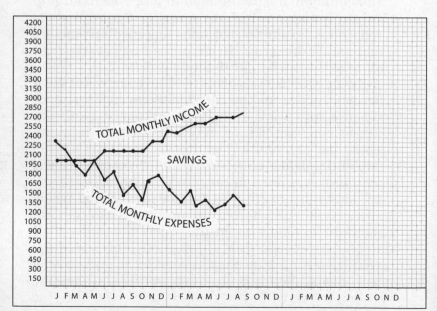

Becoming a Super Saver

How much are you saving now? Are you still going into debt? Digging out of debt? Spending everything you earn?

Your savings rate is one of the most important factors for achieving Financial Independence. Think about savings rate in this way: If you spend 100 percent of your paycheck, you will never retire. If you spend 0 percent of your paycheck each month, then congrats! You are already financially independent and no longer need to work for money. But what about all those percentages in between? As we said, on average, people who do the steps lower their expenses by 20 percent—and many don't even remember what they used to spend their money on.

Once you see this transformation on your Wall Chart, the lightbulb goes on. The more you save, the sooner you are FI. Saving more becomes like a game. For example, you discover from your grocery category that meat every meal is your biggest daily drain, so you halve your portions or the number of times a week you eat it. One financial blogger decided to not buy any new clothes for a year and found it easy. Living alone might look like a luxury you no longer want, given that adding a roommate to your house now might lasso your retirement date and pull it four years closer. Plus, it might shave off some unattractive habits from your life—grumpiness in the morning or dishes in the sink. Such adjustments tend to stick. You actually change your habits.

We once heard an advocate for the homeless say that most Americans are two paychecks away from homelessness. That seemed excessive, almost beyond belief. Yet when we talked with other professionals who have their fingers on the pulse of consumer debt, some have said that two paychecks is a conservative estimate. One paycheck or one major illness would be enough to send many people over the edge. A 2015 US Federal Reserve Board report found that 47 percent of Americans would have to borrow money or sell something to cover a $400 emergency expense.[3] How can one of the richest nations to ever exist have so many of its citizens barely making ends meet? With savings, unemployment is not a tragedy. If you lose your paycheck but have savings, you need not lose any of your possessions. What's more, you may see the opportunity to explore options you were too busy or too tired to consider before. You could pack up the family in a camper and travel around the country. You could strap on a backpack and tour the world. You could read. You could do every household project on your list. You could learn a new trade. You could explore your creative side, painting pictures or making music for the sheer pleasure of it. You could spend the whole year in a systematic job search for the work that suits you to a T. You could get your GED, BA, or MA and qualify for a whole new level in your chosen field of work. You could volunteer full-time for a cause you care about and maybe even be asked to stay on as paid staff. You could get reacquainted with your family.

Try this: Ask yourself how you would spend your time if you could take a year off with pay. Don't be surprised if you find your mind a total blank; complete identification with your job may have temporarily suppressed your true dreams and desires. But stay with the question and discover the possibilities of what you would choose to do if you had enough savings that you didn't need paid employment for one year.

How do you feel about having savings? What are your thoughts about it—for or against? Are you postponing it, thinking you'll do it later or when you've paid off your debt or when you have a better job? Does having savings compromise your self-image? Does it represent the passage of your youth or capitulation to your parents? Is it something that you'll get around to "one day"? Are you a spendthrift who thinks the term "disposable income" means you get to spend every last penny in your pocket? Does saving seem like an impossible dream, given your current financial status? What about your religious or political convictions about saving money? Should you be tithing your excess money to the church, giving it to the poor, or donating it to a cause? The point here is not necessarily to change your savings habits but to get in touch with your predisposition about savings so that you'll be able to manage, with ease and integrity, the increase in savings that comes as a by-product of doing these steps.

Later on, we'll talk about how to give these savings a life of their own. If you put your savings in a CD or a debt instrument (like a US Treasury, corporate, or municipal bond with an AA or better rating) or any matching fund option at your work and you don't touch it, it will, all by itself, make you money through the magic of compound interest (which we explain in chapter 8). The sooner you start, the more you'll have; it's as simple as that. This is why parents establish savings accounts for their children at young ages. While your savings percentage will change with time, the intentional act of allocating something to a savings account or safe investment is the same as saving money on a consumer purchase through smart shopping. In both cases, you get more for less.

Savings, then, are a form of Financial Independence. Savings can give you new courage at your job and new energy to explore the neglected parts of your life. Savings pave over the lean times in freelance or seasonal work. Savings relax any unconscious fear of homelessness. Savings keep you from making bad choices out of desperation. Saving money also builds the potential for freedom—from future emergencies, from being in debt, and from working nine to five until sixty-five.

Saving money is like building a dam on a river. The water that builds up behind the dam has an increasing amount of potential energy. Allow your life energy (money) to accumulate in a bank account and you will be ready to power anything from painting your house to reorienting your life.

ALL THIS FROM A GRAPH?

There is nothing magical about the Wall Chart. You can enter your numbers at the beginning of the month and ignore it the rest of the month and nothing will happen. But if you interact with it, keep it in plain sight, listen to what it's telling you, and keep going, you will notice changes over time. Part of Financial Intelligence is the continuing awareness of your earning, spending, and saving patterns over time.

- It is a constant *reminder* of your commitment to transform your relationship with money. It counters the "out of sight, out of mind" syndrome. It keeps you aware of your intention to change your unconscious spending habits.
- It is a *feedback system*, showing you at a glance, clearly and graphically, your current status and your progress toward your goal. You don't have to haul out your piggy bank or your Monthly Tabulations to see how you're doing. The two lines on your graph are either going up or going down.
- It can be an *inspiration*, an experience of satisfaction with the progress you're making that spurs you to even greater heights. When you are down in the weeds of daily life, a glance at the Wall Chart can remind you of the beautiful life you are seeding.
- It can be a *motivation*, a prod to keep you on track when discouragement creeps in or your energy flags. When temptation strikes, the thought of facing your Wall Chart at the end of the month might help you make a healthier choice.
- It puts your *integrity* on the line—visibly. It is hard (or at least harder) to lie to yourself about your progress in the presence of your Wall Chart.
- It is a continuing *suggestion* that you honor your life energy. Your income represents many hours of your precious tenure on this beautiful earth, and your

expenses represent ways you've chosen to use those valuable hours. The Wall Chart reminds you to steward this resource of time as well as possible.

♦ It can stimulate your *interest* in personal finance, a skill you can improve through reading books, listening to podcasts, taking courses, and talking with friends who actually know more than you do.

♦ Finally, it enlists continuing *support*. By having it on the wall where others can see it, you're inviting interest and participation. It helps to have your friends and relatives cheering on the sidelines. Think about the Money Talks you'll have!

FINAL INSPIRATION
FROM LINDA AND MIKE LENICH

Linda and Mike Lenich started the nine-step program in July 1992, soon after they heard about it on the radio. At that time, they were $52,000 in debt (car loan and mortgage). By July 1993, simply by following the steps, including the supercharged motivation that came from their Wall Chart, they were debt-free. But this isn't the total story. If you look at their chart you'll see they traced their debt back to 1986, when it was at $75,000+. That was when they were following a "surefire-make-a-million-beat-the-market" stock and commodities scheme that plunged them for a while in up to $125,000 of debt. Part of Mike's love of *Your Money or Your Life* was that this program worked because they became aware, committed, and conscious. He never again wanted to experience the gut-wrenching, face-blanching panic that struck when the surefire scheme precipitously failed.

Taking the slow and steady route, they still achieved FI many years ago. Linda has dedicated much of her time since to her great love, quilt making. Mike cultivated his guitar playing and even now makes some

FIGURE 5-3

The Leniches' Savings and Salary Chart

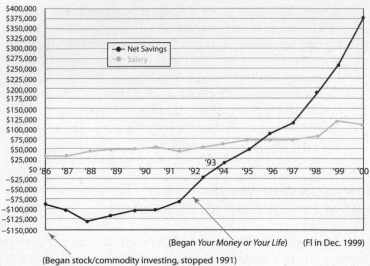

(Began *Your Money or Your Life*)   (FI in Dec. 1999)

(Began stock/commodity investing, stopped 1991)

(Debt = Loans; Home, Rental Property, Home Equity, Car, Credit Cards)

side money playing gigs in clubs. For many years he also led groups applying the steps of the program to their lives and even now uses his money smarts to help older people manage their retirement savings.

SUMMARY OF STEP 5

Make and keep up-to-date a chart of your total monthly income and your total monthly expenses. Look at it often. Share it with others.

MONEY TALK QUESTIONS

Social support is a key to behavior change. It keeps you inspired and accountable.

Using the suggestions in the epilogue for how to have a Money Talk, raise these questions in your daily reflections, with your partner, or in social groups. Remember, adding "Why?" to the end of any question will take it deeper. Adding "How has society shaped my answer?" to any question will take it wider. There are no right answers.

- How much money do you need to be happy?
- What or who can help you change your relationship with money?
- What might change if you could know what others—a friend, date, boss, stranger—earn?
- What motivates you to save?
- What helps you save money?

6

The American Dream—on
a Shoestring

It is both sad and telling that there is no word in the English language for living at the peak of the fulfillment curve, always having plenty but never being burdened with excess. The word would need to evoke the careful stewarding of tangible resources (time, money, material possessions) coupled with the joyful expansion of spiritual resources (creativity, intelligence, love). Unfortunately, you can't say, "I'm enoughing" or "I'm choosing a life of enoughness," to explain the mixture of affluence and thrift that comes from following the steps of this program.

The terms *simplicity* and *minimalism* address the lack of excess, but can seem austere or even monastic. The technique of *tidying up* adds the desire to spark joy, but is still focused mostly on stuff, and not on the deeper issues of time, money, and fulfillment. The word *frugality* used to serve that function, but by the middle of the twentieth century it seemed like a quaint notion of Depression-era grandparents.

How did frugality lose favor? It is, after all, a perennial ideal across time and cultures as well as a cornerstone of the American character. In ancient times both Socrates and Plato praised the "golden mean." Both the Old Testament ("Give me neither poverty nor wealth, but only enough") and the teachings of Jesus ("Ye cannot serve both God and money") extol the value of material simplicity in enriching the life of the spirit. In American history, well-known individuals (Benjamin Franklin, Henry David Thoreau, Ralph Waldo Emerson, Robert Frost) as well as groups (Amish, Quakers, Hutterites, Mennonites) have carried forward the virtue of thrift—both out of respect for the earth and out of a thirst for a touch of heaven. And the challenges of building our nation required frugality of most of our citizens. Indeed, the wealth we enjoy today is the result of centuries of frugality. As we said earlier, the "more is better" consumer culture is a Johnny-come-lately on the American scene. Our bedrock is frugality, and it's high time we made friends again with the word—and the practice.

Let's explore this word *frugality* to see if we can't redeem it as the key to fulfillment.

THE PLEASURES OF FRUGALITY

We looked up *frugal* in the dictionary and found "practicing or marked by economy, as in the expenditure of money or the use of material resources."[1] That sounds about right—a serviceable, practical, and fairly colorless word. None of the elegance or grace of the "enoughness" that FIers experience. But when we dig deeper, the dictionary tells us that *frugal* shares a Latin root with *frug* (meaning "virtue"), *frux* (meaning "fruit" or "value"), and *frui* (meaning "to enjoy or have the use of"). Now we're talking! Frugality is *enjoying* the *virtue* of getting good *value* for every minute of your life energy and from everything you *have the use of*.

That's not just interesting, it's transformative. Frugality means enjoying what we have. If you have ten dresses but still feel you have nothing to wear, you may be a compulsive shopper—the thrill of getting is greater than the joy of having and using. But if you have ten dresses and have enjoyed wearing all of them for years, you are frugal. Waste lies not in the number of possessions but in the failure to enjoy them. Your success at being frugal is measured not by your penny-pinching but by your degree of enjoyment of the material world.

Enjoyment of the material world? Isn't that materialism? Aren't frugal people anti-materialists? It's all in how you pay attention. For materialists, the world exists to be used, and often used up. Also, materialists may measure their worth by what they have or how other people regard what they have, leading to a "more is better and it's never enough" treadmill. Frugal people, however, make sure to get the full pleasure from everything—a dandelion or a bouquet of roses, a single strawberry or a gourmet meal. A materialist might consume the juice of five oranges as a prelude to a pancake breakfast. A frugal person, on the other hand, might relish eating a single orange, enjoying the color and texture of the whole fruit, the smell and the light spray that comes as you begin to peel it, the translucence of each section, the flood of flavor that pours out as a section bursts over the tongue . . . and the thrift of saving the peels for baking.

To be frugal means to have a high joy-to-stuff ratio. If you get one unit of joy for each material possession, that's frugal. But if you need ten possessions to even begin registering on the joy meter, you're missing the point of being alive.

There's a word in Spanish that encompasses all this: *aprovechar*. It means to use something wisely—be it a sunny day at the beach or leftovers made into a delicious new meal. It's getting full value from life, enjoying all the good that each moment and each thing has to offer. You can *aprovecha* a simple meal, a bowl of ripe strawberries, or a cruise in the Bahamas. There's nothing miserly about *aprovechar*; it's a succulent word, full of sunlight and flavor. If only *frugal* sounded so sweet.

The "more is better and it's never enough" mentality

in North America fails the frugality test not solely because of the excess, but because of the lack of enjoyment of what we already have. Indeed, North Americans have been called materialists, but that's a misnomer. All too often it's not material things we enjoy as much as what these things symbolize: conquest, status, success, achievement, a sense of worth and even favor in the eyes of the Creator. Once we've acquired the dream house, the status car, or the perfect partner, we rarely stop to enjoy them thoroughly. Instead, we're off and running after the next coveted acquisition.

Another lesson we can derive from the dictionary definition of *frugal* is the recognition that we don't need to possess a thing to enjoy it—we merely need to use it. If we are enjoying an item, whether or not we own it, we're being frugal. For many of life's pleasures it may be far better to use something than to possess it (and pay in time and energy for the upkeep). Fortunately, young people today seem less wedded to their stuff than prior generations. Due to a combination of limited incomes and growing access to on-demand, temporary use of everything from movies to audiobooks to cars, they are questioning the benefits of ownership and discovering the pleasures of the sharing economy.

Frugality, then, is also learning to share, to see the world as ours rather than as theirs and mine. "A man's home is his castle," once a promise of greater autonomy, has devolved into subdivisions of McMansions, each man a feudal lord. If we want something (or wanted it in the past, or imagine we might want it in the future), we think we must bring it inside the boundaries of the world called "mine." What we fail to recognize is that what is outside the walls of "mine" doesn't belong to the enemy; it belongs to "the rest of us."

While not explicit in the word, being frugal and being happy with having enough means that more will be available for others. This is where frugality is both practical and ethical. Sharing resources means life gets less costly and the range of things and services available to each one gets wider. Sharing resources—from lawn mowers to cars to guest rooms to our used excess, which we unload to resale shops or in online or local trading groups—means that fewer resources must be extracted from the earth, burned, or used briefly and trashed. We leave fewer plastics in the ocean, less garbage in our .dumps, and fewer toxins everywhere by sharing. From tool libraries to online groups that facilitate selling or giving away your surplus, to the loan of your lawn mower or wheelbarrow to neighbors (who might thank you with a loaf of bread or dog sitting), sharing a bit of the wealth makes life richer for both giver and receiver.

In addition to the good feeling you get when you give from your bounty to others (and others give to you), you get community through the many daily exchanges of time, helping out, gifting, and even offering a listening ear—and community is the real treasure. As part of a community, you can relax into belonging and getting a helping hand when you need it. Frugality isn't being a lone and lonely ranger, perfect in your self-reliance. It's discovering that you have more to give and more to enjoy than mere material possessions. In fact, Financial Interdependence is one key to successfully transitioning from "more is better" to "enough is enough."

Frugality is the balance we seek. Frugality is being efficient in harvesting happiness from the world you live in. Frugality is right use (which sounds, appropriately, like "righteous")—the wise stewarding of money, time, energy, space, and possessions. Goldilocks expressed it well when she declared the porridge not too hot, not too cold, but just right. Frugality is something like that—not too much, not too little, but just right. Nothing is wasted. Or left unused. It's a clean machine. Sleek. Perfect. Simple yet elegant. It's that magic word—*enough*. The peak of the fulfillment curve. The jumping-off point for a life of being fulfilled, of learning, and of contributing.

Keep this in mind as we explore ways to save money. We aren't talking about being cheap, making do, or being a skinflint or a tightwad. We're talking about creative frugality, a way of life in which you get the maximum fulfillment for each unit of life energy spent.

In fact, now that you know money is your life energy, it seems foolish to consider wasting it on stuff you don't enjoy and never use. Recalling the arithmetic we did in chapter 2, you'll remember that if you are forty years old, actuarial tables indicate that you have just 356,532 hours of life energy left in your bank. That may seem like a lot now, but those hours will feel very precious at the end of your life. Spend them well now and you won't have regrets later. Striking a balance between maximizing earning from paid employment and building other forms of wealth like friendships, networks, and skills is a lifelong process.

In the end, this creative frugality is an expression of self-esteem. It honors the life energy you invest in your material possessions. Saving those minutes and hours of life energy through careful consuming is the ultimate in self-respect.

Step 6: Valuing Your Life Energy—Minimizing Spending

This step involves the intelligent use of your life energy (money) and the conscious lowering or elimination of expenses.

Consider the sections that follow as a menu of options. Explore the ones that intrigue or inspire you, and leave the rest. There's something for everyone here—but not everything will be for you. It might be instructive, though, to ask yourself why you are discarding some ideas and adopting others. You may encounter some childhood programming, some cultural myths, and even some revealing information about your values.

Remember, these ideas are opportunities, not shoulds. Frugality is about enjoyment, not penny-pinching! Happy saving—or should we say happy frugaling . . .

ONE SURE WAY TO SAVE MONEY

Stop Trying to Impress Other People

It's an endless and fruitless waste of time and money, plus others are likely so busy trying to impress you that they will, at best, not notice your efforts. At worst, they will resent you for one-upping them.

When Thorstein Veblen published *The Theory of the Leisure Class* in 1899, it didn't make a big splash. But the term he coined, "conspicuous consumption," has made it into the heart of our culture. In the foreword to Veblen's book, social commentator and writer Stuart Chase summarized his thesis this way:

> People above the line of base subsistence, in this age and all earlier ages, do not use the surplus, which society has given them, primarily for useful purposes. They do not seek to expand their own lives, to live more wisely, intelligently, understandingly, but to impress other people with the fact that they have a surplus . . . spending money, time and effort quite uselessly in the pleasurable business of inflating the ego.[2]

But just because conspicuous consumption is a cross-cultural and evolutionary aberration of the human species doesn't mean that you have to fall prey to it. Social media makes unhooking from self-comparison even harder, as your friends are constantly posting humble-brags about their exotic vacations, their meals at upscale restaurants, or their newest toys. If you stop trying to impress other people you will save thousands, perhaps millions of dollars. If you must, impress people with how much money you saved with your creative DIY project or travel hack, or the natural beauty you experienced while camping instead of going to a resort.

TEN SURE WAYS TO SAVE MONEY

1. Don't Go Shopping

If you don't go shopping, you won't spend money. Of course, if you really need something from the store, go and buy it. But don't just go shopping.

It used to be so simple: If you didn't make the effort to physically go to a store, you couldn't buy anything. Now, with a tap on your phone, just about anything in the world can be delivered to your doorstep within days or even hours. Even if you choose not to actively shop online, being connected at all means you are constantly exposed to advertising that's increasingly targeted to your wants and needs, filling your screens, feeds, and in-boxes with "relevant" offers to help you part with your money. News content, which used to be sacrosanct, is intermingled with paid advertorials. Used wisely, these offers can help you get things you need for less, but it's also much easier to waste your money on stuff you don't need when you don't have to get in your car and drive to the mall.

In the off-line retail world, a 2014 scientific telephone survey of one thousand adult Americans found that 75 percent said they had made an impulse buy—those spur-of-the-moment purchases you didn't intend to make when you entered the store. Excitement was the biggest stimulus overall, but men tended to buy while drunk and women while bored or sad, with both genders doing it when angry. Half reported regret when the bills came due.[3] Caveat emptor! Online, with your interests and habits being tracked and shared among search engines, social media platforms, and advertisers, sophisticated recommendation algorithms are working to drive impulse buys, and since you don't even need to leave home for one-click shopping, it can be even more impulsive.

Why is shopping one of our favorite national pastimes? More than the simple act of acquiring needed goods and services, shopping attempts to fill (but obviously fails, since we have to shop so often) myriad needs: for a reward after a job well done; for an antidepressant; for esteem boosting, self-assertion, status, and nurturing; and in the case of malls, for socializing and time structuring. Consumption seems to be our favorite high, our nationally sanctioned addiction, the all-American form of substance abuse.

What to do? Don't use shopping as a reward, a relief, or entertainment. Reduce your exposure to tempting offers by opting out of promotional e-mails or at the very least filtering them out of your primary in-box. Be savvy enough about media to know who's paying for the content you're consuming, so you can recognize hidden advertising when you see it. Most important, develop a discipline of buying only what you need. It's like working a muscle—your frugality muscle. Over time, it strengthens, and soon enough you're no longer swayed by targeted advertising. You may be saving more than money. You may be saving your sanity, not to mention your soul.

2. Live Within Your Means

This notion is so outmoded that some readers might not even know what it signifies. To live within your means is to buy only what you can prudently afford, to avoid debt unless you have an assurance that you will be able to pay it promptly, and to always have something put away for a rainy day. It was quite a fashionable way to live a few short generations ago, before the expansion of credit. There are two sides to the coin of living beyond your means. The shiny side is that you can have everything you want right now. The tarnished side is that you will pay for it with your life—in interest. Buying on credit, from cars to houses to vacations, often results in paying three times the purchase price. Is going to Hawaii for two weeks this year worth working perhaps four additional months next year to pay it off? This doesn't mean you have to cut up all your credit cards—you just have to avoid using them if you can't pay them off right away. We recognize that credit cards can be a way to put food on the table for those who unexpectedly hit hard times. However, it's important to distinguish between necessity and indulgence so you have as little debt as possible to pay off.

Living within your means suggests that you wait until you have the money before you buy something. This gives you the benefit of avoiding interest charges. It also gives you a waiting period during which you may well discover that you don't want some of those things after all. The bright side of living within your means is that you will use and enjoy what you have and harvest a full measure of fulfillment from it, whether it's your ten-year-old but still-great car, your favorite coat, or your old house. It also means that you can weather the economic bad times when they come—which they will.

3. Take Care of What You Have

There is one thing we all have that we want to last a long time: our bodies. Simple attention to proven preventive practices will save you lots of money. Taking care of your teeth, for example, can save thousands in dental bills. And eating what you know agrees with your body (judging by your energy, not by your taste buds) may save you thousands in expensive procedures—not to mention your life.

Extend this principle to all your possessions. Mend ripped clothes, resole worn shoes, replace your computer's old hard drive or add more RAM. Regular oil changes are known to extend the life of your car. Cleaning your tools keeps them functioning at peak performance. (How many hair dryers and vacuum cleaners have choked to death on hair balls?) Dusting your refrigerator coils conserves energy and could save your refrigerator. One big difference between living beings and machines is that machines are not self-healing. If you ignore an occasional headache, it will probably go away. If you ignore a funny noise coming from your computer or your car, you may incur major (and costly) damage.

Many of us have lived with excess for so long that it no longer occurs to us to maintain what we have. "There's always more where that came from," we tell ourselves. But more costs money. And more may not, in the long run, be available. We need to rewire our brains to think repair rather than replace.

4. Wear It Out

What's the last item you actually wore out? If it weren't for the fashion industry (and boredom), we could all enjoy the same basic wardrobe for many years. Survey your possessions. Are you simply upgrading or duplicating last year's phone, furniture, kitchenware, and linens, or are you truly wearing them out? Think how much money you would save if you simply decided to use things even 20 percent longer. If you tend to upgrade your linens every three years, try replacing them every four years. If you trade in your car every four years, try extending that to five. If you buy a new coat every other winter, see whether every third winter would do just as well. And when you're about to buy something, ask yourself, "Do I already have one of these that is in perfectly usable condition?"

Another way to save money is to ask, before trashing something, whether there might be another way to use part or all of it. Old dishcloths and worn-out clothing become cleaning rags. Old magazines become art materials. The web is full of creative DIY life hacks that can help you reuse everyday items.

A word of caution to the already frugal: Using something until you wear it out does not mean using it until it wears you out. If you must continually fiddle with a lamp to make it work and you've already tried repairing it, it may not be worth your life energy to coax it along for another year. If your car is taking you for a ride, costing more hours in tinkering (or more money in repairs) than it's giving you in service, buy a newer one. If your knees are suffering from running shoes that have lost their bounce, it would be cheaper to buy a new pair (on sale) than to have knee surgery.

5. Do It Yourself

Can you replace a bulb or other simple part in your car? Fix a plumbing leak? Do your taxes? Make your own gifts? Change the tire on your bicycle? Bake a cake from scratch? Build a bookshelf? Refinish furniture? Plant a garden? Design your own website? Cut your family's hair? Form your own nonprofit corporation? It used to be that life was simpler and we learned basic life skills from our parents in the process of growing up. Now, for the most part, we are consumers of goods and services provided by others. To reverse that trend, just ask yourself, when you're about to hire an expert: "Can I do this myself? What would it take to learn how? Would it be a useful skill to know?" The maker revolution is putting DIY back in fashion; makerspaces—where electronics, fabric, wood, and wire can be repurposed with flair—are popping up everywhere.

Granted, our electronics have gotten so technical that a DIYer would have trouble figuring out how to even get into the guts to fix something. For example, back in the day a car was a machine that was fixable by a backyard mechanic. Now cars are rolling computers that do everything including drive themselves at times—and require professional technicians to service them.

Years ago, when **Tina U.** *was young and lived in Fiji with her doctor husband for several months, she was embarrassed by how the native Fijians seemed to revere them. She tried to diminish their respect to an appropriate level, but they would have none of it. Then she discovered that since the Fijians made—and could repair—every single thing they depended on to live, they assumed that Tina and Charles had made their transistor radio, watch, and typewriter. They were unable to understand that these things were made by others and that Tina and Charles had no idea how.*

Basic living and survival skills can be learned through websites, books, online courses, adult education classes, and the world's growing repository of how to make or fix everything, YouTube. Every breakdown can be used as an opportunity for learning and empowerment. What you can't do, or choose not to do, you can hire others to do for you and then tag along for the ride. Every bit of your energy invested in solving these breakdowns not only teaches you something you need to know for the next time, but helps prevent mistakes and reduces the bill. Sure, it's maddeningly cheaper now to replace some things rather than repair them, but if you are curious or want to be empowered or are simply revolted by the image of future generations dealing with your trashed stuff, you can hop online and learn.

One FIer tells the story of how her heating system failed one winter. Three companies sent out repair people to assess the problem and make a bid. Each one told her with absolute certainty what the problem was. Unfortunately, none of their diagnoses or solutions matched! So she did her own research, meditated on the Rube Goldberg maze of pipes, came to an educated guess, and chose the company that came closest to her analysis, thus saving herself hundreds of dollars of unnecessary and possibly destructive work. By staying with the repairman and observing his work, she also was able to avert a few more expensive mistakes and to save (expensive) time by doing some of the simpler tasks. A typical working person might have paid several times what she did to have the job done and then felt fortunate to have two paychecks "since the cost of living in the modern world is so high."

6. Anticipate Your Needs

Forethought in purchasing can bring significant savings. With enough lead time you will likely find the items you need at a cheaper price. Keep a list of things you anticipate needing in the coming year. Get to know the brands, features, and typical price ranges for those items. Use the tools from your favorite deal sites, online retailers, or classified advertising sites like Craigslist to receive notifications when the item you need becomes available or changes price. Being ready to pounce on a deal will help ensure you get the item at the sale price, since many of the best deals are gone in days, hours, or even minutes. Watch for seasonal bargains around major holidays, especially at brick-and-mortar stores that still advertise in local newspapers. For expensive items like cars, computers, or phones, waiting until next year's model is about to come out can get you a big discount on this year's model. By simply observing the poor condition of your car's left rear tire while it still has some life left, or knowing when you need to take your next flight, you can anticipate a need.

In the shorter term, shopping at the corner convenience store can be expensive. Anticipating your needs—that you'll be wanting evening snacks, that you'll run out of milk midweek, or that your supply of toilet paper is running low—can eliminate running out to the corner store to pick up these items. Instead you can purchase them during your supermarket shopping, on a run to the office supply store, or online. This can result in significant savings over the long term.

Anticipating your needs also eliminates one of the biggest threats to your frugality: impulse buying. If you haven't anticipated needing something when you leave your house at 3:05, chances are you don't need it at 3:10 when you're standing at the gazingus pin counter at the corner store. We're not saying you should buy only things that are on your premeditated shopping list (although that isn't such a bad idea for compulsive shoppers); we are saying that you must be scrupulously honest when you're out and about. Saying, "I anticipate needing this," as you're drooling over a left-handed veeblefetzer or cashmere sweater is not the same as having already anticipated needing one and recognizing that this particular one is a bargain. You may have heard of Parkinson's law ("Work expands so as to fill the time available for its completion").; The corollary is: "Needs expand to encompass whatever you want to buy on impulse."

7. Research Value, Quality, Durability, Multiple Use, and Price

Research your purchases. Read reviews, comments, and crowdsourced ratings from trusted sites and online marketplaces. Decide what features are most important to you. Don't just be a bargain junkie and automatically buy the cheapest item available. Durability might be critical for something you plan to use daily for twenty years. One obvious way of saving money is to spend less on each item you buy, but it's equally true that spending $40 on a tool that lasts ten years instead of buying a $30 one that will need to be replaced in five years will save you $20 in the long run. Versatility is also a factor. Buying one item for $10 that will serve the purpose of four different $5 items will net you a savings of $10. One heavy-duty kitchen pot can (and perhaps should) replace half a dozen specialty appliances like a rice cooker, a Crock-Pot, a Dutch oven, a deep-fat fryer, and a spaghetti cooker. So, if you really expect to be using an item, buying for durability and for multiple purposes can be a good savings technique. But if you'll be using the item only occasionally, you may not want to spend the extra dollars on a high-quality product. Knowing what your needs are and knowing the whole range of what is available will allow you to choose the right item.

You can also evaluate quality by developing a sharp eye and carefully examining what you are buying. Are the seams in a piece of clothing ample? Are the edges finished? Is the fabric durable? Are the screws holding the appliance together sturdy enough for the job? Is the material strong or flimsy? Is the furniture nailed, stapled, or screwed? You will become an expert materialist— knowing materials so well that you can read the probable longevity of an item the way a forester can read the age and history of a fallen tree.

8. Buy It for Less

There are numerous ways to get what you need for less:

Comparison-shop: Deciding where to buy something involves trade-offs between price and values such as convenience, selection, support for your local economy, and environmental and social justice concerns. You may be willing to pay more for an item from a local, independent store than you would for an item ordered online, but how much more? To decide, you need to be able to compare prices. Use metasearch sites or browser add-ons that allow you to check pricing on many sites simultaneously. For local stores that don't have their inventory online, call them to find out what's in stock, what they can order, and the best price they can offer you. Many stores, both brick-and-mortar and online, offer price matching, in which they'll honor a lower price from stores in the vicinity or from a select list of online retailers. Some retailers will even refund you the difference if you find the same item cheaper elsewhere within a specified number of days after your purchase. Especially for expensive items, being a skilled comparison shopper can save you thousands of dollars.

Bargain: You can ask for discounts when paying cash. You can ask for discounts for less-than-perfect items. You can ask for the sale price even if the sale begins tomorrow or ended yesterday. You can ask for further discounts on items already marked down. You can ask for discounts if you buy a number of items at the same time. You can ask for discounts anywhere, anytime. Nothing ventured, nothing gained. Haggling is a time-honored tradition. The list price of any consumer item is usually inflated. If you're buying a new car, you no longer need to go in and haggle blindly. The dealer's invoice cost and often other incentives they're getting that month can be found online, so you can more easily start bargaining at a fair price. For each new car I've purchased, I've called all the dealers within a hundred miles, and have gotten every car for 30 to 50 percent off the list price.

For example, in 2017 I spotted a used Sunrader camper on a car lot. Knowing the value and rarity of these classics (and that my days of tenting are over), I took it for a test drive. It sputtered and chugged up hills, but with my knowledge of old-style internal combustion engines, I knew just how to fix it. It had suffered some water damage. A latch didn't work. I drove it back with a frown. Nope, I don't want to buy this many problems. The dealer asked what price might make it worth it. I came back with half sticker price out the door. "Sold!" he said.

You have nothing to lose by asking for a discount at any store—from your local hardware store to a clothing emporium. A case in point was my recent outing to buy new running shoes. A $95 (list price) pair was sitting on the manager's special rack with no price. They fit perfectly. I asked a salesman what they would cost. "Thirty-nine ninety-nine," he replied. "Would you take thirty?" I asked. Surveying what he had left, he said, "Twenty-eight dollars." I could have pointed out that haggling etiquette suggests that his counteroffer be higher, not lower, than mine. But I was astute enough to shut my mouth, open my wallet, and take advantage of a great bargain. By the way, this strategy works best at independently owned stores where the owner has more authority to make instant decisions. So if the chain store has it for less, at least give the independent, local store owner a chance to meet the price.

You can also buy it used. Reexamine your attitudes about buying used items. Most of us live in "used" houses—someone else probably built your home and inaugurated the shower, toilet, fridge, and more. The biggest cost for a new car in its first year of ownership is the depreciation, which averages almost 20 percent of the purchase price. Buy a car that's a few years or even just a few months old and you can save thousands of dollars.

But what about everything else? Online marketplaces like Craigslist and eBay are great places to find used items to buy. Social media apps can be a marketplace for matching people with unused stuff to those with unmet needs. Like cars, new furniture loses its value quickly, so buying a mint-condition sofa or dining set used on Craigslist will certainly save you a bundle. If you wouldn't be caught dead in a Goodwill thrift store, take a closer look around your town. Thrift stores have long since become fashionable emporiums. Clothing, kitchenware, furniture, drapes—all can be found in thrift stores, and you may be surprised at the high quality you can find in many of them. As a matter of fact, donating brand-new items to thrift stores is one way that shopaholics justify excess purchases. If you just can't bring yourself to shop at thrift stores, consider consignment shops. The prices are higher, but the quality is often higher as well.

In our experience, thrift stores are best for clothing, but garage sales are best for appliances, furniture, and household items. If you're an early bird (arriving before the sellers have even had their morning coffee), you can often find exceptional buys—unless you get shooed away because you are too early. On the other hand, the later in the day you go to a garage sale, the more eager the people will be to get rid of the stuff for a song.

Swap meets and flea markets still exist in some places; there you'll find merchants of every stripe displaying their wares: shrewd hucksters (buyer beware), collectors of every kind, and families hoping to unload their excess before moving across the country. Whether you're bargain-hunting at garage sales or on Craigslist, make sure you're really saving money on something you need, rather than accumulating more junk you don't need just because "it's such a deal!"

The old saying "One man's trash is another man's treasure" also brings to mind ways to get used things without paying a penny using the Freecycle Network or the Buy Nothing Project. Large old windows removed in a house renovation become a greenhouse for a farmer instead of going to a landfill. These person-to-person hand-me-down networks are a win for both parties and for the planet.

9. Meet Your Needs Differently

The principle of substitution says that there are hundreds if not thousands of ways to meet a need. Traditional economics would have you believe that more, better, or different stuff can satisfy almost any need and is just a credit card swipe away. But who says frugal pleasures are less pleasurable because they are less pricey? For example, what's the best way to lift your spirits? An antidepressant? Running? Cognitive therapy? A change of scenery? Going to a funny movie? Helping someone in a worse pickle? Retail therapy?

Which works best for you? Do you have just one strategy or many different ones? When you feel depleted, where do you turn? Rest? Exercise? Caffeine? Therapy (retail or talk)? TV? In other words, there's a difference between needs and the strategies we use to satisfy those needs.

For example, freedom is a basic need, but if "freedom" means "travel" to me, what am I really looking for? What values or desires lie behind that core need? Often it's novelty, stimulation, and getting out of daily and sometimes deadening routines. It's needing some aimlessness and idleness in contrast to my norm of purposefulness. It's learning new languages, cultures, facts. Meeting new people. A slower pace with less stress. Swimming in a different sea of assumptions, getting jolted out of narrow-mindedness. Tasting new food. Indulging in a novel during a long flight. It's being out of town and unavailable for all the meetings and decisions that tend to whittle down my store of daily joy.

But do I need to travel to faraway places to find novel experiences? Remember, substitution as a frugality strategy isn't about downgrading pleasure. It's about ensuring that I get precisely what I am seeking for less—or nothing at all. I'm not limiting myself (waaa!); I'm focusing myself (yum!). Freedom from my daily routines might involve letting go of rigid standards (let the house be less clean), some burdensome responsibilities (don't always say yes to those requesting my help), and some entrenched habits (like never hiring someone to do for you what you can do for yourself). When gas prices are high, how about traveling more locally—seeing the sights within a day's drive—and discovering exotic people and places nearby? Even taking my camper to a park within a hundred miles puts me in the woods or at the seashore, with all the tantalizing smells and sights. Staying closer to home also reveals some hidden treasures in your own backyard or over the backyard fence—like your beautiful flower garden or your neighbor's interesting stories. Stay put long enough and the details and delights of where you are become more evident. See, substitution isn't deprivation; it's about getting creative.

Substitution, when it's creative, also reminds us that what we seek when we buy something new is to change a feeling state. We feel hungry, for example, so we eat to have a feeling of satisfaction. We feel lonely, so we join a club or make a date to feel connected. We feel bored, so we go to a movie or read a magazine or go on a trip to feel enlivened. But most of our needs are not material! Substitution says, "When you feel a desire to shop, take time to trace it back to the need and ask if creativity rather than consumption might best fill it." Donella Meadows cuts to the heart of it in *Beyond the Limits*:

> People don't need enormous cars; they need respect. They don't need closets full of clothes; they need to feel attractive and they need excitement and variety and beauty. People don't need electronic equipment; they need something worthwhile to do with their lives. People need identity, community, challenge, acknowledgement, love, joy. To try to fill these needs with material things is to set up an unquenchable appetite for false solutions to real and never-satisfied problems. The resulting psychological emptiness is one of the major forces behind the desire for material growth.[4]

Substitution isn't limitation. It's liberation. It's letting go of assumptions and habits, looking at the richness of reality, and picking from the smorgasbord of pleasures available right under your nose.

10. Follow the Nine Steps of This Program

Hundreds of thousands of people have successfully followed the steps of this program. These people have found that doing all the steps leads to a transformed experience of money and the material world. It's the transformation, not the tips, that saves them money. Mild shopping addictions evaporate. Self-denial and self-indulgence both yield to self-awareness, which ends up being a much bigger pleasure. You can use this program as a series of tips or advice, or you can let it work its magic by doing the steps. The steps are a whole-system approach to money and stuff that changes your habits by changing your way of seeing. All the steps matter. They synergize to spur you on.

SAVING ON THE BASICS

From Penny-Pinching to Smart Saving

In an earlier edition of this book we included a section called "101 Sure Ways to Save Money." But times have changed, and some of our tried-and-true suggestions aren't so true anymore.

In addition, legions of bloggers, podcasters, and YouTubers are offering new ideas and tips every day, as well as numerous books focused on frugal, simple living. This ranges from cheap travel to cheap cooking, from DIY household fixes to how to build a home from the ground up, from growing your own food to growing your own eco-village.

Finally, keep in mind that the strategies you come up with for yourself in your own life often will be much more powerful than the advice of others. Consider the following story:

> **Harry N.** *was looking at his Wall Chart and reconsidering his practice of hiring a house cleaner and gardener to take care of his home. He wasn't ready, however, to take on all that daily maintenance himself. So he came up with a surprising solution. He noticed that his family never used the large dining room. It came with the house, so they furnished it, forgot about it, and ate in the family room. But with his*

*new FI thinking he saw that he could remodel, replacing the
dining room with a studio apartment. He made the renova-
tions and found a couple who was willing to do yard and
house work in exchange for room and board.*

That kind of creative thinking could never be embodied in a "hints and tips" list! Nevertheless, a little guidance can be extremely useful in helping to break old
patterns and getting you to think creatively. So we include the following quick tips containing real-life examples of FI thinking that can save you money and buy you
freedom.

Managing Debt and Your Finances

A cardinal rule of frugality is to avoid debt. After all,
you've already done your time on the job for the privilege of having the money in your pocket. Why pay
again—and drag the ball and chain of debt around as
you hobble down the road of life?

Some people, the author included, manage to go
through life paying cash for everything, but those people with debt for large-ticket essentials (college, mortgage, car) follow the frugality rule by paying it off as
quickly as possible.

Unfortunately, the easiest ways to borrow money—
credit cards and payday loans—are also the most financially ruinous for many. We can't say enough about how
important it is to pay off any balances you currently
have on these high-interest-rate rip-offs, and to completely avoid them in the future. Use a credit card for
convenience, building credit, or to earn points, but only
if you can pay the entire balance every month. And we
mean every month! Otherwise, use cash or a debit card.
The same goes for car loans and making large purchases
on installment plans—if you get a low- or zero-interest
rate and have the discipline to reliably make the payments, consider it. Otherwise, wait until you've saved up

enough to buy it with your own money instead of paying interest and fees to borrow it from the bank.

Some forms of debt can be viewed as an investment if the money you borrow enables you to buy an asset that appreciates in value or boosts your earning power. If you can reliably make your mortgage payment every month and you live in an area where real estate values consistently rise (as opposed to boom-and-bust or stagnation), having a low-interest, fixed-rate mortgage could be a wise investment, especially if you can deduct the mortgage interest on your taxes. Many people, however, will find comfort and freedom in the idea of owning their home debt-free, and therefore should figure out the best way to pay off their mortgage early. Young people often use student loans to acquire the education they need to earn a better living. While you can view this as a kind of investment in your financial future, no one wants to start out his adult life with this huge burden hanging over his head. Get scholarships and avoid student loans if you can—or if not, pay them off quickly, and deduct the interest from your taxes.

If you do borrow money in any of these forms, it's critical that you make your monthly payments, or your credit rating will be damaged. A low credit rating could prevent you from buying a house or renting the apartment you want, and can even raise the interest rate you'll pay on credit card debt.

You should be able to do all your basic banking for free and even earn a bit of interest if you sign up for online banking at many credit unions and banks. Credit unions exist to serve members instead of generate profit for outside shareholders, so they tend to have the lowest fees and best interest rates on your deposits. Regardless of where you bank, avoid overdrawing your account or bouncing checks, as this will usually incur a sizable fee. Use the free online banking tools available to alert you about low balances, track your expenses, and automate bill paying.

Having a Place to Live

As we said in chapter 3, housing is usually the most expensive item on your Monthly Tabulation. Urbanization is putting more of us in high-cost cities, so being creative about housing can reduce your costs significantly. Consider, for example, moving to a less expensive area or finding a housemate (easier than ever thanks to social media and Craigslist). You may well be able to keep your current job and work remotely. Also consider living in a smaller home. The average square footage of a new single-family home in 1973 was 1,660. By 2015, it was 2,687![5] Ask yourself if you really need that much space. While a tiny house of a couple hundred square feet might not be for you, a smaller house might meet your needs and leave you with less space to heat, cool, and clean. Explore living in an intentional community like cohousing, where you'll be able to share your life with people who share your values while usually also lowering your expenses. If you've identified a neighborhood you like, consider finding a house to rent that isn't yet on the market. Look for telltale signs that a house isn't currently occupied such as an untended yard or uncollected mail, find the owner through the tax office, and make it easy for her to want to rent her property to you. If you already have a house, consider renting out unused space. If you're in the market for a new home, think about buying a duplex. Living on one side and renting out the other will allow you to lower your monthly mortgage payment dramatically. Finally, technology enables some people to work from just about anywhere, which allows full-time RVers and location-independent workers (digital nomads) to live in beautiful places around the world, often for less money than it costs to stay planted in one place.

Rachel Z. had a lucrative job that grated on many of her values—and lots of good ideas about what she'd do if she didn't have to report to work every day. She found herself constantly thinking through alternatives, devising escape routes from a job that was beginning to feel like a prison. The FI course gave her a tunnel out, but it was her own ingenuity that turned on the light at the end of it. She realized that she could move into the lower level of her house, rent out her bedroom, and use that rental income to handle her monthly mortgage payments. She did just that, and by implementing a few other creative strategies, she managed to leave her job with enough money to live on.

Cara and Richard M., both artists, took on a job as apartment managers. Their place was furnished and free, their commute was nil, their job costuming was a few grungy thrift-store outfits for doing the dirty work—plus they got a monthly income. All this meant they could get rid of their day jobs and spend more time on their art.

Getting Around

Consider this. For nearly all of human history people walked or rode in carts pulled by other animals. After nomadic foraging gave way to agricultural settlements, most people never traveled more than ten miles from their home in their lifetime. The internal combustion engine didn't exist until the 1860s, when Nikolaus Otto first patented the engine now in your auto. That's only 150 years ago. Only a fraction of humans on this planet today own a car. People get around and always have—but it's our curious minds, not vehicles with engines, that have propelled us around the world. So let's just get some perspective as we see how we might, in our short lifetimes, frugalize our ride.

For most people, a car is the second-most expensive thing they buy, after a house, and the annual cost of owning a car is high, including insurance, registration, maintenance, repairs, gas, and depreciation. If you have to own a car, get something that's reasonably reliable and fuel efficient, maintain it well, and keep it for as long as you can. This will nearly always be cheaper than buying a new car, even over the long run. Then find ways to drive it less to wear it out slower. Join a carpool, take the bus, live close to work, work from home some days if you can, and do errands on foot or bicycle. Ask your employer if you could work a four-day week, which would reduce your commuting costs and get you off the road during rush hour. Those who live in cities have a number of alternatives to owning a car, including public transportation, car sharing (both peer-to-peer and fleets), bike sharing, on-demand car services, taxis, and traditional rental cars. With all those options and the high cost of parking, it's often cheaper and more convenient to not own a car in a big city. Even if you don't live in a big city, see if you can find a way to avoid owning a second car. You will save a lot of your hard-earned cash, and you may find other benefits as well.

Rosemary I. did the math and with considerable trepidation sold her one and only car. Her city had a car-sharing coop, so she joined for her once-a-week stocking-up at the hardware, grocery, and other stores. She calculated that renting a car for her once-a-month weekend in the country plus her once-a-week errands cost her a fraction of what she was paying for insurance, registration, monthly payments, repairs, and maintenance on the car she owned. And sometimes she could coax a friend to go camping with her—in the friend's car—adding the advantage of human companionship to the joy of communing with nature. She paid for the gas, and for the two together the pleasure was doubled while the cost was halved. A bargain.

As a home remodeler **Ted Y.** rationalized his two extra vehicles (an old pickup truck and another beater) as useful for hauling tools and materials to his jobs. Since they weren't worth much on the open market, he'd assumed it was cheaper to keep them. Not true. Doing his Monthly Tabulations showed him the high cost of the convenience of having—and maintaining—these backup vehicles. After calculating the cost of the new transmission, the insurance, and licensing, Ted found that he could just rent an extra truck for less money when he needed it. He sold off both extra vehicles.

Taking Care of Your Body

Medical costs are extremely high, so staying well is good for your wallet as well as for your body. Your best basic health insurance is a healthy diet, exercise, good rest, and low stress. Although new medical studies are always coming out that seem to conflict with the previous ones, keep up on health recommendations that gain credibility. Prevention is key. Take full advantage of the benefits of your health insurance, including preventive visits and screenings, life coaching, mental health screenings, and health club membership, if they offer that. Some employers also offer savings accounts that allow employees to save, invest, and spend tax-fee earnings for qualified health expenses. If you're paying for your own health insurance, shop carefully and see if you qualify for any state-run, more affordable plans. If you're generally healthy, you can opt for health insurance with a higher deductible and a lower premium, potentially saving you money. Prevention also avoids one of the costliest ways to access a doctor: the emergency room. Nip illnesses in the bud and you can nip ruinous medical expenses in the bud as well.

If you don't have health insurance, prevention and comparison shopping are even more important. Keep an eye out for health fairs, where you can often get basic blood work and tests done free or for a minimal fee. If your teeth need care, consider visiting a dental school in your area, where student dentists often provide excellent care at a fraction of the usual cost. Also, remember that many doctors have privileges at several different hospitals—find out which ones your doctor can use and comparison-shop for the lowest price. You'll be surprised at how much the daily rates and operating room costs vary from one hospital to the next.

Because of the high cost of surgery and health insurance in the United States, millions of people a year travel to other countries to get expensive medical procedures done. Organizations like Patients Beyond Borders help these medical tourists find the care they need in other countries, where it can cost anywhere from 20 to 90 percent less than the same procedure in the States. Caveat emptor in neon letters, though. If you have complications once you are home, you may have to pay hometown prices for help, thereby negating your savings. Be sure to do your research before embarking on this journey.

Sharing/Bartering

Studies consistently show that one of the paths to happiness (and frugality) is being involved in community. One quick way to build community and save money is sharing your stuff, as we said earlier about cars, either by renting or lending it. There are systems designed specifically for brokering trades, like alternative local currencies, babysitting coops, and time banks. Neighborhood listservs create nearby mutual aid networks. With time banks, people swap hour for hour—for example, giving a haircut can be exchanged for accompanying someone to doctor visits or helping with their computer. Think of a skill you have and a service you need. Get creative! Sharing is a win-win, and you get the bonus of community in the process.

Eating

No matter how frugal we become, almost all of us have to spend at least some money on food. Once you begin tracking your expenses, you'll see how much eating out can cost. Making the time to enjoy cooking meals at home and even entertaining friends that way instead of going out is a sure way to save money and improve your health. Starting a garden can help keep the cost of the produce you eat down, especially if you're used to buying organic.

There are many ways to save money on groceries—some are obvious and some are not. Obvious tips include making a list and sticking to it, knowing what's on sale at your local store, clipping (or getting online) coupons, avoiding convenience foods, and buying in bulk. Eating with the seasons also saves money. By not insisting on peaches in February and strawberries in September, you can lower your grocery bill significantly and enjoy food that is both tastier and much more sustainably produced. The most expensive items on most people's weekly grocery bill are meat, alcohol, and coffee. Look carefully at your consumption of these, and see if you can reduce them, or make a special effort to get them at a cheaper price. Michael Pollan's pithy seven-word food rule, "Eat food, not too much, mostly plants," has helped people rethink meat as more of a condiment than an entrée. Look into joining a bulk-buying coop with friends and neighbors to save money on many of your staples.

We so identify food with what is sold in the store that we don't realize how much of it grows wild all around us. You can glean a willing farmer's fields, ask your neighbors if they are OK with you taking their extra fruit, or eat berries from wild bushes (in the Pacific Northwest our untamable blackberries make gluttons of us all). Good food and community—for free.

Staying Connected, Informed, and Entertained

Look at how much you spend every year on your phone plan, data package, cable and Internet at home (and maybe that old standby—a landline?), subscriptions to music and video streaming services, your favorite news sites, and maybe even a newspaper and a few magazines. What was once relatively simple has become very complex—and expensive. How can we rein this monster in and still get what we need?

First of all, if you're locked into a traditional, expensive phone contract, don't renew it. There are phone plans that can cost you a quarter of what you're paying, saving you thousands of dollars a year if you have a family of phone users. Pay-as-you-go plans mean you're not paying for minutes or megabytes you don't use. If you spend most of your day at home or at work, where you have Wi-Fi, leave data off and just turn it on when you need it, and use Internet messaging and calling apps instead of phone and text messaging. No-contract plans allow you to shop around and switch anytime you find a better deal, with no penalty. Plans that allow you to bring your own device means you can buy used phones. Last year's flagship phone sells for a couple hundred dollars less now. Don't need the latest? An older smartphone in good condition can be found for around $100. Once you've accepted a mobile phone as part of your daily life, consider ditching that expensive landline if you still have one.

What about television and movies? Follow the example of "cord cutters" who have found they can replace their expensive cable or satellite package with a combination of an old-fashioned over-the-air (OTA) antenna and streaming services. Depending on where you live, an OTA antenna can deliver local channels with a picture and sound quality that exceeds cable and satellite, and it's free! There's lots of free streaming content available, and you can always rent a movie or series to supplement that. If you must subscribe to a paid streaming service, do some research and try to choose just one that best fits your needs and tastes. The same goes for streaming music services.

While it's important to support journalism sites,

magazines, and newspapers you care about with paid subscriptions, be sure to consider the cost of these, especially when much of that information and perspective is available elsewhere for free. Speaking of print, public libraries are an even better resource now than they were a generation ago. The ability to easily get books from other branches in your local system has increased the selection of books you can borrow. Most libraries have also added digital services, allowing you to borrow downloadable e-books and audiobooks from home. And it's still all free to you, already paid for with your tax dollars.

Getting Away

As your handling of money gets clearer and your life becomes more satisfying, you will have less of a need to "vacate." Consider relaxing closer to home. You might even enjoy taking a vacation in your own house—a "staycation." Given the amount of time you work for the privilege of owning or renting your abode, you are entitled to relax and appreciate it for a week. If you do want to get away, any change of location might do—three miles or three hundred miles are both "away." Reflect on your true needs and you may find that a day trip and a new (used) hammock for the backyard would be just as satisfying as the traditional week away. Camping is also an inexpensive way to get away, relax, and experience nature's beauty on a shoestring.

If you do decide to travel farther afield, there are numerous ways to do this on the cheap. If you're flying, use the most effective travel search engines to find the cheapest fares. Be flexible on dates, times, and locations, and subscribe to sites and price alerts that can uncover unpublished, deeply discounted flights. These can easily be half the cost of a normal fare. If you have the discipline, you can try travel hacking—opening and closing credit cards to amass airline miles, hotel points, or cash. For accommodations, consider couch surfing, apartment or room rentals, and hostels—all of which can add a more personal connection with locals or fellow travelers versus a hotel. You could also try WWOOFing (World Wide Opportunities on Organic Farms), in which you volunteer your time working on an organic or sustainable farm in exchange for lodging and food. Wherever you go, avoid the tourist traps, eat where the locals do, and walk or use public transportation whenever possible—you'll get a more authentic experience of the place you visit and spend less.

If you want to travel somewhere exotic, there just might be someone there who considers your hometown exotic. Home exchange sites broker house swaps, so you could trade Provence, France, for Providence, Rhode Island. Also consider volunteer vacations with scientific research or service groups. Better to live in a village and help build a school or find a cure for a disease than to whiz through on a shopping excursion, taking pictures, buying artifacts, and leaving the people in the dust. You can house-sit and there are matchmaking sites for that.

Some clever FIers actually live in low-budget countries for part of the year to refill low coffers without having to go back to a job. Major costs such as housing, transportation, and food are all considerably cheaper, plus you get the joy of traveling rolled right into daily life!

Protecting What You Own

As you practice the steps in this book, you will invariably become a much more conscious consumer. While this skill will serve you well in all aspects of your purchasing life, it's particularly important when it comes to buying insurance. Before you spend any money in this category, be sure you understand what you are buying. For example, does the current blue-book value or condition of your car warrant the comprehensive and collision insurance you are carrying? Are you insuring heirlooms that you would never replace if they were stolen? If you have no dependents to support, do you really need life insurance? Review each of your insurance policies carefully to ensure that you are getting maximum value. If you don't understand your policy fully, a reputable insurance agent should be more than willing to explain it.

Kathy and Langdon L. paused in doing their Monthly Tabulations and evaluations when they got to homeowners insurance. They were paying $6 a month to insure some heirloom jewelry from Kathy's grandmother. Applying FI thinking, they realized that they would never be able to replace these priceless treasures. They wouldn't even want to. What made them special was the connection with their past. So what was the $6 a month for? Consolation money? Langdon, with his penchant for figuring things out, calculated how much principal would be required to yield $6 a month in interest by the time they planned to be financially independent. The figure ($1,000) was so convincing that they dropped the insurance.

Speaking of dropping insurance, **Irene and Quentin** did it before paying a penny. They looked at the cost of long-term-care insurance to manage the uncertainty of outliving their money, but the expense had them think again. Instead they chose to self-insure and reduce their risk by "aging in place"—that is, staying home and staying healthy, connected, and active in mind and body. Not having children, they chose to live in a large, multigenerational cohousing community in a place that would work even if they ended up in wheelchairs.

Michael Phillips and Catherine Campbell's book *Simple Living Investments for Old Age*[6] dispels the myth of aging as a decline into decrepitude and suggests four strategies for living well while living long. The first is to be active in pursuit of health (don't just be a pill-popping, insurance-dependent senior). The second is to cultivate new friends, especially younger ones, and to participate in community—both of which remind you daily that you are alive and valued. The third is simplifying possessions while regarding inevitable changes within and around you as the next adventure rather than the last straw. Finally, attend to traditional investments like owning a house and having enough—but not more than enough—income. Their advice reminds us that protecting what you own—be it your car, house, or body—isn't a more-is-better matter. Some things take too much time, worry, and money to merit protecting. Choose well what you must protect—and how to protect it.

It's never too late to think about aging gracefully and frugally—or too early.

Raising Children

The US Department of Agriculture estimates that it will cost the average American family over $230,000 to raise a child to the age of eighteen (not including any college expenses). Although the numbers are staggering, there are plenty of FI parents who are successfully reducing those costs.

In general, it's important for parents to model frugal living. If you curb your own spending, your children will almost always follow suit. If your child is resistant, you might want to give that child a larger-than-normal allowance—but explain that this fund will now have to pay for clothing and other essentials. Many FIers have reported that when their children realized they would have to spend their own money for the stuff they wanted, they became frugal and entrepreneurial quite quickly.

Assuming the great outdoors is dangerous—or wet— parents too often let their children turn to TV and computers for fun. Connecting children with nature gives endless hours of fascination—and is largely free. Cultivating a love for the outdoors is a lifelong gift and one that fewer and fewer of us are instilling in our children.

Another tip is to substitute creativity for money in as many aspects of your life with children as you can—including planning birthday parties (homemade cakes and old-fashioned games like potato-sack races and water-balloon tosses are charming and inexpensive) and Halloween celebrations (handcrafted costumes are fun to make and much more memorable). If you have tried all forms of creativity and your child still wants something you don't really want to buy, then suggest that you talk about it again in a few days. Most passing fancies are just that—they pass. But if your child keeps asking for a particular item, then you know it is likely a legitimate desire. You can then determine together if and how your child might eventually pay for it.

Clothing swaps and giveaways can whittle the cost of kids' clothes down to a pittance. Hand-me-downs now transcend the boundaries of families. Online sharing networks and mom groups facilitate moving clothes around as kids outgrow them. This goes for the full kit of baby needs—cribs, toys, baby bathtubs, and more.

These days, a babysitter for a date night (even a sitter who's barely older than the child he or she is taking care of) can easily cost more than the dinner out. Find another couple with similar-aged children and try doing a weekly date-night swap. One night a week you watch their kid(s), and the next week they watch yours. You get a date every other week, pay nothing for babysitting, and the kids will likely love playing with their friends every week. Another option is to join a babysitting coop.

Then there's the biggest child-rearing expense: college. The book *Frugal Living for Dummies* has a solid section on how to reduce college costs. Among the recommendations: Have your child take AP or CLEP tests to get early college credits and thereby get through college quicker. The tests cost less than $100 and can save thousands of dollars per credit earned. With enough credits, your child could even enter college as a sopho-more. He or she could also attend a community college for two years (taking advantage of the cheaper tuition) before transferring and graduating from a four-year school. The Running Start program lets motivated high schoolers complete up to two years of college before they graduate, entering college at the junior level.

> **Kathy and Langdon L.** *economized on college for their two children. "Is it reasonable," they wondered, "for us to work another decade to put them through whatever school they want?" In the end they decided to offer their children tuition for a four-year in-state college. If they wanted to go out-of-state or Ivy League, their children would earn the dif-ference, either by working or through scholarships.*

Years ahead of time, tell your children that affordabil-ity will be a key factor in choosing which colleges they apply to, and which one they can choose to attend. One of the hidden benefits of living a frugal lifestyle is that being content with less income and fewer assets qualifies you for more college financial aid. Many FIers find that the better-endowed private colleges will offer enough need-based aid to make the cost similar to that of a pub-lic university, and sometimes even less. Knowing this, use colleges' net price calculators to get a sense for how much need-based aid each school might offer you, and how much of that will be in the form of grants and work-study versus loans. It may turn out that an Ivy League college provides the cheapest education you can get, if your child has the grades to get accepted!

Throwing Stuff Away

Of course, if you are doing the steps of this program, very little of what you bring into your house goes out again as trash. Many people at the beginning of trans-forming their relationship with money have lucrative yard sales to weed out the unwanted items unearthed in their step 1 inventory. Or they list them on online auction sites, or donate them (getting a tax deduction in the process).

Kitchen waste can be dug into your garden, put in a compost bin, or fed to worms that will return it to you as rich soil. In wealthier countries, tires as well as paper, aluminum, steel, glass, and cardboard waste can be recycled. Some cities, like New York City, have even instituted composting programs for food waste.

Sharing works here as well. Instead of paying for garbage pickup, one apartment renter pays for one month of her neighbor's annual trash pickup bill. She brings her little sack of garbage over for weekly pickup—and often puts the garbage can out and brings it in as well.

While the cost savings on your garbage bill might be minimal, keep looking for ways to turn your trash into treasure. Who knows? Among the possessions gathering dust in your basement there might be something worth a lot of money—if you suspect that, get it appraised.

Gifting and Celebrating

For many people, giving presents is an important way to express love. However, you can cut back on the cost of gifts without cutting back on the affection behind them. This is where question 3 from step 4 helps to reveal hidden options. If you didn't have to work for a living, would you give different (and less expensive) gifts? One of the biggest gift-giving occasions in our culture is Christmas. If holiday celebrations feel excessive, begin to set limits on what feels right to you and your family. Bill McKibben's book *Hundred Dollar Holiday*[7] may be helpful here. Some FIers promise their children one, or at most three, toys at Christmas—and let them select the ones they want.

*This had been **Amy and Jim D.**'s strategy once they observed the fulfillment curve at work on Christmas Day. The first one, two, or three presents were greeted with squeals of* *ecstasy, but from then on it was all downhill. Instead of being able to play with what they had, the kids felt compelled to keep opening all their gifts. By the end they were tired and cranky and nothing suited them.*

Other gift-giving ideas (useful all year round) include giving services—like a massage, babysitting, or a home-cooked meal—instead of material objects. You can also buy gifts at garage sales and save them for the right occasion. "Regifting"—either of gifts you received and couldn't use or new items you bought at a garage sale—is more socially acceptable now than ever. (Be sure you don't regift a present to the same person who gave it to you, though, as one very chagrined friend did recently.) Finally, a great way to recycle both new and used gifts during the holidays is to organize a "Secret Santa" party, where each attendee brings a wrapped gift and swaps it for another.

Ursula K.*'s spirits sank as the season for "goodwill to all"— Christmas—approached. With parents, siblings, in-laws, nieces, and nephew, she needed to buy over twenty gifts. After much soul-searching she saw she had a choice: her solvency and sanity—or sticking with "the way it's always been done." She took a deep breath and wrote a letter to each family member expressing her love for them and her desire to neither give nor receive Christmas presents. She steeled herself for resistance, but what she got back was respect. By the way, Ursula also hosted her own wedding, organizing her large network of friends to cater, entertain, and even perform the ceremony.*

There you have some "hints and tips," the biggest one of which is what Ursula did: Observe reality, tell yourself the truth about what you really want and need, and have the courage to buck convention with integrity and respect. This isn't scrimping and saving! It's being wise and savvy. This desire to do whatever you want whenever you want and damn the consequences seems to be an underlying current in the "free world." But as we've seen, such freedom is often quite costly, whereas consciousness often saves you far more money and thus liberates far more time.

Partnering

People who practice these frugality strategies know that life gets more interesting and delightful as you discover new ways to economize. At very least, you get great bragging rights . . . *if* you are lucky enough to find others who share your values and admire your clever tactics. Such companions can boost both your spirits and your skills, while going it alone can leave you feeling like an odd duck in a society that encourages wasteful spending. If you want to change but your partner doesn't (yet), you might seek out like-minded people or groups to support and inspire you. Luckily with the global FIRE (Financial Independence, Retire Early) community of bloggers and practitioners together with a myriad of on-line and face-to-face ways to connect, it's far easier to find like-minded friends—and lovers.

> **Ann Haebig and Fred Ecks** *met on an online simply living discussion board. Their frugal values, as well as their desires for their lives, matched. But that wasn't always the case. When he was younger, Fred, with his master's in computer science, had a garage full of "toys" and mounting debt—and he was tired of being tired all the time. That's when he read an article that mentioned* Your Money or Your Life, *bought the book, and after holing up for a weekend devouring it, dedicated himself to saying good-bye to paid work forever. He was twenty-seven at the time, and by thirty-five he was "retired" and "living cheap with style." On the way he sold his house, left his marriage, started to shop in thrift stores, lived in rented rooms, cooked for himself, and began enjoying himself more—traveling, sailing, even taking a job with an environmental*

organization in Europe at a third the pay but twice the fun. Ann had tried for years to live her environmental values but ended up, again and again, being another bored "dot-commer" for the money. Your Money or Your Life—and later Fred—confirmed her sense that life could be different, and showed her the way to make it happen. She kept whittling down her expenses while saving and saving some more, and now she works very part-time. She and Fred live on a house-boat in San Francisco, travel together, and volunteer helping others think through their own money lives. She reports, "Much of what I do now I'd do for free. I have time for triathlon training, bicycle advocacy work, and practicing guitar. We were car-free for five years here, but now have a car so we can get to farther-flung trails. Fred also works very occasionally for races for pay. He doesn't do this out of financial necessity. Fred and I have a strong relationship based on shared values and we have time for each other. Life is good!"

Fred and Ann are acutely aware that our consumption impacts the earth, and they make their spending choices with this in mind. It feeds their consciences while pulling their expense line down.

SAVE MONEY, SAVE THE PLANET?

It isn't just an odd coincidence that saving money and saving the planet are connected. In fact, in some sense your money is the planet. Here's how.

Money is a lien on the earth's resources. Every time we spend money on anything, we are consuming not only the metal, plastic, wood, or other material in the item itself but also all the resources it took to extract these from the earth, transport them to the manufacturer, process them, assemble the product, ship it to the retailer, and bring it from the store to your home. All of that activity and cost is somehow included in the price of, say, a new computer. Then there are the environmental costs that aren't included in the price, what economists call externalities: the pollution and waste we pay for in other ways—in lung disease, cancer, respiratory problems, desertification, flooding, and so on. What it boils down to is that every time we spend money we are voting for the kind of planet we want to leave to future generations.

Money is a lien on the life energy of the planet. We call this the Pogonomics Principle—economics from cartoon character Pogo's point of view. Pogo's contribution to Earth Day 1970 was the observation that "we have met the enemy and he is us." It's no mystery why the planet is polluted. We did it through our demand for more, better, and different stuff.

And that is something that we can do something about—and benefit ourselves in the process. Creative frugality is a double win—for our wallets and our world.

The point of all this is not to send you off into the desert to eat berries and wear fig leaves. It is especially important to remember the mantra: No shame, no blame. We were all born into a world where consuming is part of life, and consuming our way to happiness seemed both natural and benign. The kinds of changes we may all need to make to keep the environment viable will require some deliberate and courageous modifications of our current habits. But why wait? Start to live with these questions now. You will see many places where you can choose a nonpolluting pleasure and have twice the fulfillment—once for you and once for the planet. Indeed, enjoying nature and feeling your vital connection to the earth, the source of all life, is one of the greatest pleasures there is.

If you want to find out how to save money while saving the earth, many fine books, blogs, and websites are available that can help you reevaluate your personal lifestyle choices in light of our current understanding about human impact on the ecosystem. Getting books from your library is a great way to save a tree.

The key is remembering that anything you buy and

don't use, anything you throw away, anything you consume and don't enjoy is money down the drain, wasting your life energy and wasting the finite resources of the planet. Any waste of your life energy means more hours lost to the rat race, making a dying. Frugality is the user-friendly and earth-friendly lifestyle.

> *When we talk about preservation of the environment, it is related to many other things. Ultimately the decision must come from the human heart, so I think the key point is to have a genuine sense of universal responsibility.*
>
> —Dalai Lama[8]

1,001 SURE WAYS TO SAVE MONEY

After a year of keeping your Monthly Tabulations, you will have approximately 1,001 single entries under your fifteen to thirty spending categories. Chances are very good that you could be spending less on every purchase—from apples to zinnias—with no reduction in the quality of product or the quality of your life. It's the attitude of honoring your life energy that will show you the way, not following someone else's recipe for a frugal life. You will be as excited about the savings you discover as we have been about furnishing our home from garage sales and giveaways. The empowerment comes from your cleverness and your creativity in finding your strategies for frugality. That's why we call it creative frugality. So here's a blank slate. Write your own 1,001 tips for living on less and loving it.

1,000,001 SURE WAYS TO SAVE MONEY

Watch your thoughts. Anyone who practices meditation knows that the gray matter between our ears, like a frenetic monkey, churns out a steady stream of unrelated thoughts at the rate of at least one a second. In just 11.6 days you'll have 1,000,001 thoughts—and most of them will have something to do with desires. I want this. I don't want that. I like this. I don't like that. The Buddha said that desire is the source of all suffering. It is also the source of all shopping. By being conscious of your next 1,000,001 desires, you'll have 1,000,001 opportunities to not spend money on something that won't bring you fulfillment. Advertising doesn't make you buy stuff. Other people's expectations don't make you buy stuff. Television doesn't make you buy stuff. Your thoughts make you buy stuff. Watch those suckers. They're dangerous to your pocketbook—and to a lot more.

CHECKLIST: THINK BEFORE YOU SPEND

1. Don't go shopping.
2. Live within your means.
3. Take care of what you have.
4. Wear it out.
5. Do it yourself.
6. Anticipate your needs.
7. Research value, quality, durability, multiple use, and price.
8. Buy it for less.
9. Meet your needs differently.
10. Follow the nine steps of this program.

SUMMARY OF STEP 6

Lower your total monthly expenses by valuing your life energy and increasing your consciousness in spending. Learn to choose quality of life over standard of living.

MONEY TALK QUESTIONS

Rugged individualism is a losing strategy for figuring out ways to lower your expenses while increasing your fulfillment. Harvest attitudes and practical tips from these conversations while appreciating how consumerism makes us crazy.

Using the suggestions in the epilogue for how to have a Money Talk, raise these questions in your daily reflections, with your partner, or in social groups. Remember, adding "Why?" to the end of any question will take it deeper. Adding "How has society shaped my answer?" to any question will take it wider. There are no right answers.

- Whom are you trying to impress or please through what you have or how you spend?
- How do you economize? On what? How do you feel about it?
- Talk about one thing you own that you love. What do you love about it?
- Take us shopping with you, describing where you are, how you feel, what you buy.
- What's your gazingus pin (your "gotta have it" purchase)?
- What's the last item you actually wore out?

7

For Love or Money:
Valuing Your Life Energy—Work and Income

In chapter 6 we talked about valuing your life energy by spending your money more consciously. In this chapter we will talk about valuing your life energy by looking at how well you spend your time. Are you getting full value for selling that most precious commodity—your life? Does work work for you?

Sometimes you have to question the obvious in order to get at the truth. The question we will be exploring in this chapter is "What is work?" Common wisdom says that work is what we do to make a living. But that definition robs us of our life. Some of us honor our jobs and neglect the rest of our lives. Others of us endure our jobs and make up for it on the evenings and weekends. Some of us work from home—and never get downtime. Some piece together several jobs in the gig economy but BYOB (be your own boss) consumes every waking hour. Some of us love our work—or did once and hope to again—but find our personal vision constrained by boards, supervisors, funders, or investors. When "work = what you do for money," it means the "work" of our free time is of lesser value. We fail to value our life energy and often feel helpless about making changes. What we will be exploring now is whether our definition of work itself is part of the problem.

How well are you using your life energy both on and off the job? Is your job consuming (using up, destroying, wasting) your life? Do you love your life, using each hour—on and off the job—with care? As we said in chapter 2, our life energy is precious because it is limited and irretrievable and because our choices about how we use it express the meaning and purpose of our time here on earth. So far you have learned to value your life energy by aligning your spending with your fulfillment and your values. Now it's time to learn about valuing your life energy by maximizing your compensation—in love or money—for the hours you invest in your work.

WHAT IS WORK?

Just as with money, our concept of work consists of a patchwork of contradictory beliefs, thoughts, and feelings—notions we've absorbed from our parents, our culture, the media, and our life experience. The following quotations highlight the incongruity of our different definitions of work:

E. F. Schumacher, an influential twentieth-century economist, says:

. . . the three purposes of human work [are] as follows:

- First, to provide necessary and useful goods and services.
- Second, to enable every one of us to use and thereby perfect our gifts like good stewards.
- Third, to do so in service to, and in cooperation with, others, so as to liberate ourselves from our inborn egocentricity.[1]

The late economist Robert Theobald tells us:

Work is defined as something that people do not want to do and money as the reward that compensates for the unpleasantness of work.[2]

Studs Terkel begins his book *Working* this way:

This book, being about work, is, by its very nature, about violence—to the spirit as well as to the body. It is about ulcers as well as accidents, about shouting matches as well as fistfights, about nervous breakdowns as well as kicking the dog around. It is, above all (or beneath all), about daily humiliations. To survive the day is triumph enough for the walking wounded among the great many of us. . . . It is about a search, too, for daily meaning as well as daily bread, for recognition as well as cash, for astonishment rather than torpor; in short, for a sort of life rather than a Monday through Friday sort of dying.[3]

Twentieth-century poet Kahlil Gibran, on the other hand, tells us, "Work is love made visible."[4]

What is work? Is it a blessing or a curse? A trial or a triumph? Our task will be to redefine work the same way we redefined money—by looking for what we can say about work that is consistently true.

WORK THROUGH THE AGES

Let's begin by taking a brief look at the history of "work," for it is through looking at history that we find new opportunities to shape our own personal stories. Where do our concepts about work come from? Why do we work? And what is the place of work in our lives?

Minimum Daily Requirement of Work

As human beings we all must do some work for basic survival—but how much? Is there a "minimum daily requirement" of work? A number of diverse sources—studies ranging from hunter-gatherer cultures to modern history—would place this figure at about three hours a day during an adult lifetime.

Marshall Sahlins, author of *Stone Age Economics*, discovered that before Western influence changed daily life, Kung men, who live in the Kalahari, hunted from two to two and a half days a week, with an average workweek of fifteen hours. Women gathered for about the same period of time each week. In fact, one day's work supplied a woman's family with vegetables for the next three days. Throughout the year both men and women worked for a couple of days, then took a couple off to rest and play games, gossip, plan rituals, and visit. . . . It would appear that the workweek in the old days beats today's banker's hours by quite a bit.[5]

This suggests that three hours a day is all that we must spend working for survival. One can imagine that in preindustrial times this pattern would make sense. Life was more whole back then, when "work" blended into family time, religious celebrations, and play. Then came the "labor-saving" Industrial Revolution and the compartmentalization of life into "work" and "non-work"—with work taking an ever-bigger bite out of the average person's day.

In the nineteenth century the "common man," with justified aversion to such long hours on the job, began to fight for a shorter workweek. Champions for the workers claimed that fewer hours on the job would decrease fatigue and increase productivity. Indeed, they said, fewer hours was the natural expression of the maturing Industrial Revolution. People would pursue learning. An educated and engaged citizenry would support our democracy.

But all that came to a halt during the Depression.[6] The workweek, having fallen dramatically from sixty hours at the turn of the century to thirty-five hours during the Depression, became locked in at forty hours for many and has crept up to fifty or even sixty hours a week in recent years. Why?

The Right to Life, Liberty, and the Pursuit of a Paycheck?

During the Depression, free time became equated with unemployment. In an effort to boost the economy and reduce unemployment, the New Deal established the forty-hour week and the government as the employer of last resort. Workers were educated to consider employment, not free time, to be their right as citizens (life, liberty, and the pursuit of the paycheck?). Benjamin Kline Hunnicutt, in *Work Without End*, illuminates the doctrine of "full employment":

> Since the Depression, few Americans have thought of work reduction as a natural, continuous, and positive result of economic growth and increased productivity. Instead, additional leisure has been seen as a drain on the economy, a liability on wages, and the abandonment of economic progress.[7]

The myths of "growth is good" and "full employment" established themselves as key values. These dovetailed nicely with the gospel of "full consumption," which preached that leisure is a commodity to be consumed rather than free time to be enjoyed. For the past half century, full employment has meant more consumers with more "disposable income." This means increased profits, which means business expansion, which means more jobs, which means more consumers with more disposable income. Consumption keeps the wheels of "progress" moving, as we saw in chapter 1.

So we see that our concept (as a society) of leisure has changed radically. From being considered a desirable and civilizing component of day-to-day life, it has become something to be feared, a reminder of unemployment during the years of the Depression. As the value of leisure has dropped, the value of work has risen. The push for full employment, along with the growth of advertising, has created a populace increasingly oriented toward work and toward earning more money in order to consume more resources.

To counter all this, a free-time movement has sprung up in the early twenty-first century. A campaign called Take Back Your Time, initiated by filmmaker John de Graaf, advocates for shorter work hours and longer vacations for overworked Americans. Even with all the studies saying that reduced hours and sufficient leisure actually increase worker productivity, time advocates are swimming upstream against a cultural assumption that the eight-hour workday is next to godliness.

The emerging Slow Food movement also challenges our workaholic lifestyle. This movement suggests that eating is far more than wolfing down fast food alone at your computer, fueling the body for the next leg of the rat race; rather, it's a time of conviviality, pleasure, and conversation. In short, it's civilizing.

Work Takes On New Meaning

In addition, according to Hunnicutt, during the last half century we've begun to lose the fabric of family, culture, and community that give meaning to life outside the workplace. The traditional rituals, the socializing, and the simple pleasure of one another's company all provided structure for nonwork time, affording people a sense of purpose and belonging. Without this experience of being part of a people and a place, leisure leads more often to loneliness and boredom. Because life outside the workplace has lost vitality and meaning, work has ceased being a means to an end and become an end in itself. Hunnicutt notes:

Meaning, justification, purpose, and even salvation were now sought in work, without a necessary reference to any traditional philosophic or theological structure. Men and women were answering the old religious questions in new ways, and the answers were more and more in terms of work, career, occupation, and professions.[8]

Arlie Hochschild, in her 2001 book, *The Time Bind*, says that families now have three jobs—work, home, and repair of relationships damaged by ever more time at the office. Even corporations with "family-friendly" policies subtly reward people who spend more time at work (whether they are more productive or not). *Some* offices are even getting more comfortable, while homes are more hectic, inducing a guilty desire to spend more time working because it's more restful![9]

The final piece of the puzzle snaps into place when we look at the shift in the religious attitude toward work that came with the rise of the Protestant ethic. Before that time, work was profane and religion was sacred. Afterward, work was seen as the arena where you worked out your salvation—and the evidence of a successful religious life was a successful financial life.

So here we are in the twenty-first century. Our paid employment has taken on myriad roles. Our jobs now serve the function that traditionally belonged to religion: They are the place where we seek answers to the perennial questions "Who am I?" and "Why am I here?" and "What's it all for?" They also serve the function of families, giving answers to the questions "Who are my people?" and "Where do I belong?"

Our jobs are called upon to provide the exhilaration of romance and the depths of love. It's as though we believed that there is a Job Charming out there—like the Prince Charming in fairy tales—that will fill our needs and inspire us to greatness. We've come to believe that, through this job, we would somehow have it all: status, meaning, adventure, travel, luxury, respect, power, tough challenges, and fantastic rewards. All we need is to find Mr. or Ms. Right—Mr. or Ms. Right Job. Indeed, in terms of sheer hours, we may be more wedded to our jobs than to our partners. The vows for better or worse, richer or poorer, in sickness and in health—and often till death do us part—may be better applied to our jobs than to our wives or husbands. Perhaps what keeps some of us stuck in the home-freeway-office loop is this very Job Charming illusion. We're like the princess who keeps kissing toads, hoping one day to find herself hugging a handsome prince. Our jobs are our toads.

Young people today are swimming against an even stronger current. Our phones and laptops keep us on call to our employers and side hustles (second and third jobs that fit into the cracks of the main one) 24-7. When your primary job isn't enough, it's hard to patch together enough hustles to pay off student loans and graduate from living in your parents' basement. The fact that they've dubbed their multiple jobs as hustles indicates how much energy it takes to fledge and flourish. They know full well they are in a brave new world of endless hustle—brave as in it takes courage to move against the undertow. The old conveyor belt of job as identity as career as security and pension is now utterly shredded. Does this liberate young people from the Job(s) Charming syndrome? No. If they are always hustling, they are always "on the job." Even dating can become networking for the next job opportunity.

DID WE WIN THE INDUSTRIAL REVOLUTION?

We've come a long way since the time when our ancestors worked three hours a day and enjoyed the pleasures of socializing, rituals, celebrations, and games the rest of the time. Has it been worth it? We've certainly gained a tremendous amount by focusing our creativity and ingenuity on mastering the physical world. Science, technology, culture, art, language, and music have all evolved and brought us countless blessings. Few of us would want to turn back the clock entirely, forsaking Bach or penicillin. We do need to stop the clock, however, and evaluate our direction. Are we still on course? Let's look briefly at the modern workplace and job market. Where are we? And is it where we want to be?

❖ Some workers feel underemployed, their days filled with repetitive, menial, or unchallenging tasks that call forth very little of their creativity or intelligence. Others feel overworked, especially now with corporate downsizing shifting more and more responsibilities onto the shoulders of the lucky few who retain their jobs. The start-up field can feel like the Wild West, with new, well-funded companies emerging overnight offering young employees major perks like free office food and Ping-Pong tables to counterbalance the intensity of the work environment.

❖ The rising awareness of issues of social justice, climate change, and the toxic by-products of a consumer society is tearing some workers in two: Economically they need their jobs, but ethically they don't support the products or services their companies provide.

❖ Retirement security is no longer secure. Only 7 percent of corporations still offer defined benefit pension plans; 25 percent offer hybrids with "defined contributions," such as 401(k)s plus some cash.[10] The rest are shifting saving for retirement back onto the shoulders of workers. Some people even wonder about the long-term security of our national social security safety net. This, of course, is what brings many people to this book. You want to take your retirement fully into your own hands, and on your own timetable—no matter what happens "out there."

❖ According to a 2014 report by the Conference Board, a New York–based nonprofit research group, the majority of Americans are unhappy at work. In their first survey, in 1987, 61.1 percent of workers said they liked their jobs. But that was the high point. The all-time low was 2010, when only 42.6 percent of workers said they liked their jobs. As the prospects for long-term work with the same employer have eroded and employees have been saddled with ever-higher health plan deductibles and payroll deductions, the two categories in which workers' satisfaction fell the most were job security and health plans, both declining by at least 11 points since 1987.[11]

We've had enough, it would seem, of making a dying in such a crazy world. Even if we like our professions, even if we've lucked out in the workplace lottery, even if we are among the 50 percent not dissatisfied, we still suffer from Job Charming syndrome. We might still seek to fill needs that jobs can never fulfill. We might risk that ultimate deathbed regret: Why did I spend so much time at my job?

WHAT IS THE PURPOSE OF WORK?

Let's continue our exploration of work, this most personal and profound relationship, by reflecting on a few questions:

+ Why do you do what you do to earn money?
+ What motivates you to get out of bed to go somewhere and make money?
+ What is the purpose, in your experience, of your paid employment? (If you are supported by a working spouse or relative, you can reflect either on why that "breadwinner" works or on some work experience from your past. If you are retired or unemployed, think about a job you once had.)

Now consider the following list of various purposes of paid employment and see which ones apply to you.

Earning money
- To provide for oneself and the family
- To save for the future
- To engage in philanthropy
- To achieve Financial Independence

A sense of security
- To ensure that your place at the company is assured
- To ensure that you'll have benefits

Tradition
- To carry on a family tradition of following a particular profession
- To fulfill a duty to your family
- Because everybody works

Service
- To do your fair share
- To make a contribution to others, society, and the world
- To "be the change you wish to see in the world," aligning skills with helping others

Learning
- To acquire new skills, grow as a human, become more marketable
- To be stimulated and challenged
- To innovate and create

Power
- To influence other people
- To influence decisions and outcomes
- To assure respect and admiration from those you want to impress
- To achieve success and prominence in your field

Socializing
◆ To enjoy connecting with your coworkers
◆ To interact with other people and feel part of a larger community
◆ To engage in companywide events and parties

Time structuring
◆ To structure your time and give an orderly rhythm to your life

Have you noticed that work has two different functions: the material, financial function (i.e., getting paid) and the personal function (emotional, intellectual, psychological, and even spiritual)?

The original question was: What is the purpose served by paid employment? In reality, there is only one purpose served by paid employment: getting paid. That is the only real link between work and money. The other "purposes" of paid employment are other types of rewards, which are certainly desirable but not directly related to getting paid. They are all equally available in unpaid activities.

For middle-class workers and up, any stress, confusion, or disappointment we might feel concerning our paid employment is rarely because of the pay itself. We have already seen that beyond a certain level of comfort, more money does not bring more satisfaction. Perhaps the trouble with our paid employment, then, is that our needs for stimulation, recognition, growth, contribution, interaction, and meaning are not being met by our jobs. The Conference Board survey of job satisfaction referred to earlier supports this. **Growth potential, communication channels, interest in work, and recognition make a job satisfying—not pay.** What if we removed most of these expectations from our paid employment and recognized that all purposes for work other than earning money could be fulfilled by unpaid activities?

This observation brings us to a critical point in

reexamining our relationship with work. There are two sides to work. On one side is our need and desire for money. We work in order to get paid and afford our basic human needs. On the other side, totally separate from our wages, is the fact that we work in order to fulfill many other positive goals in our lives.

It should be noted that this may be not true for the millions who do not earn enough—even with two jobs—to support themselves and their families. The United States is the only advanced economy in the world without guaranteed paid vacation, and less than half of low-wage workers get any paid vacation time.[12]

BREAKING THE LINK
BETWEEN WORK AND WAGES

The real problem with work, then, is not that our expectations are too high. It's that we have confused work with paid employment. Redefining "work" as simply any productive or purposeful activity, with paid employment being just one activity among many, frees us from the false assumption that what we do to put food on the table and a roof over our heads should also provide us with our sense of meaning, purpose, and fulfillment. Breaking the link between work and money allows us to reclaim balance and sanity.

Our fulfillment as human beings lies not in our jobs but in the whole picture of our lives—in our inner sense of what life is about, our connectedness with others, and our yearning for meaning and purpose. By separating work and wages we actually open the door to integrating all parts of our lives, from earning money to loving our families, into one whole called "who we really are." When we are whole, we don't need to try to consume our way to happiness. Happiness is our birthright.

Whether you love or hate your paid employment, by separating work and wages you can see more clearly whether you are valuing—both on and off the job—that precious commodity called life energy.

Remember from our discussion about life energy in chapter 2 that a forty-year-old would have about 350,000 hours left? With a third dedicated to sleeping and 15 percent dedicated to the necessary activities of having a body and a roof over your head (cooking, cleaning, fixing stuff, errands), you can divide your hours bank account in half. These hours are all you've got. There is nothing in your life that is more valuable than your time, the moments you have left. Separating work from wages means all moments in your life matter, and reclaiming more moments to spend as you will, not as you must, is a worthy goal indeed.

Breaking the link between work and wages has as much power in our lives as the recognition that money is simply something we trade our life energy for. Money is our life energy; it takes its value not from external definitions but from what we invest in it. Similarly, paid employment takes its only intrinsic value from the fact that we are paid to do it. Everything else we do is an expression of who we are, not what we must do out of economic necessity. By breaking the link, we regain quality, values, and self-worth as our bottom line. By breaking the link, we can redefine work simply as whatever we do in alignment with our purpose in life. By breaking the link, we get our life back.

THE STUNNING IMPLICATIONS OF BREAKING THE LINK

From this point of view, it's clear why your paid employment may feel like making a dying. Besides earning money, you may be doing nothing else on the job that is in alignment with your purpose. Eight to ten hours a day. Five days a week. Fifty weeks a year. Forty or more years of your life. This opens up a host of questions. How much money do you need to be at the peak of fulfillment? Is your job providing that amount? Are you working for less than you're worth and bringing home less money than you need? Or are you earning far more than you need for fulfillment? What is the purpose of that extra money? If it serves no purpose, would you want to work less and have more time to do what matters to you? If it does serve a purpose, is that purpose so clear and so connected with your values that it brings an experience of joy to your hours at your paid employment? If not, what needs to change?

Let's explore together some of the implications of redefining work by breaking the link between work and wages, of seeing paid employment as distinct from work—work in the sense of fulfillment of purpose(s) in life.

People at both ends of the age spectrum are already doing this, but not necessarily in an empowered way. Many millennials began their working lives after the financial meltdown of 2008, when the stock market lost half its value. If they followed their parents' script, went to college, and took on debt, expecting their parents' results, they were greeted with an economy in free fall and fewer opportunities in the traditional job market. No wonder they are such entrepreneurs, side-hackers, and gig-economy workers. No wonder they have to brand themselves to go out into a fast-changing world where niches open, get filled, and close in a matter of months. Coders, bloggers, app designers, and entrepreneurs work long uncompensated hours and often come up empty. No wonder, as well, that millennials have revived interest in this book and the possibility of Financial Independence. They already have multiple facets to their lives—some that make money, some as hobbies, some as passions, some as quirks.

On the other end of the time scale, many boomers are

entering their Social Security years with only Social Security. They too have to figure out how to make money doing odd and not-so-odd jobs. With sufficient retirement income, they can play with their grandkids. Without, they might play with other people's children . . . for pay. If you've worked at only one company for most of your career, it takes oomph to put yourself out into the world, where ageism runs rampant. Millennials have that in abundance. Boomers, not so much.

This said, those among you in your vast middle working years, consider these advantages of separating work from income. It will inspire you on your path of transforming your relationship with money and may well lead to early retirement . . . or at least a retirement that gives you freedom rather than worry.

1. Redefining Work Increases Choices

Let's say you are a natural-born teacher but you took a job as a computer programmer because you can make more money (which you are convinced you need). In the old way of thinking, every time someone asked you what you do, you would be forced to affirm, "I am a computer programmer." What do you suppose the effect on you might be of this long-term incongruity between your inner sense of yourself and your outer presentation? You might be just mildly unhappy and not know why. You might get ill, as one friend of ours did when she gave up her dream of being a concert pianist and became a programmer instead. She developed an inexplicable illness that put her on disability for nearly a year. You might run up a credit card debt to reward yourself for doing something that doesn't suit you.

The one thing you might overlook, though, is questioning whether or not you are a computer programmer just because that's what you do to make a living. When you break the link between wages and work, another option opens up. When you're asked what you do, you can affirm, "I am a teacher, but currently I'm writing computer programs to make money." Being able to acknowledge who you really are allows you to reevaluate how you've structured your "career." You might decide to save money and go back to school for your teaching credentials. You might decide to reduce your programming hours so that you can volunteer as a teacher. You might decide to teach computer programming. You might bring in a third love, like kayaking, and teach that on weekends while you program computers for money. Disconnecting work from wages allows the various parts of your compartmentalized life to break loose, slide around, and rearrange themselves in a pattern that serves you better.

Donna O. worked her way up the ladder of success but found the grind did not suit her sensibilities. As a doctor she found herself trying to promote health in an unhealthy system, one that demanded hundred-hour workweeks, not enough sleep, and precious little time for anything else.

During her residency and early years as a physician, she found the work so all-consuming that she had no time to think about money, and no time to consider how she was spending it. Marrying another doctor only doubled the pattern of unconsciousness. Donna and her husband accumulated houses and cars and exotic investments. The thought of keeping track of their spending was beyond comprehension. They confused consciousness with worry—and they had enough to worry about in practicing medicine.

But Donna's days as a superdoc were numbered. The birth of her two children reminded her of what matters most. She wanted out of the medical business and back into a caring—and balanced—profession. With a mixture of trepidation and resolve, she left her secure medical group with all its "benefits" and opened a clinic for women, staffed by women, that would reflect her values.

About this time she listened to the original FI audio course published in 1984. In her enthusiasm she immediately went to her husband and asked him the question she was beginning to ask herself: "What would you do if you didn't have to work for money?"

"What do you mean?" he replied. "I love my work."

"But what if you never had to charge anyone to meet your overhead?"

Unable to answer that question, he promptly went to sleep. Eventually he listened to the course, but his zeal for a new way of practicing medicine did not match Donna's. She began to work on the steps of the program but still felt out of step with her husband. She finally came to the conclusion that even in a conventional marriage—or perhaps especially in a conventional marriage—a woman has to be willing to live a life of her own. She did the steps on her own.

As her personal insight grew, she began to reevaluate her clinic. None of the staff wanted to work the long and arduous hours maintained by mainstream medical professionals, but they all had trouble adjusting to earning less money. Expensive procedures are what pay the bills for most physicians. Donna preferred prevention, yet the economics of medicine kept pulling her back into the old way of working. "Either I have to do medicine differently or not do it at all."

For Donna, Financial Independence is the whole process of recovery from old ways of thinking about money, work, meaning, and purpose. "If a healthy practice of medicine means less money, so be it!"

Donna is not alone. A nationwide survey done by the Center for a New American Dream found that nearly half of Americans had made voluntary changes in their lives that resulted in making less money. Those who did so reported being happy with the changes and said that the major motivations for making less money were reducing stress, striking a balance in their lives, and having more free time.

2. Redefining Work Allows You to Work from the Inside Out

For many of us, much of life is lived from the outside in, selecting our roles and personas like dishes at a Chinese restaurant. One person might select "fireman" from the Job column, "blond hair and blue eyes" from the Wife column, "two" from the Children column, "casual" from the Style column, "Toyota" from the Car column, "Republican" from the Political column, and "condo" from the Housing column and figure he's got life pretty well squared away. Fitting our well-rounded selves into the square hole called Job reinforces this impression that life consists of selecting options from a fixed list. Unless you're an artist or an entrepreneur, most often your job consists of working with someone else's agenda—for which service you get paid. There's a kind of subtle yet pervasive irresponsibility in the work world, a sense that we are always doing someone else's bidding, angling to please someone else up the line a bit. In large corporations, most workers don't even have a clue as to who originated the plan they're diligently getting to work. And such corporations buy not only our work but our personalities as well, with their unspoken cultural norms about who talks with whom, what to wear, where people at various levels "do" lunch, how much overtime you have to put in to be "visible," and hundreds of other daily choices. It's clear that if we think that what we do to make money is who we are, we will end up adopting whatever pattern will allow us to survive best at our job. But if who you are and what you do to make money are distinct, as they can be when you disconnect work from wages, you can reclaim your lost self. As you come to know yourself, your values, your beliefs, your real talents, and what you care about, you will be able to work from the inside out. You will be able to do your job without giving up your self.

Margaret P. is in the process of shifting from living according to others' values (living from the outside in) to discovering and living her values (living from the inside out). She'd already been married, had two children, and gotten a divorce. As a single parent with a strong sense of duty, she wanted to earn as much as possible to support her family, so she gave up teaching and became a certified financial planner.

She worked on commission—and some products were more lucrative than others. The conflict between the profits and her clients' best interests gave her stomach pains and she realized she had to stop selling financial products at all costs. She stopped pursuing sales, and while her body got better, her personal financial picture got worse.

She was glad that she and **Ivy U.** had started the Financial Independence support group of twenty people committed to working with the FI program. As they followed the steps of the program, they found themselves ever more willing to follow the prompting of their hearts—and for each one of them, that looked slightly different. For example, through "honoring her life energy," one woman saw that she was wasting her talent in a bog of mediocrity. "They aren't paying me enough to stay here in this amount of pain." So she quit and lived on savings until she found other work.

All of these changes came out of the process of doing the steps of this program.

3. Redefining Work Makes Us Life Designers, Not Just Wage Earners

Before the Industrial Revolution, most people were farmers, meaning they were able to build, maintain, and fix almost everything they needed for daily life. Post–Industrial Revolution, especially post–information and tech revolutions, we learn to spend most of our time selling one small slice of our talents to pay for everything else we need. Lose your job, though, and you still have a mortgage, car payments, and credit card payments without anything coming in. Disconnecting work from wages, however, opens the door to valuing the big piece of the pie called "the rest of your time." Few go back to being Jacks and Jills of all trades such as farmers or home builders, but the more we learn to honor unpaid work, the more likely our debt will be lower. We might learn handyman skills or build that deck ourselves or host a website or launch a blog . . . When we stop working for money, we may be out of a job but we are not out of work.

It also means play might end up being pay. You might learn skills in a job that you take into your life. You may learn lessons in your life that later you'll be paid for. The skills acquired in one job may lead to another. On one job you may learn the ins and outs of a trade so you can leave that job and ply that trade for fun . . . or profit. Job becomes school. School becomes play. Work becomes self-expression. You are your boss, whether you're paid or not, and you can carve out your own path.

4. Redefining Work Adds Life to Your Retirement

Retirement doesn't mean you stop working. It means you can stop working *for money*. We all want to be useful, to be recognized by others for the contribution we make. If we think paid employment is our only admirable, respectable, and consequential way to contribute, then who'd want to retire? Nobody wants to be a has-been, washed up, put out to pasture. Disconnecting work from wages means that you are valuable in every role, task, activity—and it might free you to retire a lot earlier so you can give a lot more of yourself to others.

5. Redefining Work Honors Unpaid Activity

Nancy got tired of hearing herself say, "I don't know where my day went," each evening as she looked at how little she'd crossed off her to-do list. She'd tracked her money to get a handle on where it all went. Maybe she could do it for time as well. For a week, every fifteen minutes, she noted what she'd done in that slot. She soon realized that she spent most of her time on activities she didn't consider important: cleaning, cooking, shopping, and chatting with family members. Her "official" list had only work-related tasks—a meeting with a colleague, responding to e-mails. Everything else—which was most of her time—wasn't on her list at all. She realized if she was paid to clean a house, she'd have it on the list. Cleaning her own house—nowhere! The exercise showed her that she bestowed status only on paid employment. Now she puts everything on her list and gets to be proud of all she's accomplished, paid or unpaid.

Isn't it true that unpaid activity is often seen as worthless—as in worth less than paid activity? Isn't it true that there is an almost universal belief in our culture that if you are not working for money, not building a career, not employed, you are a nobody?

Our inner work—the job of self-examination, self-development, and emotional and spiritual maturation—is just as crucial as paid work or housework or yard work. It takes time to know yourself—time for reflection, for prayer and ritual, for developing a coherent philosophy of life and personal code of ethics, and for setting personal goals and evaluating progress.

Disconnecting work and wages does away with that painful erasure of self from our identification with our jobs.

6. Redefining Work Reunites Work and Play

Work is serious. Play is frivolous. Work is adult. Play is childish. Work is useful. Play is useless. Sometimes play may look like work, as in an intense chess game. Sometimes work can look like and even be called play, as in professional sports. And sometimes work feels so much like play that people say (somewhat guiltily), "This job is such fun I shouldn't be paid for it." So how do we tell the difference between work and play? Both play and work can be competitive as well as cooperative. They can both build skill and give a sense of achievement. With both you can enter a state of intense focus, concentration, and flow. In fact, from the outside, watching a person fully engaged in an activity, one would not know if he or she was being paid or just playing. This is the power of disconnecting work and wages—you reconnect work and play so your whole life can glow with enjoyment.

7. Redefining Work Allows You to Enjoy Your Leisure More

For the Greeks, leisure was the highest good, the essence of freedom—a time for self-development and for higher pursuits. Yet here we are in the early twenty-first century unable to really relax and enjoy our leisure. Even our language betrays us by calling it "time off," as though leisure were just a few minutes of recuperation before we're back "on," a once-again productive (i.e., real) human being. If we did not identify so strongly with what we do for money, we might honor and enjoy our leisure more. It's OK to play. It's OK to relax in the shade and listen to the birds. It's OK to take a walk to nowhere in particular. It's OK to leave your technology at home and go camping. There is no shame in taking time to do activities alone either. It's OK to take pleasure in just being rather than always doing. Leisure is not an identity crisis if you know you are not your job.

Perhaps because our jobs are so laced into every hour of our days, we take our leisure in unconscious and unsatisfying ways, like those micro-vacations consisting of secretly checking our phones while at work for texts from friends, social media, and maybe a recent skit from a late-night-TV comic. Separating work from wages reminds us to work with focus while at work and focus fully on our chosen activities when our time is our own.

8. Redefining Work Sheds a New Light on "Right Livelihood"

"Right livelihood" is the ideal of finding a way for your true work or vocation to be your paid work as well. Admirable though it is, there are pitfalls to this noble effort that the FI program neatly sidesteps.

There is no guarantee that you will find someone to pay you to do what you feel called to do. It may take many years to develop your art or your research or your social innovation or your new technology to the point where those who have money will fund you. Crowdfunding is an innovative workaround for those long waits for government or foundation money—but a 2015 report from the London-based Crowdfunding Center found that between 70 and 90 percent of the campaigns failed, depending on the platform.[13] Most often this has less to do with the real value of your work than it has to do with luck, chance, perseverance, connections, race or gender, and a host of other factors.

By giving up the expectation that you will be paid to do the work you are passionate about, you can do both things with more integrity. You can make money to cover your expenses, and you can follow your heart without compromise. You can hold a vision for doing the work you love once you have retired—and let that dream fuel your passion to do the nine-step program with integrity and determination. You can treat your paid-employment years like preparation for your full-time vocation, with each job teaching and honing important personal and work skills as well as building networks. To whatever degree you've settled for work you don't love, if you have failed at being paid to do what you love, you can know that you have not really settled, you are just setting yourself up for your next move and ultimately your Financial Independence.

New students in the martial art aikido learn an exercise called the "unbendable arm." Facing a partner with the top of one wrist resting on the partner's collarbone, the student is told to resist as the partner uses two hands to pull down on his elbow. Try as he might, the student quickly loses. Then he is instructed to relax and feel energy flowing from his center in his belly out through his arm to infinity, as if it were water rushing through a fire hose. Now the partner, try as she might, can't bend the arm.

Putting your attention on getting paid actually diverts energy from engaging in your chosen forms of service. You're doing two things, not one. As with the unbendable arm, you can focus on resisting your partner (getting paid) or extending your energy toward infinity (your calling).

Or consider what happens when commerce intervenes in the process of finding your calling, in this case making art. In *The Biology of Art*, zoologist Desmond Morris tells of an experiment in introducing the "profit motive" to apes. The first step was teaching them to be artists and to produce drawings and paintings that were decidedly lovely. Once their "art" was established, he began to "pay" them, rewarding them with peanuts for their work. Under the reward system their artwork quickly deteriorated, and they began turning out hasty scrawls just to get the peanuts. "Commercialism" destroyed the apes as artists and got them scrambling for peanuts instead.[14]

Insisting that your calling and your paid employment be one and the same can tip the balance of your focus from mission to money. Achieving Financial Independence, meaning both freeing your mind and ultimately freeing your time, gives you an unbendable arm—no matter what your employment may be.

Imagine you luck out and find that dream job, the one that marries who you are and how you earn money, but something happens—new management, your project shut down and team reabsorbed into the general pool—and you are confronted with money versus mission. If you disconnect work from wages, you stay clear on your "true work" and assess whether your situation will ultimately free you to do it without compromise. You return to the unbendable arm and choose.

Implications for Your Income

Now that we've established that the only intrinsic purpose of paid employment is getting paid (whether you love or hate your job), it makes sense to see whether you are trading your precious life energy for what it's worth. Since you know that your life is bigger than your job, it makes sense to get a job that really "does the job"—that is, pays you well. This leads to step 7 of the FI program.

Step 7: Valuing Your Life Energy—Maximizing Income

Step 7 is about increasing your income by valuing the life energy you invest in your job and exchanging it for the highest pay consistent with your health and integrity.

When you pick up your paycheck, tally up your gig checks, or tabulate all your combined income, are you really getting a fair exchange for your investment of valuable life energy? The key to freedom from the making-a-dying world is valuing your life energy. We have seen that money is just something you trade your life energy for. We have also recognized that the purpose of paid employment is getting paid. Don't reason and self-respect both suggest, then, that when you are working for pay, you should make the most money per hour possible, consistent with your integrity and your health? While that may sound like good old-fashioned greed, follow along and you'll find yourself headed in another direction altogether.

In following steps 1 through 6 you have defined what *enough* is for you, including your best guess of how much will be enough in the future. Instead of defining *enough* as "more than I have now," thus condemning yourself to the experience of perpetual poverty, you are discovering that enough may be less—and closer—than you imagined. And remember, enough is not the minimum amount for survival; it is the exact amount that gives you fulfillment without excess. As we pointed out in chapter 5, this enough often falls far below your income. By spending less money than you earn, you can spend less time on the job and still have enough. It's basic math. If enough is $2,500 a month and you earn $25 an hour, you must work 100 hours a month to meet your expenses. But if you could earn $50 an hour, you could conceivably work 50 hours a month at your paid employment. Or save 50 percent of your income!

Now we're moving back toward the lifestyle human beings enjoyed before the Industrial Revolution. You could work two or three hours a day as an independent contractor for money and spend the rest of the time doing what you want to do for relaxation, fun, self-development, human interaction, community involvement, or world service. If you chose to work more hours at your paid employment, you would do it only for good reason, since you place a high value on your life energy. You might be doing it to support someone or something else. You might be doing it to get out of debt and experience that particular aspect of financial freedom. You might be doing it to develop savings so that you can be secure no matter what the economic climate. Or you might be doing it so that you can achieve some other life goals, like going back to school or traveling around the world or even becoming financially independent. The size and intensity of your goals will determine the time and vigor you invest in the workplace. You might even be so eager to reach a financial goal that you end up with several side gigs alongside your job—joyfully. Unlike the behavior of a workaholic, however, working extra hours is now connected with and serves your purpose.

> *Disconnecting work from wages for* **Rosemary I.** *meant that she could move toward pursuing other goals beyond her job—goals that ranged from travel to writing to working on projects that might help the planet. While she enjoyed her job as an activities director at a retirement home, she didn't plan to devote her whole life to it. She saw clearly that the more she earned now, the sooner she could get on with her other goals. Rather than searching for a higher-paying job—with the possibility of more stress—she decided on another strategy. She got a second job working on call with a small audio duplication and distribution company, putting in several hours a week on evenings and weekends. The schedule was flexible, the people congenial, the stress minimal, and her hourly pay was just as good as what she was getting at her full-time job. Even though she's working far more than forty hours a week, her goal keeps her energy up and her spirits high.*

Valuing your life energy and seeking the highest pay possible has nothing to do with the "more is better" mentality. If money = life energy, then by increasing your income you increase the amount of life available to you. Depending on your actual hourly wage, a new car could cost a month, six months, or a year of work. And you don't want more money so that you can have more status, prestige, power, or security. You know that money doesn't buy those things. You want more money so that you can have more freedom to be yourself without worrying about the money. Likewise, you don't want more money to boost your self-esteem. You want more money as an expression of your self-esteem, of valuing your life energy.

NEW OPTIONS FOR PAID EMPLOYMENT

You have several creative options to explore at this point, including increasing your pay so you can work part-time, enhancing your current job, or changing jobs altogether.

Higher Pay: A Matter of Attitude

Many people are passive, even fatalistic, about the size of their earnings. They act out of a victim mentality, totally at the mercy of outside forces—the boss, the wage scale, the unemployment situation, the recession, the poor local economy, the president's economic policy, competition from low-paid workers in developing countries, and on and on. The attitude is one of "I can't find a good job—and it's because of Them. They are keeping me in a low-paying job."

While economic realities may at times be harsh, it is also the nature of the human mind to make real the thoughts and beliefs that we hold (a fact that should encourage great care in how we think about ourselves). One important factor limiting your earning potential is attitude: attitudes about yourself (e.g., "I'm not good enough"), about your job or employer ("They're out to get me"), and about current circumstances ("There just aren't any jobs"). If you see yourself as a victim, you may well be too busy feeling sorry for yourself to notice the many opportunities to change your dismal destiny.

To be successful, cultivate positive attitudes of self-respect, pride in your contribution to your workplace, dedication to your job, cooperation with your employers and coworkers, desire to do the job right, personal integrity, responsibility, and accountability—and do it just because you value your life energy.

Think how valuing your life energy might transform your experience and performance on the job, as well as your ability to get another job should you want one.

Wherever you are working, you are working for yourself. You are committed to excellence at your job because you're committed to 100 percent integrity, no matter what you're doing.

You'd be surprised at the degree to which job satisfaction lies in the worker, not in the work.

Ted Y., *the carpenter we met in chapter 6, found that one of the gifts of the FI program was the chance to reconnect with his aspirations as a writer. He'd grown up in an air force family and had kept moving as an adult. He finished high school in Gulfport, Mississippi, and then moved to Austin, Texas, where he employed eight people in a remodeling business until the oil crash ripped the rug and floor out from under him. That and a divorce pared his possessions down to a van load (making step 1 very easy), and he took off, eventually landing in Oregon. Within a year of putting the FI program into practice, Ted had enough money saved to support himself for a year, allowing him to back away from the financial edge. He decided to try writing some stories that had been with him for years, stories based on his experiences in Mississippi in the early 1970s, when he built a Baptist church with some old African American carpenters. To free up more time for writing, Ted started bidding his remodeling jobs a lot higher, assuming that most of those contracts wouldn't come through. What happened was a big surprise. Many people had been so impressed with his work in the past that they were willing to pay whatever he asked. He had all the work he wanted, at much higher wages. Wanting to deliver the quality they were paying for, he put even greater care into his carpentry. His reputation for superior craftsmanship spread, bringing in more work. His hours of paid employment went down, his income went up, his anxiety went down, his peace of mind went up, and his time to write seemed boundless. He was surprised, but he wasn't going to question his good fortune—or was it his good self-esteem?*

Financial Independence as a Part-Time Job

Ted Y. chose what we usually refer to as part-time work. However, this new way of thinking about money and work puts that term in a new light. In the world of job = identity, part-time work makes you only a part-time person, who has only part-time worth. As a part-timer, this thinking concludes, you would be sacrificing many of the benefits of full-time employment. You'd lose out on health insurance and whatever retirement plan your company provides. You'd lose out on opportunities for advancement. In the new way of thinking, however, you are working part-time on someone else's agenda for money so you can work as much time as possible on your own agenda. You give your employers their money's worth, but you don't define your self-worth by what you do on the job.

People have adopted a number of variations on this theme of part-time work. Some work a shorter workweek. Some work six months a year for money and do their art, travel, volunteering, or play the other six months. Some work four hours a day so that they can be available for their children before and after school. Some ask their boss for what they need. Why not? Nothing ventured, nothing gained. Consider renegotiating your vacation time, asking your boss to let you work twenty-four hours per week, or detailing why telecommuting will make you a better employee.

But What If I Like My Job?

If you like your job, this new perspective (valuing your life energy) will only enhance your experience—and your earnings.

Maddy C. (who is partners with Tom C., the propane-truck driver) loves her work as a "holistic accountant," empowering people to become responsible with their money. Upon doing the FI course she discovered the blind spots in her own personal finances. When she calculated her real hourly wage, she found that out of her $90-per-hour fee, she netted $7.50. Her husband did better delivering propane during the winter in rural Maine. Where was all that money going?

Because she had wanted to provide service for people who couldn't afford it, she offered discount rates to low-income people and was always the one to do unpaid overtime and go the extra mile. Doing the Monthly Tabulations showed her that she wasn't making any headway economically. She had forgotten the simple lesson of valuing her own life energy.

She decided to raise her rates by 23 percent and to limit her staff to one secretary. In addition, she decided to limit both the number of clients, concentrating on those who wanted to learn to help themselves, and the number of hours she worked. After making these changes she found herself with exactly the number and type of clients she wanted, and she now works fewer hours while earning more money.

But What If I Don't Have—or Want—a "Job"?

There are many reasons people don't have or want a "job" in the traditional sense. They can be self-employed, entrepreneurs, on call as handymen and dog walkers, artists of every ilk who might gig on the side, partners who tend to home and family, off-the-grid homesteaders, and on and on. Some now in the gig economy might long to return to having just one job for one boss and benefits, but others have adapted to the fluidity of freelancing and short-term work. Among these are coaches and consultants who have clients instead of jobs—getting 1099s instead of W-2s. And then there are those who have truly independent means—family wealth or other luck of the draw—and spend their time on their creativity or curiosity or service. Some, of course, are among the growing legions of FIers! Any of these will benefit from separating work from wages and seeing if this new mind-set influences their choice of paid employment.

Increasing numbers of people, though, are intent on building their wealth the way the wealthy often do: using their money to make money. From day traders to stock pickers to personal portfolio managers to real estate flippers, these people use their time and attention to maximize return as in any other job or business. In terms of this book, being a day trader is no different from being a heavy equipment operator or a scientist in a lab or a classroom teacher or a rock star. They are all jobs. Sometimes these investors do better than everyone in their high school class—and so there! Sometimes they come out ahead of at least what they would have earned in their planned profession. Sometimes they crash and burn.

Making your money through investing is no more aligned with FI than making your money as a nurse practitioner or a real estate agent. No matter how you make money, there is a trade-off of time—of life energy. You should still evaluate your job—investing—the way you'd evaluate any other job: Ask yourself, "What is my real hourly wage?"

Chapters 8 and 9 cover an approach to investing aligned with FI: intelligence, integrity, and independence.

How to Get a High-Paying, High-Integrity Job

As we have seen, there is no Job Charming. The people we've met in these pages had to do a lot of soul-searching, risk taking, experimenting, and challenging of old beliefs in order to move forward into jobs with higher pay and high integrity. They had to see that their lives are bigger than their jobs. The parts of them that were suffocated by their paid employment had to be given room to breathe again. Visions from childhood of how life could be had to be excavated from under the status, seriousness, and self-importance that masquerade as adulthood. They had to tell themselves the truth about whether their current paid employment was really doing what paid employment is supposed to do: earn money.

There are a number of excellent job-hunting guides and blogs on the market. Just one word of caution: As P. T. Barnum once said, there's a sucker born every minute. Be as sharp a shopper for a job as you would be for a car or a refrigerator.

Nina N. had left her marriage and raised four children as a single mother ten years before she started doing this program. Then she listened to the audio course and even though she was living with friends, exchanging labor for room and board, she started tracking her few expenses. Determined to become financially independent, she applied for a job as a maid at a nearby motel—and got it. She hurried home, ecstatic to tell her housemates, only to realize she forgot to ask how much she'd be paid.

Several months later Nina moved to Seattle to look for a job that paid more than the minimum wage. Within weeks she was out on assignments from a temporary employment agency. Right away she put her Wall Chart up, and within a few months she had wiped out several thousand dollars in debt. Her progress spurred her on. For every temporary position she calculated her real hourly wage. Soon she'd doubled her income, but she didn't stop there. Temping at a hospital, she learned of an opening as a full-time administrative assistant to a department head. She went for it. Her pay shot up above $17 per hour, and she now had benefits. Sure, she'd never had a job like this before, but she'd raised four children—how hard could one doctor be?

But she didn't give up looking. Her Wall Chart was a daily reminder that the more she sold her life energy for, the sooner her time would be her own again. One weekend, while volunteering at a conference on a topic of interest, the whole staff walked off to protest a policy—and Nina stepped up. When the board went looking for a new executive director, Nina was the clear choice. By the time she retired, her annual salary was over $48,000, a figure that had been so unthinkable to the hotel-maid Nina that she now had to tape extra graph paper to the top of her Wall Chart to even enter her monthly income. Her earnings had literally gone off the chart! (See Figure 7-1.)

FIGURE 7-1

Nina's Wall Chart—with Income

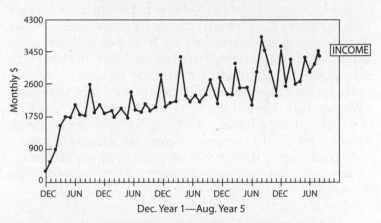

Because of her focus on valuing her life energy, Nina quadrupled her income. Her self-image went from "minimum-wage worker" to "executive director."

Step 7 is simply valuing your life energy and increasing your income—because the only purpose of paid employment is getting paid. You do this not out of greed or competition but out of self-respect and an appreciation for life. As a by-product you might well find yourself with less debt, more savings, more free time, more energy on the job, more energy off the job, more satisfied clients, a more satisfied family, and more peace of mind.

SUMMARY OF STEP 7

Increase your income by valuing the life energy you invest in your job, exchanging it for the highest pay consistent with your health and integrity.

MONEY TALK QUESTIONS

Stories around a circle—be it a campfire or Money Talk—teach us so much about how to make better choices, not just for our money lives but to have more meaning and happiness. Enrich yourself by inviting others to speak and listen in this unique way.

Using the suggestions in the epilogue for how to have a Money Talk, raise these questions in your daily reflections, with your partner, or in social groups. Remember, adding "Why?" to the end of any question will take it deeper. Adding "How has society shaped my answer?" to any question will take it wider. There are no right answers.

- ◆ How could you double your income without selling your soul or compromising your health?
- ◆ What was your first job? Best job? Worst job?
- ◆ What would be your dream job—whether or not you were paid for it?
- ◆ What is work and why do we do it?
- ◆ What is your life's work?
- ◆ What do you like—and dislike—about the work you do for money?

8

Catching Fire:
The Crossover Point

So far the by-product of doing the steps has been mini-mizing your expenses, maximizing your income, paying off debt, and having your bank account start to grow. In the old days, you'd consider those savings spending money: a vacation, technology upgrades, a down pay-ment for a new house. But now that you've done the steps, your old habits of spending everything you have—and more—on new stuff or experiences has quieted down. You know that money is your life energy, and you are determined to spend it only on what brings you joy and serves your purpose. Most of your old gazingus pins no longer grab your attention, and those few that make it past the cash register often look like fool's gold very soon afterward. You've started to feel the freedom of "enough."

What's next?

This is the moment when, if you are lucky, your successful uncle Louie or tía Rosalita or cousin Archie sits you down for the "magic of compound interest" talk—the concept in which your money starts to work for you. They say, "You're young. If you start saving now, by the magic of compound interest you will be rich by the time you're fifty."

Me? Rich?

Consider this chapter *that* talk—and then some.

Doing steps 1 through 7 transformed your relationship with money. Now steps 8 and 9 will transform your relationship with your future.

Enter your successful tía Rosalita or uncle Louie or cousin Archie, who explains that if you invest your savings rather than spending them, you will build wealth. Your money makes money for you. Store it in the bank and you get interest. Buy bonds and you get even more interest. Conservatively invest in the stock market and you get dividends. Reinvest all your interest and dividends and build more wealth. "Eventually, my [boy/girl], your money will do all the work for you. You'll be financially independent."

This relative is actually right by your side now. It's your Wall Chart. More powerful than you may realize, this simple snapshot of your financial life will help transform your life in profound ways. Pay attention. It's simple once you see what's going on. Notice that once your expense line goes down, your income line goes up, your debt disappears, and you start to have savings.

In chapter 7 we saw Nina N.'s Wall Chart with her

FIGURE 8-1

Nina's Wall Chart—with Income and Expenses

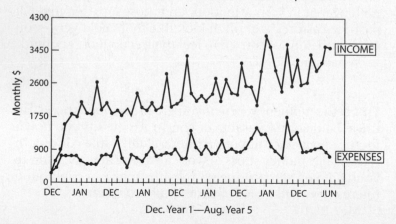

Dec. Year 1—Aug. Year 5

income line going off the top. Let's take a look at it again, this time adding the expense line (see Figure 8-1). You'll notice that it settles into a groove.

Having lived on the edge of poverty for so many years, **Nina N.** *didn't have a lot of "big spender" habits to contend with, so her expense line soon settled in at around $950 a month. What doesn't show up on the chart is the change in her "discretionary" spending from "entertainment to fill the void" to "activities in support of my purpose," and the fact that her feeling of inner peace went steadily up. Her income line, as we said in chapter 7, went off the chart, not only from her professional work but also from some part-time piecework she did for a small local company. Nina's chart is fairly typical for a dyed-in-the-wool frugal person whose earning power goes through the ceiling.*

Elaine H.*'s chart (see Figure 8-2) is typical of a fairly steady earner and heavy spender who diligently applied the principles of this program and cut her spending in half, while, she claims, adding to both the quality of her life and her self-esteem.*

FIGURE 8-2

Elaine's Wall Chart—with Income and Expenses

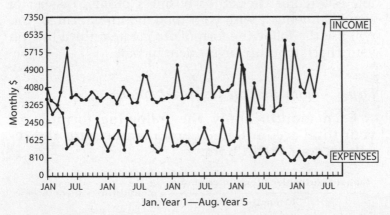

Jan. Year 1—Aug. Year 5

Capital

What you see in both these charts is a growing gap between income and expenses—that is, savings. Before FI thinking, this gap means more spending money. After FI thinking, these savings are seen in a different light. FI thinking calls that gap "capital."

Capital is money that makes money, as opposed to sitting in the bank. Whether $50 or $500, your capital can start producing an income. Doing steps 8 and 9, you will see that Financial Independence isn't just for the 1 percent or the 10 percent. It's for anyone and everyone who chooses to transform their relationship with money and accumulate *enough* wealth, which, when invested wisely, can provide a lifetime of passive income. With step 8, the possibility of complete Financial Independence opens up.

Let that sink in.

A New Line on Your Chart: Monthly Investment Income

The income you receive from your capital is of a different nature than your job income. It comes in whether or not you go to work, e-mail clients a final project, or hit your monthly sales goal. This money continues to flow from all your investments in the form of dividends, interest, rental checks, or business profits. Instead of simply lumping it with your total monthly income, you will use the following formula to create a third line on your chart: monthly investment income.

Step 8: Capital and the Crossover Point

Each month, apply the following formula to your total accumulated capital and record the result on your Wall Chart:

$$\frac{\text{capital} \times \text{current long-term interest rate}}{\text{12 months}} = \text{monthly investment income}$$

Simply put, when your monthly investment income line on your Wall Chart "crosses over" your expense line, you "cross over" into Financial Independence. Here's how.

Your total accumulated capital is simply the money you have (usually in a savings account) that you are not planning to spend. For the current interest rate, don't use what you get on your checking account; instead use the current yield of long-term (thirty years) US Treasury bonds or, perhaps, certificates of deposit (CDs). The US Treasury bond figure is one of the best reflections of prevailing interest rates on debt instruments (we are not saying to buy them; just use the interest rate). It is a conservative estimate of the return you can expect from such a long-term investment. *Applying this percentage to your capital doesn't mean you now have that income. It simulates the kind of income you will have later from your FI portfolio (we'll talk more about this in chapter 9), thus allowing you to do this crucial step of projecting what your FI income will be.*

For mathematical simplicity we will use 4 percent, but this is a convenience for our discussion only and not a prediction or a promise about what interest rates will be when you are ready to invest. When you do, there are a variety of investments you can own, which will ultimately determine your estimated return on investment (ROI). Regardless of what those investments might be, what we know for sure about the financial world is that even the safest investments go up and down. At the moment, don't worry too much about your number—just use the current rate.

Interestingly, in traditional financial planning 4 percent is also a key percentage for calculating retirement income. It's known as the "safe withdrawal rate." With a blended portfolio of stocks and bond funds, withdrawing 4 percent of your capital each year is considered a safe allowance to pay yourself once you no longer work for income. This 4 percent rule preserves your capital, protects against inflation, and gives you an annual income to cover your expenses. The concept is somewhat

"Goldilocks" in nature. If you were to estimate 3 percent annual withdrawals, it may not be enough money to cover your expenses. However, withdrawing 5 percent of your capital each year may dry it up too quickly.

Remember, this is a general example and not specific financial instructions. Because both the safe withdrawal rate and current long-term bond interest use the same percentage, 4 percent is a reasonable choice for the following examples.

Let's say you have $100 in savings. If you were to invest that $100 of capital in a bond that pays 4 percent interest, the equation would look like this:

$$\frac{\$100 \times 4\%}{12} = \$.33 \text{ month}$$

For every $100 invested, you will get $.33 each month, for the life of the bond or CD. The original $100 remains untouched and you will eventually get it back. But this is only the beginning!

So if on the first month of your chart you have $1,000 in savings and the current interest rate is 4 percent, your equation will read:

$$\frac{\$1,000 \times 4\%}{12} = \$3.33 \text{ monthly investment income}$$

This simply means that the $1,000 you now have in *savings* has the power to bring in $3.33 every month—if you consider it *capital* and invest it in a bond or other equivalent investment. In this example you would post $3.33 on your Wall Chart. (We'll see in a moment how that looks on Nina's Wall Chart.)

Sure, it's a tiny figure compared to the towering income spikes on your Wall Chart, but it's still $3.33 a month ($40 a year) for the life of that bond. For fun, try translating that into something tangible, some expense you consider necessary for survival. It could be the pounds of rice you use in a month. Or a couple of weeks' worth of coffee beans. Or part of your cell phone bill.

Keep applying the equation to your total accumulated savings each month. For example, if you save another $500 during the second month, add it to your previous total of $1,000 and your equation for that month will look like this:

$$\frac{\$1,500 \times 4\%}{12} = \$5.00 \text{ monthly investment income}$$

Post this figure and connect it to the previous one. After a number of months your chart will show a third line creeping up from the bottom. This line represents monthly investment income (see Figure 8-3).

Once your income and expenditures become consistent, you can calculate your "finish line," or how much you would need to save and invest to make employment optional. To do this, think about the preceding equation in reverse. Let's say your average annual spending is $36,000, or $3,000 per month, and you want a safe withdrawal rate of 4 percent after retiring. Based on these numbers, you can calculate how much you would need in assets to declare Financial Independence.

$$\frac{\$3,000 \times 12}{4\%} = \$900,000 \text{ total assets}$$

Mr. Money Mustache summarizes this rule of thumb as follows: Your *Crossover Point* comes when you have 25 times your annual expenses—which functionally gives you a 4 percent withdrawal rate indefinitely. For example, an annual expense of $36,000 requires $900,000 in total assets ($36,000 × 25) for becoming financially independent.

In chapter 9, we'll help you decide when to make the leap from savings to investing. When you're finally

FIGURE 8-3

Applying the Formula to Capital to Get Monthly Investment
Income and Entering on Wall Chart

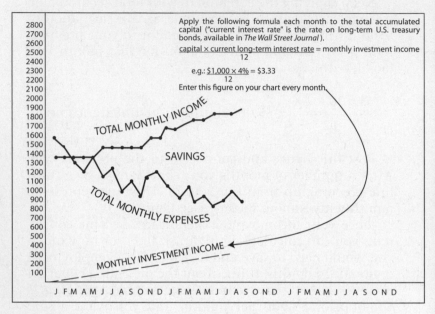

comfortable, let's say you begin by investing $5,000 in a
long-term bond. The income from that investment will
become part of your monthly investment income figure.
The next $5,000 you accumulate will be invested in a
similar way, and the next and the next and the next.

Let's go back to Nina's chart and see how that looks
(see Figure 8-4).

Since she started out with some debt, **Nina***'s monthly invest-*
ment income line didn't even show up until about a year
after she took the hotel-maid job. Once she started accumu-
lating savings and converting them to capital, however, her
monthly investment income kept going up. In January of
year 4, for example, Nina has a monthly investment income
of $215, while her expenses are $845. By the next January

FIGURE 8-4

Nina's Wall Chart—with Monthly Investment Income

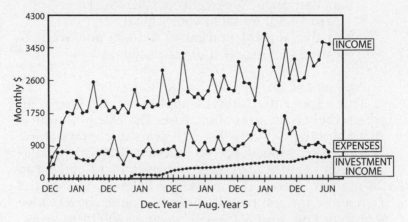

Dec. Year 1—Aug. Year 5

her monthly investment income is $350 and her expenses are still less than $1,000. Now look at February of year 5. Her monthly investment income is $545, and her expenses are still within the $950 range. What you are seeing at work here is not only Nina's increasing investment income but also what's known as the magic of compound interest.

Even if the amount added to your capital each month is a constant increment (e.g., your monthly savings are always $500), compound interest makes sure that the monthly investment income line on your chart curves upward rather than remaining straight. This is the magic of compound interest your relatives would have talked to you about. Compound interest means you add your interest income to your capital and apply the percent return to the combined total, not just to the original capital. For example:

Year one you earn 4 percent on $100, adding $4 to your capital.

Year two apply 4 percent to your capital, now $104, and you earn $4.16. Add it to your capital.

Year three apply 4 percent to $108.16 and you earn $4.33. Add it to your capital.

Year four apply 4 percent to $112.49 and you earn $4.50. Add it to your capital.

Year five apply 4 percent to $116.99 and you earn $4.68. Apply it to your capital.

And on and on.

This exponential growth applies to any system in which there is an annual increase. The rule of thumb is that anything will double in 10 years if it grows at a 7 percent rate. Money you've invested. Human population. Your debt! (Cards today range from 12 percent to 24 percent interest if you carry a balance. You do the compound interest math.) Given our more conservative 4 percent rate, your $100 will become $200 in 18 years.

You can see this upward trend developing in Nina's Wall Chart. That modest yet ever-increasing monthly investment income line is steadily gaining on the fairly stable monthly expenses line. We'll see the significance of this in a moment. But for now all we need to notice is that simply doing the steps, month in and month out, has caused Nina's investment income to head up. This will also happen to you.

WHERE DO YOU
ACTUALLY PUT YOUR SAVINGS?

During your wealth accumulation years, you'll first want to build up liquid (readily available) cash in a bank account. Common wisdom says you should have three (ideally six) months of expenses in liquid cash stashed in your bank. It is risk-free because Federal Deposit Insurance means that Uncle Sam has you covered up to $250,000 per account if the bank fails. But even "the bank" isn't as simple as it was a few decades ago. You have choices. Do you consider your bank's track record in bankrolling companies that pollute or discriminate? Do you choose the one closest to your house? Do you choose a credit union, a local member-owned financial cooperative? Do you choose an online bank accessible anywhere in the world to eke out a fraction more interest?

We call this liquid cash your "cushion." Many call it an "emergency fund" because it's there if you have to fly home to see a sick parent or buy a new (to you) car if your old Volvo blows a head gasket. It's where you store your daily life money, depositing income and paying bills. If you're currently living paycheck to paycheck, the thought of saving up a half year of expenses may seem impossible, but don't fear! Following this program will prepare you to do that and then some.

Beyond Your Cushion

In chapter 9 you'll learn about investment vehicles that are most likely to conserve capital while generating income. Joe Dominguez recommended US Treasury bonds for this purpose, but as we will see, the golden opportunity of Treasury bonds is long gone . . . and we don't know when or if it's coming back. Because of that, chapter 9 will also discuss other strategies FIers have used in the years since *Your Money or Your Life* was first published in 1992.

For now, focus on increasing your liquid cash and then purchasing laddered CDs (certificates of deposit with staggered maturity dates) or, if you follow current FIRE (Financial Independence, Retire Early) theory, index funds (explained in chapter 9).

Some of you may be lucky enough to already have savings opportunities at your fingertips. If your company offers a retirement plan such as a 401(k) or similar, take advantage of it because many employers will match your contributions—essentially giving you free money for investing—at an average of 6 percent of each paycheck. Receiving this match instantly doubles your money and is, by far, one of the best returns on your investment. Plus, it grows tax-free. Most 401(k)s now are managed by large brokerage houses that offer you a variety of options, from mutual funds to bond funds. For those self-employed readers, you too can open a 401(k) or an SEP and contribute through your business.

If your employer doesn't offer such a plan, consider an individual retirement account, or IRA. Anyone can open one, and much like an employer-provided retirement account, an IRA also provides tax advantages and grows tax-free. Both a 401(k) and an IRA are excellent accounts that all working people can take advantage of in some way.

There are plenty of other options; this is simply an overview of some of the common places people choose to turn their savings into income-producing investments.

It may seem strange, but for now, your monthly investment income line is not influenced by where or how you currently save your money, as long as you keep saving it. Later, when you are FI and investing for passive income, this will no longer be needed. As we mentioned before, this is a way you can *project* the income you will have from your FI portfolio. Whether it's in a checking account, CDs, or retirement account, you apply the 4 percent formula to your capital to generate the projection of returns.

THE CROSSOVER POINT

One day, while you're looking at your Wall Chart, you will realize that you can project your monthly investment income line into the future.

Because you have established a fairly steady trend in your total monthly expenses, you can reasonably project that line into the future as well. If your expenses stabilize in a range—like $2,800 to $3,200 a month—pick the higher number just so you feel very safe projecting what your post-FI expenses will be. That will quiet the fears some might have about unforeseen expenses.

You will notice that at some time in the not-too-distant

FIGURE 8-5

The Crossover Point

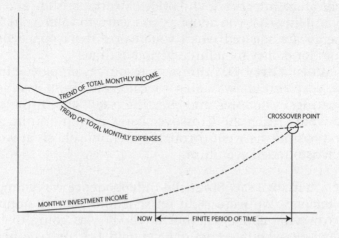

future those two lines (total monthly expenses and monthly investment income) will cross. We call that the *Crossover Point* (Figure 8-5). Beyond the Crossover Point, income from your investment capital will be higher than your monthly expenses—and your employment officially becomes optional!

The Crossover Point provides us with our final definition of Financial Independence. At the Crossover Point, where monthly investment income exceeds your monthly expenses, you will be financially independent in the traditional sense of that term. You will have passive income from a source other than a job.

THE POWER OF A VISIBLE TIME HORIZON

This realization has had a powerful impact on many people. Think about it. If you see your life as bigger than your job and can conceive of having to work for money for only a finite and foreseeable period of time, then you are likely to be an even more highly motivated, high-integrity worker. The qualities of self-assurance, high motivation, dedication, integrity, joyful pride of workmanship, and responsibility that you adopt as you learn to value your life energy are squared when you realize that you need to work for money for a finite period of time.

When **Larry D.**, a human resources employee in a big corporation, was able to calculate, from years of tracking, evaluating, and charting (see Figure 8-6), that he would reach the Crossover Point within a finite period of time, he went through a metamorphosis at work that astounded even him.

"Finally I saw Financial Independence was going to happen. We were right on schedule for it. I stopped worrying about whether anybody was going to fire me or whether I would get laid off, or whether I stepped on toes, and it was extremely empowering." (His wife said he'd come home from work saying, "I'm bulletproof! I'm bulletproof!")

"I just started going gangbusters at work. It was kind of scary from just about everybody else's perspective too because I had phenomenal energy and incredible confidence. . . . I negotiated some of the toughest settlements that I've probably ever negotiated during those six or eight months, and I did not lose. Not only did I not lose, I prevailed big-time on everything. . . . If a manager really screwed up bad on something, I said, 'OK, send them to me and I'll fix it.' It worked out really well for the company and for me."

Take a minute to think about what would happen if you knew that you would have to work for money for a limited, foreseeable length of time instead of that vague limbo of working until traditional retirement. You would still *appear* to be working for your boss, but you would know you were working for your own freedom. If you are close to retirement age, how does it feel to consider

FIGURE 8-6

Dorothy and Larry's Financials

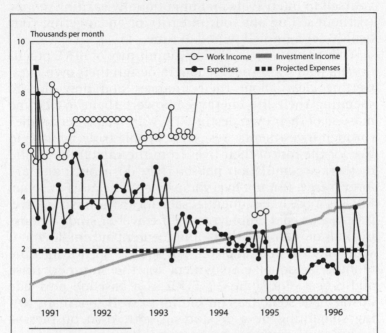

Note: Dorothy and Larry determined that $2,000 per month was their post–financial independence income requirement (also known as their point of "enough"). As you can see, their steadily growing "investment income" line crossed their "projected expenses at FI" line back in 1993, and then crossed their "expense" line in late 1994. The big drop in work income came in January 1995 when Dorothy left paid employment, and again in April, when Larry quit. Also, note that their *actual* post-FI expenses have been considerably lower than their estimated target of $2,000/month—the result of learned frugal thinking and continued use of *Your Money or Your Life* principles. Source: Jacqueline Blix and David Heitmiller, *Getting a Life* (New York: Viking, 2007), p. 172.

shaving off a few years in the workplace and adding them to your retirement years? If you are in your forties—or even thirties—imagine having half your life ahead of you to fill as you *will*, not as you *must*.

One of the cornerstones of this program, for those wishing to go all the way to Financial Independence, is concentrating on making money now so that you don't have to make money later. You are thus committing yourself to intensively and intentionally earning money (without selling out your integrity or endangering your health) for a limited period of time.

There is now a worldwide community of FIRE practitioners who want the freedom to design their own lives. Getting clear about their finances and how they're spending their life energy empowers them to become masters of their own destiny. They aren't *all* "set for life" through investments. Yes, some people truly manage to live for the rest of their lives from the capital they build in their accumulation phase. They do it once and are forever free. But not everyone, by any means. For some, FIRE is more like sequential sabbaticals: You work, save, invest, exit paid employment for travel or study or raising kids or retooling skills, and reenter paid employment some months or years later. For some it's FIRE for nine months, seasonal employment for the summer, rinse and repeat. For some it's FIRE as a baseline plus side hustles. For some it's continuing to work—perhaps trying something new or starting your own business— knowing it's optional because you have an FI baseline from investments, retirement plans, or Social Security.

Even if your freedom leads you to another career, another irresistible business idea, or another lifestyle choice that costs more money and you return to paid employment, your first finite period of time changes you forever. You know you can do it again. You're savvy and empowered, resilient and knowledgeable.

Sam is a homesteader who wants us to reinhabit the heartland of this country. When he and his wife, **Donna**, decided to try to align their personal economy with the planet's ecology, they returned to their hometown in Kansas. They bought some land from a friend, tore down an old barn for lumber, and built a passive solar house with the help of sixty friends and Sam's father (a carpenter and stonemason). At the same time, Sam worked for his father hauling trash, while Donna went to nursing school to learn a consistently marketable skill. In everything they did, they tried to embody their values—self-sufficiency, household economy, energy efficiency, and eating what grew in their own garden or was locally grown. They took things slowly, being careful to pay as they went and not get in over their heads. Ideally, they hoped to eliminate over half of the standard expenses (like rent, as well as most food and utilities) and live below taxable levels. Collecting trash took only five hours a day. Meanwhile, Donna worked two days a week as a nurse.

Life was sweet and they were getting ends to meet—almost. But several things happened on their way to Eden: two children, health insurance, buying the trash business from Sam's father, a car that quit and a house that just kept crying out for small improvements. Underneath the trappings of living simply, they were caught in the classic "too much month at the end of the money" and "where does it all go?" syndrome. Eden, it seemed, could be as much of a trap as the suburbs.

It was then they discovered the Your Money or Your Life program. When Sam saw the implications of the finite period of time, his life opened up. Garbage collecting was all well and good, but the thought of doing it for the rest of his life was not attractive. What really fired his imagination was the possibility of being financially self-sufficient and dedicating himself to developing a sustainable-yield homestead on their four acres and helping his neighbors to discover the right mix and rotation for sustainably raising cattle, wheat, feed grains, and other crops in the semiarid grasslands of western Kansas.

He wanted to do this not only for himself but for the larger community. He could see the small farmers disappearing. Every year the population in his part of the country goes down while the average age goes up. He wanted to change that through his own example. Perhaps, he mused, young people could go to the city for ten years to become financially independent, return to the heartland with their cash needs taken care of, and then regenerate subsistence farming and small-town living. Perhaps his small efforts could create a good life not only for his family but for other families and rural America as well.

The finite period of time opened Sam's options from years of garbage collecting to a future filled with other projects. Four years after doing the FI course, he reached his personal Crossover Point. His investment income matched his trash income. He could stop working for money—and start working for his dreams.

CACHE

Looking at that crossover point, you might wonder if you could really be financially secure on passive income for the rest of your life. That's a very long time. The what-ifs and what-abouts will start scratching at the back door of your mind, looking to get in.

This is where a third element of your financial security comes in: your cache.

Cache (pronounced "cash") is savings in addition to core capital or cushion. In pioneer days a cache was a hole in the ground where travelers buried provisions for later use that were too heavy to carry. In your FI program, your cache is a store of extra money (beyond your capital or your cushion) that builds up for future use.

Rosemary I. *found herself getting increasingly uneasy as her projected Crossover Point approached. She was used to her job, and the thought of turning off that trusty faucet and depending on bond income alone was scary. Rationally she knew her bond income was enough and then some, but she still had* *irrational fears of not being able to reenter the job market if FI somehow didn't work. "Maybe this is what trapeze artists feel when they are assessing when to let go of their bar so they can swing over to the other one," she thought. Her safety net (cushion) was in place, but it felt very far away. She decided to bring the net closer and beef it up by building up her cache. With those extra thousands in the bank, she found it easy to face down the inner worry wart who kept asking, "But what if you total your car and have a major illness and your house burns down all in the same year?"*

But if you no longer work for income, where does cache come from?

Most people find that their expenses go down significantly when they leave paid employment. No more commuting expenses, no more dress-for-success expenses, no more restaurant-lunch expenses—and many more such reductions. So since the Crossover Point is based on your total expenses while you are engaged in paid employment, you might find investment income piling up post-FI. This is what we referred to in the definition of FI as having enough and then some.

In addition, your FI habits don't end. What you learned during your money transformation will stay with you for life. Your expenses go down through careful, conscious, and creative spending. Finally, many things you bought during your accumulation phase (like your sturdy car or ultimate camping gear or off-the-grid house) will never need to be replaced—they were part of your pre-FI expenses. Further savings. Further cache. Taxes on post-FI income are—and should continue to be—far lower than your high-earning years. More cache. Finally, you can grow your cache for unanticipated expenses or increased capital through side hustles, part-time work, gifts, inheritances, or even a new career that happens to come with a paycheck. (No one ever said you can't choose to return to work, did they?)

The initial function of the cache may be psychological.

It proves to you that you do have enough and then some over time, helping to quell any lingering what-ifs.

It is from cache that you can replace major items necessary to your chosen lifestyle when they finally do wear out—things like a car, a bicycle, or crowns for your back teeth. Your cache is a living resource, not a onetime bundle that you will deplete.

Capital. Cushion. Cache. The three pillars of Financial Independence.

There are, however, three other pillars of wealth that you rely on—possibly more than money.

NATURAL WEALTH AND FINANCIAL INTERDEPENDENCE

Imagine your savvy uncle Louie or your shrewd tía Rosalita have the kind of partners who provide the glue in any family. Auntie Rachel and Tío Manolo exude love. They make food, make music, make jokes, make everyone comfortable and at ease. They hug you and say, "Money isn't everything. If you have self-respect and love and family and help others, that's your true wealth."

This isn't either-or. *All* your relatives have a point. This program works because it walks on two legs: your dollars-and-cents life and your love (in the widest sense) life.

One is national currency, the money we all use to trade and invest.

The other is natural currency, the endless shuttling of giving and receiving between people (and all living things) who recognize one another as kin.

National currency is a relatively recent human invention, controlled by financial institutions like banks, doled out by people and institutions we don't control.

Natural currency came into being with the first living organism, which created a mutually beneficial exchange with other organisms. For any life-form to continue, it needs to provide some benefit for the life-forms around it.

The more we weave our lives beneficially with others, the less money we need to have access to everything we could possibly want. You know this because you've done steps 1 through 7 and discovered that spending less is both possible and pleasurable once you enter the sharing economy—whether it's using public services like the library or using the secondary market of peer-to-peer exchange like Craigslist—or the DIY economy, in which saving is the by-product of empowerment. You spend less not just because you are a tightwad. You spend less because you become a more skillful, loving, sharing, caring, giving, receiving human—and simply need less of your own stuff to get by. Whittling down your expenses and piling up money isn't an end in itself; it's a by-product of doing the steps.

This is natural currency. This is the *relational* rather than *transactional* economy. This is *Financial Interdependence*, which in fact is the wealth most of us depend on. It is the wealth we all share when we coexist together. You don't have to believe in this for it to be true. Clean oxygen will still flow into your lungs. The endless roads and bridges and institutions of civilization will still be there for you. Those who learn how to prosper in this interdependent love economy, though, will also be more financially independent—that is, less dependent on finances to meet their needs.

Auntie Rachel and Tío Manolo would say that real wealth is what you know, who walks with you in life, and the society where you give your best and receive your due. They are as simple as A-B-C. . . .

ABCs OF NATURAL WEALTH

Abilities includes your skills and knowledge—what you know how to do.

Belonging is who walks with you in life.

Community is the society you live in (in real life and even online)—your neighbors, your city, your environment—and nature.

Abilities, Belonging, and Community are the three forms of natural wealth you build intuitively in the process of aligning how you earn, spend, and save money with your purpose and fulfillment. As you take your eyes off the false prize (of more, better, and different stuff), you put them on the real prizes: friends, family, sharing, caring, learning, meeting challenges, intimacy, rest, and being present, connected, and respected. In other words, those best things in life that are free. Like all things natural, building this wealth takes time, attention, patience, and reciprocity (that volleying of giving and receiving that builds relationships).

Build natural wealth during your financial accumulation phase and your FI may come sooner, last longer, and be happier by far.

Abilities

Abilities are the do-it-yourself skills that save you lots of money—and can make you money if you need it. As we've pointed out in earlier chapters, your determination to be more self-reliant comes as you realize how much of your life energy goes to paying a plumber for a house call when for less than a dollar and the time it takes to watch a free fifteen-minute online video you could have fixed the faucet washer yourself. A few DIY wins and you look around for what else you could learn. You fix the vacuum cleaner (just a ganglion of cat hair in the hose). Then your car stereo (just a loose wire). Then you replace the defunct garbage disposal yourself by following the instructions that came with it. You might graduate to DIY deck building or remodeling and be endlessly and lucratively (if you want) useful to other people. All along the way you are saving money, empowering yourself, and building a wealth of skills that you could actually monetize should you need extra national currency in the future.

Maybe becoming Ms. Fix-It isn't your cup of tea, but you like cooking. Perhaps discovering how much life energy goes into restaurant meals inspires you to cook from scratch. Maybe you and your partner take ethnic cooking classes together and making meals becomes one of your favorite forms of play. Not only does this mean nourishing meals for less money, this ability could be monetized by becoming a caterer, a chef in a restaurant, or a personal chef with a raft of clients.

Photography can be a hobby, an art form, or a job— and if you love it, all of these will blend into one pleasure. Bicycle repair, house painting, website building, social media marketing, accounting, and on and on all save you money and make you valuable to others. Sometimes it makes more sense to invest in yourself by attending a training or getting certified in such skills rather than investing in a financial instrument. Get certified as an emergency medical technician and you will be a sought-after volunteer or a paid professional, and a better role model for your kids.

Post–Financial Independence, you will still be part of the economy. Keep building skills and you'll stay FI and also be able to make money again should the need arise. Having diverse skills and abilities is one key to resilience—the capacity to thrive no matter what happens in the financial markets. Honing your skills gives you leverage, freedom, and choice. This diversity of abilities is one form of wealth that you can build over a lifetime to challenge yourself, to do for others, to be of use in your community, to make money if needed, and to meet life with courage.

Damon S. *was following the traditional path of a university education and a lifelong career with a single company from which he would retire in "old age." While he valued the* *income, a life of wage slavery seemed unappealing, insecure, and difficult to break out of. In a flash of insight, he saw that he had no skills to meet his basic needs—food, water, shelter—without money. On a mission, he cut expenses, saved, and started his own business. With the surplus time and money, he enrolled in a wilderness college, learning how to live self-sufficiently, survive with nothing in the wild, forage, and grow his own food. He invested national wealth in building natural wealth and sees before him a rich life of community, love, and happiness, with enough money for what money is good at.*

What could you learn to do for love—and money? What have you always wanted to know or never thought you could master? Could you set a goal to do it? What did you love doing as a kid that you could train in now for a side gig or a survival skill? Lifelong learning is a key to happiness. Invest in your ability to survive and thrive and help others and you will never be bored. It will keep paying off in an alert mind and a secure place in society, long after your years of paid employment come to an end.

Belonging

Whom can you turn to when you need help? Who will listen to you with compassion? Who would bring you meals when you are sick? Who will celebrate your joys? Our human bonds of love and loyalty have always gotten us through the night—and life. Mobility, urbanization, and careerism have sucked the time out of our lives for what award-winning author Riane Eisler calls the caring economy—but FIers are reversing that trend. Not only does this caring economy make life less expensive, it makes life richer in precisely what life is truly for: giving and receiving. Maybe Uncle Harry came over to fix the faucet. Later you go to your friend Lily's house to pay the favor forward with what Uncle Harry taught you. Then you get sick and Lily drops off some get-well-soon soup. And on it goes, in this currency of belonging.

At one time church and family connected our lives in these mutually supportive ways, but more and more people are now outside such traditional webs of caring. Of the 40 percent of Americans who *say* they belong to a church, less than 20 percent actually attend.[1] In its most recent survey of religion in America, Gallup reports that it is less and less important in our lives.[2] According to the US Census Bureau's Fertility and Family Statistics Branch, in the 40 years between the 1970 census and 2010 census, the portion of households with two married parents and children fell by half, from 40 percent to 20 percent, while the number of single-person households grew from 17 percent in 1970 to nearly 28 percent in 2012.[3]

Aging boomers are acutely aware of how thinly populated their circles of mutual aid have become, how poor in sturdy relationships they are at the same time as the social safety net is weakening. It's sobering, frightening, and, for many, motivating. Death and dying groups, aging-in-place groups, and book groups are focusing on this gap and weaving local caring networks. Estranged families are having "the conversation" about what to do with aging parents. It's a scramble. This is why a lifelong practice of building belonging wealth is crucial to any FI program.

What relationships from your past need repair—and can you repair them so that kindness can flow? It's no accident that most spiritual paths—including Alcoholics Anonymous and other recovery programs—suggest an honest look at your relationships: whom you've harmed, whom you still resent, whom you need to make peace with. Loneliness is epidemic—and expensive. The currency of belonging has both natural and financial benefits: Being able to distribute and exchange chores, errands, and needs helps save everyone time and money. Those with strong relationships will always have someone to cook dinner with, drive them to the airport, help them move across town, or introduce them to future employment opportunities. This is sometimes referred to as "social capital"—that is, the wealth you create through your networks of mutually beneficial relationships.

While dating and mating is one way to build "belonging wealth," cultivating enduring friendships and relationships in your local community is also key. Just as dancing is a skill, belonging is a skill you can build through listening, acts of kindness, and simple rituals like a weekly call, a monthly women's or men's circle, or book or craft groups.

Community

Widen the circle of relatedness and you are in the third pillar of natural wealth: community. Community is a natural human currency. It is currency because it facilitates trade within communities that share and care outside the money economy. My community recently adopted a mutual-aid model to help people age in place—a big savings when you consider the cost of long-term care! The more trusting the community, the more resources are shared freely. Proximity plus clear communication can free up a lot of underutilized stuff so that many people can benefit from the same item. Isolation is expensive; sharing is wealth—sometimes literally, through services that will rent your car, home, or RV to others, but also more deeply, as in the myriad of daily exchanges that have nothing to do with financial transactions.

Community is also about choosing wisely the "location, location, location" where you plant your roots—the shops on your block, the social services you can draw on, the culture that's yours just by going downtown, the productivity of the farms, and the quiet of the forests. If you are picking where to settle, consider the context as well as the specific house with the specific features. Where do the food, water, and electricity come from? Can you get what you need without getting in the car? How about cultural life? Night life? Look at a climate map (whatever your beliefs). How will it be in twenty years? Fifty?

If you've already found your place on earth, wherever that may be, you can build this wealth by meeting friends in local cafés, serving on nonprofit boards, running for city or county government, writing letters to the paper, singing in a choir, joining a church, and on and on. It's the totality of the social and natural systems that will hold you safe, nourish your soul, inspire your service, and provide you with what you need over the long haul.

The ABCs of Inflation

Joe Dominguez was fond of saying, "Consciousness grows faster than inflation." In other words, you can "inflate" your skills, competencies, knowledge, close companions, and community connections faster than money. Learning to partner-dance can be a hedge. Singing in a choir. Building websites. Once you are FI you'll have more time to learn. More time to DIY. More time to bond with others. More time to find just what you need for a fraction of the cost. More time to volunteer in your community or join a church. Your travels can be cheap and leisurely rather than expensive and rushed. Unlike in your working years, convenience now has far less influence on your decisions.

What about the *s* in those ABCs of wealth? That's your "stuff," your financial and material wealth. Notice it's not capitalized—that's because it's only a small consideration in the caring economy. Your Financial *In*dependence is simply one corner of your foundation of security and freedom. Financial *Inter*dependence includes all four corners: abilities, belonging, and community, along with your hard-won stuff; these constitute your total nest egg. Together, your national wealth and natural wealth will make you rich beyond measure.

Understanding the ABCs of wealth adds a deeper

dimension to the Crossover Point. It isn't just the end of the need for paid employment; it is stepping across a threshold into a more loving, fulfilling, and interesting life whether you're at family dinners with Rachel and Louie, volunteering with Rosalita and Manolo, learning to fish with Archie, running for public office, or meditating in a cave for forty days.

Reaching your Crossover Point is a mighty accomplishment. You haven't been turned out to pasture by someone else. You've restructured your life around what is most fulfilling and valuable to you. You have dedicated yourself to replacing financial fiction with financial facts, challenging many old beliefs about yourself, your money, and your life. You have woken up from the dream that more is better and defined what is enough for you. You have become accountable with your life energy, tracking and evaluating the flow of money into and out of your life. You have developed an internal yardstick for fulfillment, liberating yourself from the sway of advertising and peer pressure. You have explored your values and personal purpose, and have increasingly oriented your life around what really matters to you. Your life is yours to create.

Crossover Point Jitters

Such passages, though, can be unnerving.

One day I got a call from an enthusiastic, creative man who'd kept us abreast of his journey to FI for years.

"I'm there. I'm FI."

"Congratulations!" I said and went on effusively about his achievement.

"You don't get it! I'm terrified. What am I going to do with all this freedom?"

If this creative man was terrified, what about others? In fact, we discovered many hit a strange wall of angst just before they "crossed over." No, not dying, but for some, crossing over into freedom can feel that way.

Joe Dominguez quelled those possible post-FI jitters

by spending his weekends doing what he imagined he'd do full-time once he was free. He knew he wanted to travel the country in a motor home after he retired, so he spent his wealth-accumulation years designing his camper and going out to a state park in New Jersey on the weekends. By the time he crossed over, Joe was ready to use his free time well.

Now that the FIRE movement is raging, we know more about how to adjust to "all that freedom"—whatever your age. Here's some advice culled from the blogs and discussion boards, as well as our own correspondence.

At first you may be jumpy. Or bored. Or you may be like a hyperactive kid in a candy store, wanting to gobble experiences. You'll get over it. You'll settle into a routine run not by a clock but by what makes you tick inside.

Whatever carrots you dangled in front of yourself to keep going—you'll start eating them. Travel. Sleep. A week at the beach. Political activism.

Many find that personal or physical issues they'd put on the back burner flare up. These problems have waited in line a long time for your attention. They don't mean you made a mistake; they mean you are getting in shape—body and soul. Whether you are thirty, forty, fifty, or older, your body will likely need attention, and that can be an adventure all its own.

You may learn to play a musical instrument, paint, sing in a choir, tap-dance, or fish; join an ultimate Frisbee team; get hooked on community theater; go conference hopping; get lost in multiplayer online fantasy games; get in better shape than you've ever been; meditate; or serve meals on wheels.

You might even tinker in your shop or at your computer and come up with some amazing solution to a gnarly problem—and spread it, giving you more influence than you ever imagined possible.

Nonprofit organizations will offer you seats on their boards. You'll have a chance to ask, "How many boards or committees are enough?"

FIers have done all of these and more.

And if you're like such FIers, you will find you have no idea how you had time for a job. Breaking the link between work and money in actual fact will exponentially expand the possibility of discovering your true work, of reintegrating the disparate pieces of your life, and of being truly whole. Your days will be brimming, even those days you just putter, tidy, cook, or wander. One activity folds into another without pressure (unless you like pressure!). Nothing is trivial because you put your full attention on it, from meditating to folding laundry to making an important speech to a packed auditorium. It's what economist Juliet Schor calls "plenitude."

You will be free to work for fun, for giving back, for inspiration or aspiration or self-transformation or . . . whatever you choose.

Choice is the true heart of Financial Independence. It's not about the money. It's about the choice of where you direct your most precious resources: your time, your attention and your life.

There is no formula for how you live after the Crossover Point. And that's the point. You are free to invent your life. You are free to explore what Buckminster Fuller meant when he said, "We are called to be architects of the future, not its victims."

SUMMARY OF STEP 8

Each month apply the following equation to your total accumulated capital and post the monthly investment income as a separate line on your Wall Chart:

$$\frac{\text{capital} \times \text{current long-term interest rate}}{12 \text{ months}} = \text{monthly investment income}$$

When you begin investing your money according to the guidelines offered in the next chapter, start entering your actual interest income for your monthly investment income on your Wall Chart (while still applying the formula to your additional savings). After trends become clear, project that line to the Crossover Point; you will then have an estimate of how much time you will have to work before reaching Financial Independence.

MONEY TALK QUESTIONS

Get inspired by hearing others' thoughts and stories. Freeing ourselves isn't the same as going it alone. Others can accelerate our path to all four FIs: Intelligence, Integrity, Independence, and Interdependence.

Using the suggestions in the epilogue for how to have a Money Talk, raise these questions in your daily reflections, with your partner, or in social groups. Remember, adding "Why?" to the end of any question will take it deeper. Adding "How has society shaped my answer?" to any question will take it wider. There are no right answers.

- What ideas—practical to wild—do you have about how you'd pay off all your debt?
- What do you want your legacy to be?
- If you didn't have to work for a living, what would you do with your time?
- If you could take a year off work, how would you spend it?
- What skills or social networks could you build now to depend less on money to meet your needs?

9

Where to Stash Your Cash for Long-Term Financial Freedom

Step 9: Investing for FI

This step will help you become knowledgeable and sophisticated about income-producing investments that can provide a consistent income sufficient for your needs over the long term.

This is the chapter about where to stash your cash as you approach—and go beyond—the Crossover Point for your FI3 (Financial Independence) years. If you got here before reading the rest of the book, expecting some hot new investment scheme, please go back to page 1. This chapter is for those of you who've accumulated sufficient money—through jobs, running your own business, inheritance, or even successful investing—that you are able and eager to free up your time for what matters more than making more money.

EMPOWER YOURSELF

One of our primary missions in this book is empowerment—allowing you to take back the power that you have inadvertently given over to money. In the previous chapter, we made it clear that your capital produces monthly investment income and in doing so effectively frees you from working for a dying. Knowing that money can work for you, this chapter focuses on common investment options that FIers around the world use to maintain wealth, generate "and then some" money, and enrich the communities in which they live.

An investment is simply somewhere you put your money hoping to make more money. FIers typically turn to one or more of these:

You can invest conservatively in bonds (essentially loans to institutions with a guarantee of repayment with interest) or revolving loan funds, which put your money to work in your region or in developing countries.

You can invest within your IRA, 401(k), or brokerage account in a wide range of mutual funds or exchange-traded funds (ETFs) that are bundles of stocks or bonds, picked by a manager or by an algorithm.

You can invest in real estate—both to live in and rent out.

You can invest in businesses—through becoming a partner or lending.

There are plenty of ways beyond these to invest, but they are either riskier, require more day-to-day attention, or are dubious ethically. Day traders can make (and lose) lots of money, but by definition, that's how they spend their days. Financial products like derivatives— bundles of subprime mortgages, for example—promised great returns . . . until they nearly brought the US economy down. You are free to invest your capital any way you want. This chapter simply offers some guidance about investment opportunities that fit the *Your Money or Your Life* FI model.

"Investing" does not mean readopting the "more is better" mentality and learning how to "make a killing" with your capital. Having followed the steps of this program, you know how much is enough for you, and the purpose of your investment program will be to assure you that you will have that amount—and then some—for the rest of your life.

This is about becoming knowledgeable and sophisticated about investment instruments that can provide sufficient income over time to assure that your basics are covered. Becoming knowledgeable and sophisticated means learning enough to free yourself from the fear and confusion that pervade the realm of personal investments—from your uncle Mervin's hot tips to the barrage of bad advice that comes through all your devices.

Nothing in this section is to be construed as specific investment advice, but is simply to highlight common ways to store wealth for the long run. The information here, like that in the rest of this book, is based on personal experience and popular FI community strategies, and is intended as guidelines, principles, and educational information.

A Brief Glossary

You will not learn anything about playing the market in this chapter, just some guiding principles for FIers to help you make informed, conservative choices. Here's a glossary of a few common terms you'll want to understand:

Risk Tolerance

How much *risk* (of losing money) can you tolerate before your investments cost you sleep, leaving you awake at night worrying about whether losses will send you back to work to rebuild wealth? The spectrum ranges from conservative investors who do not want to risk their capital at all to aggressive ones who are willing to risk all their capital for the promise of significant returns. FIers will inherently avoid the latter choice. Before the Crossover Point, some of you may risk more for greater returns, others not. After the Crossover Point, you want to maximize passive income while minimizing risk so you can pay the least attention possible to your money. Your risk tolerance may have to do with your age, your personality, how marketable your skills are, life experiences—yours and those of the people who raised you—and your attitudes toward money and credit in general. There are great online tools to help you determine your risk tolerance.

Asset Classes and Diversification

The standard types of assets are: stocks, fixed income (bonds), real estate, commodities (minerals, fossil fuels, crops), and foreign currencies. Often when one asset class is going up, another is going down, so diversifying across asset classes is one way people manage risk. FIers often diversify across asset classes through investing in a range of funds: bonds, stocks, gold, and so on. In recent years, new asset classes have emerged, including peer-to-peer lending, loan funds, equity crowdfunding in companies, and green-energy-related opportunities.

Income

There are five ways you can earn investment income:

1. *Interest* refers to periodic payments from fixed income investments such as bonds, notes, CDs, or savings accounts.
2. *Dividends* are a share of profits paid out to owners of stocks, mutual funds, ETFs, or private corporations.
3. *Capital gains* are the proceeds from the sale of investments or real estate beyond the amount originally invested. (Capital losses happen when proceeds from a sale are less than the amount originally invested, reducing your passive income.)

4. *Rents* are from owned real estate (minus expenses like taxes, insurance, mortgage, repairs, etc.).
5. *Royalties* are payments to owners of intellectual property, natural resources, franchises, and so on, by their users.

Time

What's your *time horizon*—do you have twenty more years to make mistakes and recover, or are you already retired and needing your money to last longer than your life?

Conventional wisdom (CW) suggests that when you are young, you should risk more for greater wealth accumulation; as you age, you shift to a focus on preservation of capital for a stable income. According to CW, a young person with decades until retirement should invest 90 percent stocks and 10 percent bonds because he or she can withstand booms and busts and still come out ahead. More conservative investors or those simply trying to stabilize their wealth, such as soon-to-be retirees, may opt for 20 percent stocks and 80 percent bonds. As always, though, FIers tend to be more conservative than conventional wisdom would suggest, because they are aiming to retire much earlier and retain a high confidence that they'll stay above the Crossover Point even during market declines.

Fees

The more middle-people involved in your buying and selling of investments—and the more you buy and sell—the more transaction and management costs can add up and rob you of anticipated gains. Actively managed mutual funds need to pay their managers, who presumably (but don't, on average) do a better job at picking stocks than throwing darts. Fee-only financial advisers can skim a percentage off your whole portfolio to pay for their services, or simply charge per hour for advice. Index funds have become a favorite of FIers because of low fees and—recently but not always—good performance.

Financial Advisers

Investing does not have to be a DIY mountain—unless you want it to be. You can hire an adviser to help, or even use one of the online services or brokerage houses where they survey your goals, risk tolerance, values, and so on, and put together a portfolio for you. Be sure you aren't being corralled by unscrupulous brokers into buying products that pay them handsome commissions. Fee-only advisers work only for you—and add value for many of us by doing nitty-gritty work we may not feel qualified or inclined to do, including monitoring performance, rebalancing holdings as market conditions change, and bigger-picture financial planning. Be sure to shop around!

Socially Responsible Investing

Are some of your values so important to you that investing in funds that include companies whose policies or products you abhor would cost you sleep? You're not alone, but fortunately, there's a growing sector of investment offerings that screen out companies with objectionable (to some) practices like pollution, weapons manufacturing, or gender bias, to name a few. Over time, socially responsible investments have generally matched or beaten the performance of unscreened investments.[1] However, it typically costs slightly more in fees to tack on this extra layer of social and environmental research. A good FI response to this could be to examine the fee differential and ask yourself if, over the years, it will be worth paying the difference to support, and be supported by, investments that have all passed social, environmental, and governance checks.

My own advisers at Natural Investments have kindly provided a brief explanation of socially responsible investing (SRI):

> Because aligning money with values is a core of the FI program, (SRI) deserves serious consideration by FIers. None of us can escape the ethical implications of our financial choices—in earning, spending, saving, and investing. In the world of finance, nothing is squeaky clean and fully laundered, but we can do our best to have our investments do the least harm and most good.
>
> In the nearly fifty years since its humble beginnings during the Vietnam War, when investors recoiled at their money supporting the war machine, SRI has become a $23 trillion industry globally. In the United States, 22 percent of all professionally managed money is in SRI.
>
> To put it simply, SRI seeks to:
>
> • Avoid negative impacts
> • Seek positive impacts
> • Influence the policies of the companies you've invested in
>
> How? SRI uses research into social and environmental impacts to avoid investments with objectionable or irresponsible policies and practices and to seek those that generate positive change for communities, society, and the environment. SRI also practices shareholder activism, which aims to hold companies accountable and improve corporate behavior, and incorporates community investing to foster local economies and the expansion of economic opportunities in the developing world.
>
> Today, a wide array of environmental, social, and governance (ESG) factors are assessed by SRI and conventional money managers. The financial world

increasingly recognizes that environmental and resource-related concerns can be risks to the corporate bottom line. Pragmatism, not virtue, is driving some investors toward greener industries for a better long-term return. For example, some corporate investments in coal and oil may never be recovered through future profits, and investors have serious questions about the viability of fossil-fuel companies over the coming decades. While society may be dragging its feet on the climate debate, insurance companies and the military have already incorporated climate change into their projections.

SRI does not mean sacrifice of returns, though it still holds this reputation stemming from its early days. From the early 1990s on, returns of SRI and ESG investments have matched or exceeded those of traditional, unscreened investing. In addition, SRI investors reap social, environmental, and what could be called conscience returns. In a time of great uncertainty about climate and political stability, many people feel powerless. SRI is one way they find to put their hands on the wheel of the future.

This glossary is meant to be informative but not definitive or exhaustive. In the original version of this book it was not needed since Joe had developed a set of criteria for FIers and one sort of investment that fit the bill.

TREASURY BONDS: JOE'S PLAN

When Joe Dominguez retired just past his thirty-first birthday, in 1969, there were fairly sturdy "set it and forget it" passive-income opportunities through both pensions and investing in US Treasury and agency bonds to ensure maximum safety of capital and stability of monthly investment income. Interest rates on these bonds were above 6.5 percent and inflation was below

3 percent—meaning a healthy annual profit for any investor. The next 30 years were the halcyon days of high interest rates, which spiked to nearly 15 percent during the recession of 1981 and floated back down to 6.5 percent in 1997, the year Joe died. The strategy he designed for himself in the 1960s and stood behind until he died took advantage of this rare opportunity.

The chart in Figure 9-1,[2] developed by J. P. Livingston, founder of the website the Money Habit, is eloquent in illustrating why Joe chose and recommended Treasury bonds.

When Joe began teaching in 1980, he naturally recommended US Treasury bonds as the place to stash your cash. Tens of thousands of us did just that and have remained FI ever since. Mike Lenich, whom we met earlier, in chapter 5, is one of them; he's done the program faithfully and to the letter since 1992.

Readers since the turn of the millennium have sometimes looked at Joe's investment strategy with a

FIGURE 9-1

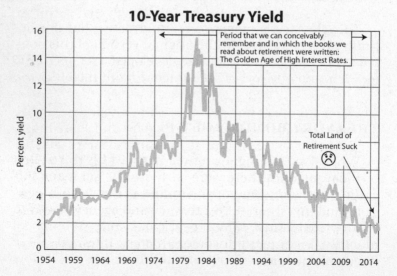

10-Year Treasury Yield

combination of envy and disdain. Envy for those rates of return; disdain for slowpokes who invest in bonds when the stock market offers such juicy alternatives for wealth creation. "Oh, that's the book about investing in Treasury bonds," they'd say dismissively. In fact, it has never been. It's been about considering options, given your current circumstances, for having a safe, steady income throughout your life, apart from what you do with your time. For Joe, T-bonds fit that to a T.

Joe set criteria for himself when it came time to stash his cash in 1969. He'd amassed $75,000, which would be $225,000 in today's dollars. With an average of 8 percent on his money, that provided just under $20,000 a year in today's dollars. Given his lifestyle, that was plenty. At today's interest rates, he would have needed four times that amount (close to that magic number of $1 million) to supply his frugal FI income.

Even though Joe's strategy might no longer be applicable, it's still worth learning about for what it says about good principles of FI investing. His criteria were these:

- Greatest safety of capital
- Greatest safety of interest ("full faith and credit of the US government" guarantees protection of principal and interest)
- Exemption from state and local taxes
- Noncallability (most Treasury bonds can't be redeemed early by the issuer)
- Greatest negotiability, absolute liquidity, global marketability—they can be bought and sold almost instantly, with minimal handling charges and in convenient denominations (such as $1,000, $5,000, and $10,000)
- Easiest availability—directly from the federal government (TreasuryDirect) and through most brokers and many banks anywhere in the world
- Cheapest availability—no middlemen, no commissions, no loads

- ◆ Duration—the range of maturities available is extensive; you can buy a note or bond that will mature in a few months or one that won't come due for thirty years.
- ◆ Absolute stability of income over the long run—ideal for FI; avoids the income fluctuations that would occur with money market funds, renting out real estate, etc.

Primer on Treasury Bonds

A bond is simply an IOU. The bond issuer promises to pay back to the holder of the bond the amount printed on the bond (face value) by a certain date (maturity date). Most bonds also pay interest at a specific percentage rate (coupon rate). This amount, though quoted as an annual percentage rate, is usually paid in two semi-annual installments.

Treasury bonds are the government's way of borrowing money. A new bond is issued for purchase every few months, with maturity dates ten, twenty, and thirty years into the future. The first thing that each new issue does is pay off the holders of old issues coming due. The remaining monies are used to make up the deficit in the federal budget. The national debt is the most senior obligation the government has; principal and interest on Treasury securities must be paid when they come due, before paying for anything else. Not to do so would destroy the "credit rating" of the US government in world markets.

Back when Joe and I invested, the world was sufficiently nervous about the ability of the US to repay, meaning our government had to pay a high interest rate to attract the loans it needed to stay afloat. Ergo, those amazing opportunities for FIers. Thirty-year Treasury bonds were a golden opportunity for a "set it and forget it" FI strategy.

Bond prices fluctuate with prevailing interest rates. Therefore, if you sell a bond before maturity, you may get more or less than you paid for it (market risk). If you hold it until maturity, you will receive exactly its face value, regardless of the interest rates prevailing at that time.

Treasury bonds, when they are newly issued, can be bought directly from the Federal Reserve, with no commissions whatsoever, through a program called TreasuryDirect. This cuts out the middleman: no broker, no added brokerage house fees. You can also buy existing Treasury bonds through a broker (for a minimal fee).

The other way for an individual to buy treasuries (any issue, not just the most recent one) is through the "secondary market" from a willing seller. You might pay more—or less—than the face value, given prevailing interest rates. You might also pay a minimal fee or commission upon purchase. Some people prefer to buy bonds on the secondary market instead of directly from the US government because they prefer to trade with a "real person" who owns the bond rather than financing the US debt.

While interest rates on US Treasury bills, bonds, and notes fell to a low point of under 2 percent in 2012 and are still very low, there is no telling whether or when this tide will turn and you will return to this section. If you like the low risk of bonds but don't want to bet on just one, you can buy bond funds, which will be described later.

Joe did not recommend corporate bonds, but some FIers may find them attractive if they are trying to eke out a bit more interest. Like US Treasury and agency bonds, they are debt instruments, interest is paid quarterly or biannually, and at maturity you get your principal back. Like government bonds, they have a credit rating from Standard & Poor's or Moody's or one of the other rating agencies. Look for BBB or better.

SRI investors who still want to benefit from the safety of the "full faith and credit" of the US government may want to look to US agency bonds instead of Treasury bonds. Agency bonds support a specific sector you might care about (farmers, students, homeowners, small businesses), while Treasury bonds fund the overall priorities of the federal budget, heavy with military and debt-repayment obligations.

A Caveat

Joe always tried to give novices the minimum information needed to invest with assurance. But with his advice he always delivered a warning: Nothing is certain. Nothing. That's life. If you don't like it, you're out of luck. If someone tells you he or she has a foolproof method for making money effortlessly and you follow it, Joe would have said that you are the fool. Here's a cautionary tale:

In the old days, when Joe taught only interested friends his FI approach, he would give them a gift when they reached FI3. He'd give them a bond. A yellowing Russian czarist bond. Before there were online brokerage accounts or registered bonds, bonds had coupons that you actually clipped and brought to the bank to get your semiannual interest. The coupons on Joe's gift bonds were clipped all the way until 1917—when the Russian Revolution rendered them worthless. Fifty years later, Joe bought a box of these bonds for a penny or so apiece—thinking at the time they'd make amusing wallpaper. Giving them to newly minted FIers was his reminder that no investment you make guarantees that geopolitical or economic conditions will not shift or protects you from finding that the nest egg you thought would give you a comfortable income for life . . . won't. Buyer—of investments—beware.

LOW-COST INDEX FUNDS: THE FIRE PLAN

If not Treasury bonds, then what? The majority of FIRE bloggers rely on and recommend investing in some form of index fund. John Bogle, who founded investment management company Vanguard in 1975, struck on a revolutionary principle that made investing accessible and simple: returning net profits to its shareholders in the form of lower costs. By eliminating sales commissions and minimizing operating expenses, Vanguard opened the door to the "little guy" and to other companies like Fidelity and Schwab. For FI investors who have learned when enough is enough, particularly in terms of their money, index funds are as close to "set it and forget it" as you can get outside of bonds.

Legendary investor Warren Buffett said, "A low-cost fund is the most sensible equity investment for the great majority of investors." He explains, "By periodically investing in an index fund, for example, the know-nothing investor can actually outperform most investment professionals."[3]

Index funds are mutual funds or exchange-traded funds (ETFs) designed to track the performance of stock market indices (such as the Dow Jones Industrial, the NASDAQ Composite, and the S&P 500) or bond market indices. In using index funds to invest your capital, you are not trying to beat the market. There is no attempt to use traditional "active" money management or to make "bets" on individual stocks. Indexing is a passive investment approach emphasizing broad diversification and low portfolio trading activity. Instead you are looking for enough of a return to meet your short-term as well as long-term goals while taking as little risk as possible. This is why index funds, with their low fees and potential for diversification, can work well for the FI investment program.

However, unlike bonds, stock index funds are invested in a pool of stocks that do fluctuate with the market. Millennial FIRE fans use stock index funds like boomers used banks, keeping a little liquid cash on hand and investing the rest in these funds. People who've lived through boom-and-bust cycles may cringe at the idea of treating a stock market product (inherently risky) like a bank (inherently safe), but for young people who've only seen the Dow go up and up, not investing in index funds seems dumb, considering the upside rewards and the tax advantage when it's done inside an IRA or 401(k). However, remember Joe's "buyer beware" warning: Over the past ninety years, the stock market has taken five big hits (32 to 86 percent drops) with recovery times afterward ranging from four to twenty-seven years. At the risk of finger wagging, here's some data:

◆ Great Depression: Down 86 percent, 27 years to recover
◆ Mid 1970s: Down 46 percent, almost a decade to recover
◆ Late 1987: Down 32 percent in just 3 months, 4 years to recover
◆ Great Recession, 2007–09: Down 50 percent, 6 years to recover (or 14 years if you count from the matching dot-com peak in 1999, which had just been regained in 2007)

The two events within the lifetime of young investors, the dot-com crash and the 2007–09 crisis, were exceptions in that they took less than a decade to recover—but that doesn't mean the cyclical nature of the market has been suspended. By contrast, bond funds are far less volatile, losing only a few percentage points when they falter.

The Index Fund Philosophy

Bogleheads—as followers of John Bogle call themselves—believe they can successfully manage risk and achieve greater returns than the average investor, many of whom are trying to time the market or make it big on the next hot tech stock. Their advice boils down to the following philosophy: Invest in low-fee index funds diversified over a few asset classes and hold them for many years.

So how do people ensure the funds are low-fee? Index funds by their very nature are passively managed, as opposed to more expensive actively managed investments. With index funds, there's no picking and choosing. For managed funds, like mutual funds, a manager picks the investments, trying to outperform the market index. Because there is less administrative management for index funds, fees are lower and more attractive to investors. These fees, or expense ratios, are charged as a percentage of your wealth. (Note that there are SRI options in the index fund realm as well; the fees [0.22 to 0.50 percent] are much lower than those of mutual funds, but higher than non-SRI index funds.)

The last element you should consider is diversifying your index funds across asset classes. While many index funds are low-cost and simple, investors still have a few choices to make. For example, there are stocks and bonds, domestic and international, large, medium, and small capital funds, and any combination of the above. It can be a US bond index fund or international stock index fund. These combinations allow you to expose yourself to various parts of the world market and reduce your overall risk.

Take Every Advantage of Company Plans

For those in their earning years, many employer retirement plans or individual IRAs will offer low-cost index funds. If your employer offers a retirement plan, review your options for passively managed, low-cost index funds. Always be sure to get the full employer match if you can—it's worth it. By contributing to retirement accounts during your working years, recall that you're reducing your overall taxes while saving for your future. If you don't have an employer plan, you can still invest in an IRA through a brokerage house. This is similar to opening a checking or savings account, but with the potential for long-term growth. As you'll soon find out, following the aforementioned advice will narrow your fund choices down to only a few options. If this is starting to sound boring, then you're doing it right. Long-term investing is not a get-rich-quick scheme or something to micromanage.

Companies like Vanguard pioneered the way with simple, no-strings-attached investing. What was once more expensive and convoluted is now accessible to anyone. Nevertheless, there are now many other companies to choose from. The most important thing is understanding that no one—and we mean no one—can time the market or predict the future. Understand your risk tolerance and diversify into stocks, bonds, and domestic and international index funds to reduce your overall risk. Since landing the perfect mix of asset classes is impossible, the most important thing is reducing exposure to one single government or company. Review the expense ratios, or fee, of each fund. As with most long-term investments, stay the course and tune out twenty-four-hour financial media. The only days you care about an investment's value are the day you buy it and the day you sell it.

Do People Really Do This?

Many popular FI luminaries have rocketed to the forefront of mainstream media with flashy headlines: WANT TO RETIRE EARLY? HOW ABOUT YOUR EARLY 30s? and SAVING 50% OF YOUR INCOME WILL LEAD TO EARLY RETIREMENT. It's no surprise these links get so many clicks. But when you dig right down, you find that many people popularizing the FI movement are following some form of the strategy we've outlined.

J. L. Collins, author of *The Simple Path to Wealth*, writes about this financial approach in a series of letters to his daughter. Through those conversations he is smacked with the reality that people like money, but they also like it simple. He boils his fatherly advice down to short

bullet points, including sensible policies like "Avoid fis-
cally irresponsible people" and "Save a portion of every
dollar you get." More pointedly, he advises her to spend
far less than she makes and invest the remainder in Vanguard's Total Stock Market Index Fund (VTSAX)—one
account, one fund. Can it really be that easy?

Possibly the biggest star in the FI-blogger heavens—
and the author of the foreword to this book—is Mr. Money
Mustache. He has touted his relationship with index
funds for years, even calling individual stocks a "sucker's
bet." On his blog he advises his readers to spend ten to
fifteen years working and living the good life off less than
50 percent of their income while also shoveling money
into index funds and long-term, low-cost investments.
Contrary to most, he thinks of market crashes as a blow-
out sale on stocks. While acknowledging real estate and
other income sources, he encourages readers to continue
making money work for them through index funds.

The Minimalists, Joshua Fields Millburn and Ryan
Nicodemus, are bloggers and authors of a popular book
Minimalism: Live a Meaningful Life. They walk the walk
when it comes to simple investing. They document their
financial tool of choice as, you guessed it, index funds—
flexible, low-cost, and reliable. They highlight huge savings in switching to low-cost money-management
brokers such as Vanguard and Betterment, another
investment-management firm offering strong competition to the world of simple investing in the form of auto-
mated investing.

And finally, Mr. and Mrs. Frugalwoods identify their
"low cost, no fuss money management system" as investing excess cash in index funds. Hmmm, sure sounds
familiar! In a post describing their strategy, they hit the
nail on the head with this one: "Our culture has a shroud
of mystery surrounding investing, which is completely
uncalled for. There's no need to pay someone to 'manage' your investments, because—get this—low-fee index
funds often outperform managed funds."[4]

If there are a few simple rules to remember from the Bogleheads, it's the following:

* Pay off debt and avoid it in the future.
* Live below your means by spending less than you earn.
* Invest the rest in low-cost index funds.
* Hold on to funds for many years.

Puzzling through these options, through the risks and rewards of different paths, **Tammy I.** *decided to split her investment portfolio using the "enough and then some" description of the nest egg you have at Crossover. She invests the bulk of her money in Treasury bonds so she knows that no matter what the world throws her way, she has enough income to cover her basics. But the "and then some" is her cache, which she invests in mutual and index funds much like the strategies we've outlined. More risk, but potentially more reward . . . and more cache. Should she lose it all, she's still FI, and she can slowly, over time, build her cache back up.*

REAL ESTATE

The next strategy we'll explore is investing in real estate. After putting down roots in your favorite community, purchasing an income-producing asset such as a duplex or quad can be an excellent FI plan. Not only do you manage property for people in your community, but tenants pay your mortgage and provide a steady stream of income for years.

Scott Trench, author of *Set for Life*, is a real estate adviser, broker, and blogger. He says, "Folks all over the country are learning that if they can buy a home, they can buy an investment property. Often, small duplexes, triplexes, and quads can be had for right around the same purchase price as a single-family home. At four units or less, folks with solid credit and income can use

FHA or low down payment (as low as 3.5 percent) to purchase income-producing property, so long as they live in that property for at least a year. The experience for many, including myself, can be phenomenal, as those that do their homework and learn the basics of tenant management can select quiet, friendly neighbors that are financially well qualified to rent the property and have a strong credit score. It's just like living in a home, and yes, you complete the small maintenance issues that every single homeowner in the country is responsible for. The difference is that you are paid thousands of dollars from tenants to take care of your home."[5]

Here's his checklist for evaluating a multifamily building:

* Is the property in a location that you are comfortable with being a part of your life for the next few years, or indefinitely?
* Is the property in a location that you believe has good prospects? Is it likely to appreciate? Is the neighborhood likely to stay attractive and safe?
* What is the property expected to generate in terms of gross rent?
* What are the expected expenses? Common ones are repairs, utilities, any homeowners association fees, taxes, capex (capital expenses), those months between tenants when units are vacant, and any management fees if you don't choose to do it yourself. This adds up to needing a substantial kitty—in the tens of thousands—going into the purchase.

Unlike other investments, real estate ties up a lot of your wealth in one investment that is not very liquid; if you are in a hurry to sell to get your money out and the housing market is weak, you might lose. There's risk, but if you are willing to do the hard work yourself and have picked well, your rental properties can be a safe, steady income for life.

A caution: There's a subset of real estate investors who make money by "flipping" properties: buying fixer-uppers, fixing them up, and selling at a hefty profit. This may be a strategy for some FIers in their wealth accumulation phase, but it fails the test for an FI portfolio. There's too much work, too much risk, and, frankly, the possibility of displacing fixed-income, poor tenants who might not be able to afford to stay in their familiar neighborhood with its well-formed social networks.

Another kind of real estate investing is investing in your own home and land in ways that are integral to your FI vision. Investing in renewable energy for your home and in farmstead infrastructure (gardens, barns, coops, and pens) will pay dividends for decades. While their money may be in index funds, Mr. and Mrs. Frugalwoods, for example, are building a rural homestead:

Kent and Beth *were both highly paid professionals when they met. Part of their attraction to one another, though, wasn't a shared high life. Kent, a PhD who'd read the huge handwriting on the wall about climate change, was a green energy consultant for a city in the South. He'd banked on making his city a model of sustainability, but he became increasingly distressed when few of his ideas made it through the bureaucracy. Beth knew that her corporate job was part of the problem, and it troubled her. They'd saved enough to leave their jobs and run a small farm outside the city to get their feet dirty. Then a drought hit. The deepwater wells ran dry. The crops wilted. The climate modeling Kent had studied in grad school was suddenly very real. They decided to head west in a motor home to find a climate-safe(r) place to settle. After many months they finally found "it": an undervalued, run-down house being consumed by blackberry bushes on eight acres of lush forestland in the Pacific Northwest. A portion of the property line bordered on a main highway, so the whole property was zoned commercial. They decided to make homesteading and raising a family their full-time job—with a twist. Living in their motor home, they rescued the house* *from the blackberries. Then they renovated a ground-floor mother-in-law apartment, the rent from which pays their mortgage. Once the main floor was livable, they rented out their motor home. Then they fixed up an outbuilding for another rental. The income from that will go into a building closer to the highway for commercial use. They'll flatten their mortgage in six years rather than twenty or thirty and consider their fertile soil, plentiful water, and rentals their natural and enduring wealth. They had one child when they bought the property, another when they'd settled in. They believe with all their hearts that raising woods-wise, conscious children, providing affordable housing, liberating all their time for parenting and service, and networking locally to make their community a lifeboat are the best things they can do for their future—and the planet's.*

In another vein, real estate doesn't have to mean a place to live. It can, as George Carlin once said, be "a place for your stuff."

Todd T. *did his own version of real estate investing by purchasing a self-storage facility and having on-site and off-site managers run the project on a daily basis. Yes, of course, this is in part profiting from consumer excess—having more stuff than house to put it in. Irony aside, Todd and his family collect enough per month that they've been able to live and save enough to buy a second facility. He's chosen a life of community service, occupying roles of significant responsibility (the school board, for example). He is able to be bold in his service because he has that passive income to actively support his life.*

Real estate can also be part of a larger investment strategy.

Dorothy E. *and her husband,* **Larry D.***, whose story encompasses the full range of this program's values, "crossed over" in 1995 with $400,000 in assets. They had, on and off,* *up to three rental properties, leveraging the value of their house. They also rented out part of their main residence as a mother-in-law apartment. Beyond their stable real estate investments and income, they made a hobby with their "and then some" money of investing in individual companies as well as mutual funds.*

To become knowledgeable and sophisticated about equity investments, they educated themselves through NAIC (National Association of Investors Corporation) and helped found several different investment clubs over the years. These are the principles they follow: 1) invest a set amount regularly; 2) reinvest earnings, dividends, and profits; 3) invest in quality growth stocks and equity mutual funds; and 4) diversify your investments. Larry said, "Joining an investment club was a safe and fun way to educate ourselves about investing in individual stocks. The point of investment clubs is learning about investments, not getting rich. We took the insights and knowledge gained at club meetings and applied them to our own investments."

The next profit area was plugging the drain in their nest egg caused by taxes. Having learned the ins and outs of the tax code, Larry notes, "More than half of our investments are in tax-deferred vehicles [IRAs, 401(k)s, etc.] as a way to keep more of what we earn—and have earned. To that end, we keep a spreadsheet that forecasts our cash flow through the next ten years or more and that's when we can access the tax-deferred accounts without penalty. And if hard times hit before then, we still have access to our money if we're willing to accept the penalties."

Their final cache stream is pure *Your Money or Your Life*—they always live below their means. The upshot: They've tripled their nest egg. Larry has worked on volunteer projects that have sometimes produced income and Dorothy has chosen to work part-time at a job she enjoys, doing it not so much for money as for love.

MY CHOICES: MULTIPLE SOCIALLY RESPONSIBLE INCOME STREAMS

Luckily, I bought the majority of my bonds from 1981 through 1997. I had one bond with a coupon rate of 15 percent. My lowest rate was 8 percent. All but the last have matured (I hated to see them go); the thirty-year term was up and the US government returned my money for me to invest again—at 5 percent and under. Until the turn of the millennium, bonds were my only investments. Since then I've diversified—without compromising my values. Even if your values aren't exactly the same as mine, I hope my example will help you make your investments reflect your own.

For me to be happy and free, my investing has to align with my values. I have worked to end overconsumption in North America for thirty years, in light of what I know about the toxicity, pollution, and climate cost of our industrial growth economy. I'm not such a purist that I eschew making money on my money, but I try to invest with my values. I drive an electric car and invest in solar industries. I buy from local farm stands and invest in local farms. I work to build a more diverse local economy and I invest in local businesses. I see my community graying and want to reverse that trend, so I often will trade with younger people for partial rent in apartments I own. Where I put my money reflects who I am—as it will for you, whatever your choices. This is inescapable.

Real Estate

In 1986, Joe and I and some friends bought a sprawling house in Seattle for $137,000. For twenty years it housed our nonprofit, the New Road Map Foundation, and over a half-dozen people. I owned a portion of the house and by the time we sold it, I'd lived rent-free for twenty years—and tripled my money when we sold. This way of investing, while accidental (we needed a stable place to live in Seattle), impressed me. Had we rented, my portion over twenty years would have been, easily $75,000. Plus, I collected rent from other house-mates along the way. Plus, I had something tangible and tradable—a house with seven bedrooms. Plus, I provided a home to dozens of people over the years. Plus, I lived in a great part of the world. Plus, I had community, one of the pillars of wealth, where a lot of internal horse trad-ing went on—haircuts for health advice for tax help. For me this constitutes socially responsible investing!

After the sale I was able to buy a house in the com-munity where I live on Whidbey Island, a story worth telling.

With that Seattle house money sitting in the bank at 1 percent interest (at best), I considered whether buying more Treasury bonds was a good choice, given the 3 per-cent coupon rate at the time. Thinking about my Seattle house, I searched for an equivalent, perhaps a duplex where I could live in one side and rent the other. One snowy winter day when my village was at a standstill, I saw a reasonably priced house listed online just half a mile up the hill from the apartment I was renting. I trudged up in my Sorel boots to find a conventional "people box": a split-entry, light green three-bedroom house, looking quite large—and ugly. Circling around back I found a deck, climbed the stairs, and looked through a sliding glass door to a view of Mount Baker, the North Cascades, and the waters of Puget Sound. A view home in a village that often ranks among the top seaside towns—my mind started to whir! Still, I'd need to take on debt to buy it. I'd paid cash my whole life and wasn't eager to break my no-debt track record.

This place would need to be a site of production rather than a site of consumption. It needed to be a money source, not a money sink; to fill my coffers, not empty them. I thought of the possibilities. I could rent the ga-rage to a woodworker or to a boat or motor-home owner. I could rent the large family room with a bathroom on the ground floor to someone without losing privacy on the main floor. My mind, like a cash register, ka-chinged away, figuring out how I'd swing it, while I trudged back home. I was already mentally dickering, shaving $5000 at a time off the price of the house and rehearsing how I'd make my pitch to the real estate agent.

In short order, two things happened. First, I called an acquaintance who'd just taken a job on Whidbey to ask if she'd like to rent the family room. "Why don't I buy the house with you instead?" she responded. We each, it turned out, had enough cash from the sale of our prior homes to pay for half. Second, the bank decided the house had been on its books too long and dropped the price by $40,000, making it a bargain. The inspection revealed some maintenance problems, but it was still doable and we nabbed it.

Nine years later, my co-owner first converted the family room to a private apartment . . . and then, because she had to move back home to take care of her mother, I bought her out. I've converted the garage to another studio apartment. Each fetches a rent that is more than fair to both tenants and landlady. I have a big garden in the backyard that gets full southern sun, and I rent my guest room in the summer on Airbnb (living in a tourist town helps). By my calculations, I realize 8 percent annually on my investment, an excellent return in this era of low interest rates. In a pinch when I'm older, I might be able to turn the house into a bank, using it as collateral for a loan to cover replacing one or another body part. I also figure that a caregiver could live in one of those apartments for free as a partial trade for a couple of hours a day keeping me washed, dressed, and fed.

Social Security

Social Security is a third income stream. I began receiving my Social Security two years early, calculating that it would take twenty years for the wee bit more I would get by waiting to equal the amount I'd get for two years by starting. Would I last that long? Would Social Security? It was right after buying my current house and I was cash poor, so I chose to start. Unlike many boomers, I have no additional pensions from long-term employment with benefits. Luckily, also unlike many other boomers, I have a diversity of investments and am not relying on the meager check I get each month.

Local Lending

My fourth income stream income after bonds, real estate, and Social Security comes from local lending. "In community I trust" isn't just a philosophical accessory I wear; it's an ethic I live, and I've found a way to do it relatively safely.

In a neighboring community, a group of practical visionaries set up a unique network called LION (Local Investing Opportunities Network), which helped connect investors with local small businesses and nonprofits that had business opportunities but lacked cash. In this model, the network simply invites people with new or existing businesses to submit letters of interest, backed later by business plans, to a secretary who distributes these opportunities to members. Any interested member can meet the business owner, learn about his or her opportunity, and negotiate an investment for whatever amount on whatever terms. Since community and relationships are core to my wealth, I have my own little revolving local loan fund, through which I have put to date close to $80,000 in local businesses. I ask for 5 percent interest on all my loans, some of which I take in product—cat litter, vegetables, a chicken coop, eggs . . . the stuff rural life is made of. In almost all cases, my borrowers are grateful and become my friends. When they flourish, my community flourishes—important because rural communities have to have a flourishing economy to stay vital and prosperous.

Green Energy

When a local group jumped through many hoops to install a large bank of solar panels on our island, I jumped at the opportunity to buy into the LLC (limited liability corporation) they'd formed for the deal. With government incentive payments plus sale of the electricity, I am profiting in three ways: I'm supporting a solar installation on my island—an investment in an energy-self-sufficient future. I'm realizing 3 percent on my money with almost no risk. And our LLC hired a local company to install made-in-Washington panels—supporting local economic development.

My ability to find and invest in other green energy and socially responsible businesses has not been quite so simple. For this reason, I engaged a "fee-only" financial adviser who specializes in this area. Since I have little interest in actively managing my money, the small percentage he takes every year is more than worth it. If I paid myself for the hours I'd invest in researching socially responsible (or at least not socially noxious) investment opportunities, plus paying for the health toll for the stress (I'm quite risk averse), it could well exceed his fee.

My adviser is uniquely attuned to my investment philosophy. He was instrumental in developing the local investing strategy in a neighboring town that my community adopted. Also, his company, Natural Investments, has a road map for investing that matches my approach. With part of my money—what's come back to me from those deliciously high coupon bonds—I've decided to take more risk than normal to invest in companies he's identified that will sell shares to small investors; I own a stake in two solar companies and a coffee cooperative. For the rest, my money is in socially responsible stocks and bond funds. If you decide to hire a financial adviser, make sure he or she's not only high integrity but also has values that match yours.

Side Hustles

Like many FIers these days, I also make a bit of money from what are currently referred to as "side hustles," which are simply additional ways of bringing in income. There is no end to the creativity of these micro-jobs, from having an online store to selling products on eBay, from keeping a few consulting and coaching clients even after FI to walking dogs to staging houses to writing blogs to tutoring kids to being a tour guide in the summers to, as I do, occasionally keynoting a conference. While writing a book is an elephant of a side hustle, it also fits here because it's episodic, snugs into my diverse life activities, and could disappear without crashing my Financial Independence.

CHECKLIST OF THINGS TO CONSIDER WHEN INVESTING

1. Is this investment in line with my values?
2. Is this investment in line with my tolerance for risk?
3. Does this provide overall diversification for my investments?
4. Does this provide the current and future income I need?
5. How easily can I liquidate (sell out of) all or part of this investment?
6. What sales charges or penalties (if any) will I incur in getting into or out of this investment?
7. What are the federal, state, and local tax implications of this investment for me? (Is it tax efficient for my income bracket or situation?)

You will construct an FI portfolio that matches your ways of thinking and of living, your tolerance for risk, and your creativity in applying consciousness rather than money to meeting your needs. It's truly up to you.

In Conclusion

You are well on your way to taking back the power you have given over to money—and to money "experts." You are ready to become a conscientious, loving, and knowledgeable steward of your life energy. Our greatest hope is that you will apply these steps to your own finances and apply your life energy to the challenges that face our species and our planet. We wish you great success.

SUMMARY OF STEP 9

Become knowledgeable and sophisticated about long-term income-producing investments and manage your finances for a consistent income sufficient for your needs over the long term.

MONEY TALK QUESTIONS

Watch out for relinquishing your power by taking advice from others. Filter everything through your own values and research. At the same time, we learn so much by hearing how others develop multiple income streams from a range of investments.

Using the suggestions in the epilogue for how to have a Money Talk, raise these questions in your daily reflections, with your partner, or in social groups. Remember, adding "Why?" to the end of any question will take it deeper. Adding "How has society shaped my answer?" to any question will take it wider. There are no right answers.

- What are you putting in place now to keep you afloat as you age?
- In a pinch, what could you do to make extra money?
- Whom or what would you trust to help you invest your money?

- What's been your experience to date with investing? What are your hopes?
- What values and beliefs do you bring to investing?
- What is your risk tolerance—in money *and* life?
- What does Financial Independence mean to you?

Quick Reference
for the 9-Step Program

There are no shorter shortcuts. This entire book, with all nine steps, *is* the shortcut. The steps are summarized here for review, reference, and reminders. This is a whole-systems approach; conscientiously applying all the steps automatically makes your personal finances an integrated whole. These are also very basic, fundamental practices for any business—and you are a business. You are in the business of maximizing the return you get in happiness for every hour of life energy spent.

Step 1: Making Peace with the Past

A. How much have you earned in your life? Find out your total lifetime earnings—the sum total of your gross income, from the first penny you ever earned to your most recent paycheck.

B. What have you got to show for it? Find out your net worth by creating a personal balance sheet of assets and liabilities—everything you own and everything you owe.

Step 2: Being in the Present—Tracking Your Life Energy

A. How much are you trading your life energy for? Establish the actual costs in time and money required to maintain your job, and compute your real hourly wage.

B. Keep track of every cent that comes into or goes out of your life.

Step 3: Where Is It All Going? (The Monthly Tabulation)

- Every month, total all expenses within categories generated by your own unique spending pattern. Then total income.
- Convert dollars spent in each category to "hours of life energy," using your real hourly wage as computed in step 2.

Step 4: Three Questions That Will Transform Your Life

On your Monthly Tabulation, ask these three questions of each of your category totals expressed as hours of life energy and record your responses:

1. Did I receive fulfillment, satisfaction, and value in proportion to life energy spent?
2. Is this expenditure of life energy in alignment with my values and life purpose?
3. How might this expenditure change if I didn't have to work for money? For each question in each category, evaluate whether the expense should increase, decrease, or stay the same for your optimal fulfillment. This is the heart of the program.

Step 5: Making Life Energy Visible

Create a large Wall (or Online) Chart plotting the total monthly income and total monthly expenses from your Monthly Tabulation. Put it where you will see it every day.

Step 6: Valuing Your Life Energy—Minimizing Spending

Learn and practice intelligent use of your life energy (money), which will result in lowering your expenses and increasing your savings. This will create greater fulfillment, integrity, and alignment in your life.

Step 7: Valuing Your Life Energy—Maximizing Income

Respect the life energy you are putting into your job. Money is simply something you trade your life energy for. Trade it with purpose and integrity for increased earnings.

Step 8: Capital and the Crossover Point

Each month apply the following equation to your total accumulated capital, and post the monthly independence income as a separate line on your Wall Chart:

$$\frac{\text{capital} \times \text{current long-term interest rate}}{12 \text{ months}} = \text{monthly investment income}$$

Step 9: Investing for FI

This step will help you become knowledgeable and sophisticated about income-producing investments that can provide a consistent income sufficient for your needs over the long term.

Set up your financial plan using the three pillars:
- ◆ Capital: The income-producing core of your Financial Independence
- ◆ Cushion: Enough ready cash, earning bank interest, to cover six months of expenses
- ◆ Cache: The surplus of funds resulting from your continued practice of the nine steps

For additional resources,

visit yourmoneyoryourlife.com.

Often.

Epilogue: Money Talks

"Money talks!" This phrase, as far back as Euripides, has eloquently expressed the power of money to get things done—in business, politics, commerce, and even romance. Unfortunately, once money talks, the conversation usually ends. Money "closes the deal," conversationally speaking, and we shut up. We live in a money-soaked culture, yet talking about our personal finances is often taboo. It's time to do something about that.

The purpose of these Money Talks is to break the silence about our relationship with money and open up a new conversation. When was the last time you openly discussed your debt? Or your income? If you're like most of us, playing the game by yourself, you're sifting through books, news stories, and advice columns and ping-ponging between methods—alternately trying to save or spend or speculate our way to happiness.

In Money Talks we daylight our assumptions, fears, crazy strategies, regrets, and lies through conversations in a spirit of "no shame, no blame." Don't you want to know what goes on in other people's minds about money? Wouldn't you like to hear about their stupidest mistakes and smartest strategies so you can break out of your rut and get sane about money? Wouldn't you like a safe way to swap stories about and ponder the mysteries of money, work, jobs, income, saving, investing, giving, and hoarding?

> *"Like many [young] people,"* **Donita S.** *says, "I was stuck in a typical nine-to-five job that wasn't right for me. I wanted to feel like I was making a difference, but sitting behind a computer for eight hours wasn't cutting it—I craved something more. Around this time a friend introduced me to a simplicity community group. I found it to be a safe place where people shared their desires, fears, values, and life goals. We discussed current events relating to finance, technology, sustainability, and mindfulness, just to name a few. I became more and more inspired to live a life of meaning, purpose, and adventure. Finally, one day, it hit me: My life wasn't going to change if I didn't take action. I had always dreamed of traveling but told myself every excuse in the book. [Soon] I quit my job and booked a plane ticket to the other side of the world, solo with a single backpack."*

Money Talks are deceptively simple, yet they can change your life. A few guidelines, a potent topic or question, a process that lets everyone have a turn. While it may seem scary-exciting to open up with others the can of worms that is our relationship with money, years of experience using such a simple method lets me guarantee with confidence that you will feel:

- Relieved
- Empowered
- More at ease with your choices
- Motivated to continue transforming your relationship with money

In Money Talks there are no experts because it's not about fixing ourselves, it's about understanding ourselves as people caught in a consumerist money culture that may feed our greed but not our real needs for being connected, respected, and protected. Discussing your relationship with money in this manner is different from talking with a financial adviser about investing or a debt-payoff plan. Our relationship with money has to do with the thoughts, feelings, attitudes, beliefs, and life experiences we've woven into a unique, personal tapestry. Solving some of your money problems might be a by-product, but it's not the purpose. Money Talks are designed to surface those surprising discoveries that come unbidden in open, inquisitive conversations.

Rules for Money Talks

Try an experiment: Ask someone to swap stories with you about one thing you've each bought in the past six months that you didn't really need. Everyone has those, guaranteed. It's a money-related question, but it isn't too personal, so it's a good way to put a toe in the water.

When I first did this in a workshop, I was stunned. No one wanted to stop their dyads to listen to me again. I could have left the room for the duration and everyone would have given the workshop rave reviews.

You could pose the topic with your partner or housemate. You could post the question on your social media feed and see what your friends say. You could bring it up over lunch with a coworker. You could even enroll a friend to cohost a Money Talk in your home or at a café. It's easier and more fun with a friend—and at the very least you'll have one person to talk to about the topic of the week. At best, it could even be a way to meet new people and broaden your community.

Since money is such a charged subject, we suggest using the following guidelines and tips to have deeper and possibly ongoing Money Talks. These suggestions are adapted from the Conversation Café process, a low-bar entry dialogue method now used around the world by people who gather to make sense of the events of the day or the big questions of our times. In the context of *Your Money or Your Life*, the topic is our ever-fascinating and confusing relationship with money. If you are following the steps, engaging in Money Talks isn't necessary but will surely accelerate your transformational journey and the very practical process of debt reduction, saving money, and redesigning your money life to reflect your values and dreams. Getting out of your head and into a "no shame, no blame" conversation really is the hottest tip for changing your relationship with money.

Who and Where

Anyone willing to engage with you in a candid, curious, "no shame, no blame" spirit is a perfect partner for a Money Talk. It could be between you and your journal, with your partner cozied up in bed, with your family around the dinner table, with your friends in a café or living room, with participants in a workshop or students in a classroom. Do it with anyone you trust and anywhere you can speak freely without being interrupted before everyone feels complete. If you are with people you don't know, the following guidelines should assure enough safety to open up.

Once you get the hang of Money Talks, you can adapt to many circumstances, but for now here are suggestions for three possible scenarios:

Process for Journaling (1 Person)

If you keep a journal, you know that writing can be a process of discovery. You can augment that quality by writing the money question you want to consider on the top of a page, taking a breath, and inviting your wiser self to write an answer. Give that wiser self freedom to scribble for at least five minutes uninterrupted. You'll be surprised by your answer. You can repeat this with another question—or the same one—as often and as long as you like.

Process for a Dialogue (2 People)

This might be a more personal and even intimate circumstance, perhaps with your partner, best friend, or teenager. It's good to affirm that you're changing the subject, so to speak, shifting from ordinary conversation to an intentional dialogue. Half a minute of silence works wonders. Then use the guidelines that follow.

Process for Small Groups (3–8 People)

Having no more than eight participants ensures that everyone gets enough time to express themselves. If more show up, you can split into two groups. People may insist they want to stay together, but guaranteed, you'll have better conversations with fewer people in the circle.

Do whatever helps everyone have a voice and helps the conversation stay personal, lively, exploratory, and safe.

It works well to open with each person around the circle having a minute or two to speak on the topic without interruption or feedback, and to close the conversation with another round of each person speaking for a minute or two about what they are taking away.

It helps for someone to function as a "host" to shift the group from chatting to the topic at hand. The host may get the ball rolling by starting the first go-round and also initiate the final go-round about ten to fifteen minutes from the agreed ending. Hosts are part of the conversation. They don't lob in firecracker questions from the edge to see what happens, or offer advice. They stay curious, inquisitive, and open along with everyone.

Don't try a Money Talk on the fly. Give it at least half an hour for two people—more with more people.

Agreements

No shame, no blame: Keep a nonjudgmental attitude, as best you can, toward yourself and others. This doesn't mean everyone has to be polite or agree—just be open to other points of view.

Confidentiality: What's said in the group stays in the group.

Presence: Arrive on time, stay till the end, and give full attention to everyone who speaks.

Brevity: Go for honesty and depth, but keep things concise so everyone has a fair amount of airtime.

Commercial-free zone: Do your marketing, advice giving, and lengthy lectures elsewhere and else-when. We don't come to be fixed. We come to learn about ourselves, one another, and our world.

Topics

An open-ended question or suggestion that everyone can answer from their own experience works best. Use the questions at the end of each chapter, and then try to come up with your own. Remember, implied in many questions and topics is ". . . and why?" Don't be afraid to go there. A great way to drive a question deeper is for someone to say, "Tell me more about that," or "What led you to that point of view?" Be careful, because your tone matters. "Why do you think that?" can sound truly interested or quite snarky.

Since society shapes our thinking, feelings, and behavior around money, you can widen any Money Talk by asking, "How has society influenced your answers?"

The questions at the end of each chapter in *Your Money or Your Life* are only examples of what can be raised in a Money Talk. In fact, your topic can be just one word—like Money, Work, Meaning, Purpose, Priorities, Simplicity, Stuff, Debt, Borrowing, Lending, Tithing, Taxes, Insurance, and so on—followed by three questions:

What do you think about it?

What do you feel about it?

What are you doing about it?

Posing a question this way gives everyone a point of

entry. Some people are thinkers, some feelers, and some doers, and each needs a door to enter the opening round with no feedback or cross talk. After that, go wild in a free-flowing conversation until the closing round.

Let's talk!

In the word *culture* is the word *cult*. If we keep a cult of silence about our relationships with money, we all stay in the grip of that shame-and-blame, more-is-better-and-it's-never-enough, greed-is-good, whoever-dies-with-the-most-toys-wins story we're taught.

We can both accelerate our own journeys and be radical culture changers by changing the subject of our conversations from small talk (trivia, gossip, complaining) to BIG talk about money and life. Not only that, we will be giving our conversation partners a profound gift: liberation from their own prisons of fear and confusion and their own blindness.

Use the questions and topics in the preceding chapters, or make up your own. Let the conversations begin.

Acknowledgments

This book is now more than twenty-five years old. Throughout these years, many hundreds of people have contributed to its reach and longevity. Here I want to single out just a few. Monica Wood edited every version of this book until it came out in 1992. Rhoda Walter was an impeccable researcher and supporter in that same period of time. The New Road Map Foundation, staffed entirely by volunteers, is the educational and charitable organization we created in 1984 to disseminate this—and other—transformational tools; the NRM team dedicated itself to bringing the nine-step program to hundreds of thousands of people in myriad ways.

For this *Your Money or Your Life* makeover, there are several heroes I want to thank by name.

Chris Ryba worked as my trusty and indispensable assistant editor throughout 2017. When we met we discovered several shared passions: *Your Money or Your Life*, for starters, smart personal financial strategies in general, and the power of conversation to transform lives. His millennial's-eye view on the world has been indispensable. We've wrestled this update into shape together, and he has edited every version of every rewrite of every chapter with clarity, intelligence, and good cheer.

Cole Hoover, another supersmart, kind, and wise millennial, helped me understand how and why his generation needs what this book can offer. Anne Tillery, Cecile Thomas, and David McNamara also offered sustained encouragement, believing fiercely in both me and this work.

Beth Vesel, my longtime agent and cheerleader, worked with me, as she has from day one, to take the seed of an idea and make it clear, compelling, and relevant enough to win the favor of my publisher, Penguin, and particularly Kathryn Court, a stalwart ally for many years.

Rod Arakaki, formerly of *Yes! Magazine*, offered his services when he learned of this makeover, and adeptly did the first reworking of chapter 6.

The team at Natural Investments—James Frazier, Christopher Peck, Michael Kramer, Hal Brill, and Jim Cummings—helped me pour just the right new wine into the old skins of chapter 9, expanding the range of ways to invest for passive income.

Thirty-year-old Grant Sabatier parachuted in out of nowhere in February 2017 with a well-crafted online article about how *Your Money or Your Life* was the most helpful book in his process of going from broke to a million dollars in about five years. It sent the earlier edition once more to number one on Amazon and began a creative partnership between us that will carry this makeover powerfully to a new generation.

At the same time, I discovered the FIRE (Financial Independence, Retire Early) movement that the original *Your Money or Your Life* seems to have influenced greatly. Pete Adeney, a.k.a. Mr. Money Mustache, and other luminaries in a very large community of FIRE leaders and bloggers, welcomed me back into the fold warmly and I look forward to years of mischief making, myth busting, and world changing together.

Finally, my local editor, A. T. Birmingham Young, and my Penguin editor, Sam Raim, have saved me from errors and excesses galore. You have them to thank for how fine this turned out.

Writing is a solitary process, but I want to also acknowledge the setting of my life—my Whidbey community, with friends who inspire, listen, laugh, and help in concrete ways, and landscapes that nourish my soul. Belonging here, with you and to you, is, in the deepest sense, my true wealth.

Notes

INTRODUCTION

1. Seventeen percent of "units" age sixty-five or older in 2014, although Social Security accounted for at least half of total income for 52 percent of units age sixty-five or older (see Table 8.A1). Source: Social Security Administration (US), *Income of the Population 55 or Older, 2014* (Washington, DC: Office of Retirement and Disability Policy, 2016), https://www.ssa.gov/policy/docs/statcomps/income_pop55/.
2. Bureau of Labor Statistics (US), "Number of Jobs Held, Labor Market Activity, and Earnings Growth Among the Youngest Baby Boomers: Results from a Longitudinal Survey" (March 31, 2015), https://www.bls.gov/news.release/pdf/nlsoy.pdf.
3. "integrity." Merriam-Webster.com. 2017. https://www.merriam-webstcr.com (September 9, 2017).

CHAPTER 1.
THE MONEY TRAP:
THE OLD ROAD MAP FOR MONEY

1. Douglas LaBier, *Modern Madness* (Reading, MA: Addison-Wesley, 1986), as discussed in Cindy Skrzycki, "Healing the Wounds of Success," *Washington Post*, July 23, 1989.

2. Organisation for Economic Co-operation and Development, *How's Life? 2015: Measuring Well-being* (Paris: OECD Publishing, 2015), http://dx.doi.org/10.1787/how_life-2015-en.

3. B. Cheng, M. Kan, G. Levanon, and R. L. Ray, *Job Satisfaction: 2015 Edition: A Lot More Jobs—A Little More Satisfaction* (The Conference Board, 2015), https://www.conference-board.org/publications/publicationdetail.cfm?publication id=3022&centerId=4; https://www.conference-board.org/press/pressdetail.cfm?pressid=6800.

4. David Walker, *A Look at Our Future: Retirement Income Security and the PBGC*, National Academy of Social Insurance Policy Research Conference, January 20, 2006, http://www.gao.gov/cghome/2006/nasrevised12006/nasrevised12006.txt.

5. More than $11,000 per person based on the $3.7 trillion debt divided by the US population of around 325 million. Board of Governors of the Federal Reserve System, "Consumer Credit—G19," December 11, 2017, http://www.federalreserve.gov/releases/G19/Current/.

6. Robert Ornstein and Paul Ehrlich, *New World New Mind* (New York: Doubleday, 1989).

7. Benjamin Kline Hunnicutt, *Work Without End: Abandoning Shorter Hours for the Right to Work* (Philadelphia: Temple University Press, 1988), 44.

8. Ibid., 45–46.

9. Victor Lebow, in *Journal of Retailing*, quoted in Vance Packard, *The Waste Makers* (New York: David McKay, 1960), as excerpted in Alan Durning, "Asking How Much Is Enough," in Lester Brown, *State of the World 1991* (New York: W. W. Norton & Company, 1991), 153.

10. D. J. Holt, P. M. Ippolito, D. M. Desrochers, and C. R. Kelley, *Children's Exposure to TV Advertising in 1977 and 2004* (Washington, DC: Federal Trade Commission Bureau of Economics, 2007), 9.

11. Michael Sebastien, "Marketers to Boost Global Ad Spending This Year to $540 Billion," *Advertising Age*, March 24, 2015, http://adage.com/article/media/marketers-boost-global-ad-spending-540-billion/297737/.

CHAPTER 2.
MONEY AIN'T WHAT
IT USED TO BE—AND NEVER WAS

1. Elizabeth Arias, Melonie Heron, and Jiaquan Xu, "United States Life Tables, 2013," *National Vital Statistics Reports* 66, no. 3 (2017): 1–64.
2. Kira M. Newman, "Six Ways Happiness Is Good for Your Health," *Greater Good Magazine*, July 28, 2015, http://greater-good.berkeley.edu/article/item/six_ways_happiness_is_good_for_your_health.

CHAPTER 3.
WHERE IS IT ALL GOING?

1. Bob Schwartz, *Diets Don't Work!* (Galveston, TX: Breakthru Publishing, 1982), 173.
2. "Footwear Industry Scorecard," NPD Group, https://www.npd.com/wps/portal/npd/us/news/data-watch/footwear-industry-scorecard/.
3. Belinda Goldsmith, "Most Women Own 19 Pairs of Shoes—Some Secretly," Reuters, September 10, 2017, http://www.reuters.com/article/us-shoes-idUSN0632859720070910.

CHAPTER 4.
HOW MUCH IS ENOUGH?
THE QUEST FOR HAPPINESS

1. George Bernard Shaw, "Epistle Dedicatory," *Man and Superman* (New York: Penguin Classics, 2004).
2. Joanna Macy, Presentation at Seva Foundation's "Spirit of Service" conference, Vancouver, BC, May 1985.
3. Viktor E. Frankl, "The Feeling of Meaninglessness: A Challenge to Psychotherapy," *American Journal of Psychoanalysis* 32, no. 1 (1972): 85–9.

4. Purpose-in-Life Test. Copyright held by Psychometric Affiliates, Box 807, Murfreesboro, TN 37133. Permission must be granted to use this test.
5. Medard Gabel, "Buckminster Fuller and the Game of the World." In Thomas T. K. Zung (ed.), *Buckminster Fuller: Anthology for the New Millennium* (pp. 122–128). New York: St. Martin's Griffin, 2002.

CHAPTER 5.
GETTING IT OUT IN THE OPEN

1. According to the National Association of Insurance Commissioners, the average expenditure for auto insurance in the United States in 2013 was $841.23. *Auto Insurance Database Report 2012/2013* (2015), http://www.naic.org/documents/prod_serv_statistical_aut_pb.pdf.
2. Drazen Prelec and Duncan Simester, "Always Leave Home Without It: A Further Investigation of the Credit-Card Effect on Willingness to Pay," *Marketing Letters* 12, no. 1 (2001): 5–12. One of the landmark studies on the subject.
3. Neil Gabler, "The Secret Shame of Middle-Class Americans," *Atlantic*, May 2016.

CHAPTER 6.
THE AMERICAN
DREAM—ON A SHOESTRING

1. *The American Heritage Dictionary of the English Language*, Fifth Edition (New York: Houghton Mifflin, 2016).
2. Thorstein Veblen, *The Theory of the Leisure Class* (New York: Modern Library, 1934), xiv.
3. Martin Merzer, "Survey: 3 in 4 Americans Make Impulse Purchases," Creditcards.com, November 23, 2014, http://www.creditcards.com/credit-card-news/impulse-purchase-survey.php.

4. Donella H. Meadows, Dennis L. Meadows, and Jorgan Randers, *Beyond the Limits: Confronting Global Collapse, Envisioning a Sustainable Future* (White River Junction, VT: Chelsea Green Publishing Company, 1993), 216.
5. US Department of Commerce, *2015 Characteristics of New Housing*, https://www.census.gov/construction/chars/pdf/c25ann2015.pdf.
6. Michael Phillips and Catherine Campbell, *Simple Living Investments for Old Age* (San Francisco: Clear Glass Publishing, 1984, 1988).
7. Bill McKibben, *Hundred Dollar Holiday: The Case for a More Joyful Christmas*, reprint ed. (New York: Simon & Schuster, 2013).
8. The Dalai Lama and Galen Rowell, *My Tibet* (Berkeley and Los Angeles: University of California Press, 1990), 55.

CHAPTER 7.
FOR LOVE OR MONEY: VALUING
YOUR LIFE ENERGY—WORK
AND INCOME

1. E. F. Schumacher, *Good Work* (New York: Harper & Row, 1979), 3–4.
2. Robert Theobald, *The Rapids of Change* (Indianapolis: Knowledge Systems, 1987), 66.
3. Studs Terkel, *Working* (New York: Ballantine Books, 1985), xiii.
4. Kahlil Gibran, *The Prophet* (New York: Alfred A. Knopf, 1969), 28.
5. Marshall Sahlins, *Stone Age Economics* (Chicago: Aldine-Atherton, 1972), 23.
6. Benjamin Kline Hunnicutt, *Work Without End: Abandoning Shorter Hours for the Right to Work* (Philadelphia: Temple University Press, 1988), 311.
7. Ibid., 309.
8. Ibid., 313–14.

9. Arlie Russell Hochschild, *The Time Bind: When Work Becomes Home and Home Becomes Work*, 2nd ed. (New York: Holt, 2001).

10. Jonnelle Marte, "Nearly a Quarter of Fortune 500 Companies Still Offer Pensions to New Hires," *Washington Post*, September 5, 2014.

11. B. Cheng, M. Kan, G. Levanon, and R. L. Ray, *Job Satisfaction: 2014 Edition*, Conference Board, June 2014 [September 2015], https://www.conference-board.org/publications/publicationdetail.cfm?publicationid=3022&centerId=4; https://www.conference-board.org/press/pressdetail.cfm?pressid=6800.

12. R. Ray, M. Sanes, and J. Schmitt, "No-Vacation Nation Revisited," Center for Economic and Policy Research, http://cepr.net/publications/reports/no-vacation-nation-2013.

13. Catherine Clifford, "Less Than a Third of Crowdfunding Campaigns Reach Their Goals," *Entrepreneur*, January 18, 2016, https://www.entrepreneur.com/article/269663.

14. Desmond Morris, *The Biology of Art* (New York: Alfred A. Knopf, 1962), 158–9.

CHAPTER 8.
CATCHING FIRE: THE CROSSOVER POINT

1. David Olson, *The American Church in Crisis: Groundbreaking Research Based on a National Database of over 200,000 Churches* (Grand Rapids, MI: Zondervan, 2008).

2. "Religion," Gallup, http://www.gallup.com/poll/1690/Religion.aspx.

3. Susan Heavey, "U.S. Families Shift As Fewer Households Include Children: Census," Reuters, August 27, 2013, http://www.reuters.com/article/us-usa-families-idUSBRE97Q0TJ20130827.

CHAPTER 9.
WHERE TO STASH YOUR
CASH FOR LONG-TERM FINANCIAL FREEDOM

1. A. Desclé, L. Dynkin, J. Hyman, and S. Polbennikov, "The Positive Impact of ESG Investing on Bond Performance," Barclays, https://www.investmentbank.barclays.com/our -insights/esg-sustainable-investing-and-bond-returns.html #tab3.

2. "10-Year Treasury Yield," The Money Habit, https://i1.wp .com/themoneyhabit.org/wp-content/uploads/2016/09/10 -Yr-Treasury-Yield-Augmented.jpg?resize=1024%2C717. Source: Board of Governors of the Federal Reserve System (US), "10-Year Treasury Constant Maturity Rate," Federal Reserve Bank of St. Louis, https://fred.stlouisfed.org/series /GS10.

3. John C. Bogle, *The Little Book of Common Sense Investing: The Only Way to Guarantee Your Fair Share of Stock Market Returns,* 2nd edition (Hoboken, NJ: Wiley, 2017).

4. Mrs. Frugalwoods, "Our Low Cost, No Fuss, DIY Money Management System," *Frugalwoods: Financial Independence and Simple Living,* January 24, 2017. http://www.frugal woods.com/2017/01/24/our-low-cost-no-fuss-diy -money-management-system/

5. Scott Trench, email message to the author, April 10, 2017.

Blessing the Hands That Feed Us

Lessons from a 10-Mile Diet

Taking the local food movement to heart, bestselling author Vicki Robin pledged to eat only food sourced within a 10-mile radius of her Whidbey Island home in Puget Sound for one month. Featuring recipes as well as practical tips on how readers can locally source their own diet, *Blessing the Hands That Feed Us* is a candid, humorous, and inspirational guide to the locavore movement and a healthy food future.

"[A] call-to-action plan to buy local and live healthier and more responsibly." *–Kirkus Reviews*